OXFORD MONOGRAPHS ON MUSIC

Handel's Muse

HANDEL'S MUSE

Patterns of Creation in his Oratorios and Musical Dramas, 1743–1751

DAVID ROSS HURLEY

OXFORD
UNIVERSITY PRESS

OXFORD

UNIVERSITY PRESS

Great Clarendon Street, Oxford OX2 6DP

Oxford University Press is a department of the University of Oxford.
It furthers the University's objective of excellence in research, scholarship,
and education by publishing worldwide in

Oxford New York

Auckland Bangkok Buenos Aires Cape Town Chennai
Dar es Salaam Delhi Hong Kong Istanbul Karachi Kolkata
Kuala Lumpur Madrid Melbourne Mexico City Mumbai Nairobi
São Paulo Shanghai Singapore Taipei Tokyo Toronto

and an associated company in Berlin

Oxford is a registered trade mark of Oxford University Press
in the UK and in certain other countries

Published in the United States
by Oxford University Press Inc., New York

British Library Cataloguing in Publication Data

Data available

Library of Congress Cataloging in Publication Data

Hurley, David Ross, 1958–
Handel's muse: patterns of creation in his oratorios and musical dramas, 1743–1751/
David Ross Hurley.
p. cm.—(Oxford monographs on music)
Includes bibliographical references and index.
1. Handel, George Frideric, 1685–1759. Oratorios. 2. Oratorio. 3. Dramatic music—18th
century—History and criticism. 4. Composition (Music) 5. Vocal music—History and
criticism. I. Title. II. Series.
ML410.H13 H87 2000 782.23'092 21—dc21 99-046012
ISBN 0–19–816396–7

3 5 7 9 10 8 6 4 2

Typeset in Bembo by
Cambrian Typesetters, Frimley, Surrey
Printed in Great Britain
on acid-free paper by
Biddles Ltd, Guildford and King's Lynn

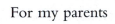

For my parents

ACKNOWLEDGEMENTS

A NUMBER of individuals and institutions have contributed to the making of this book, whose origins date back to my graduate school years. My scholarly interest in Handel's music began in Professor Ellen T. Harris's seminar on Handel's Italian cantatas given in spring quarter 1982 at the University of Chicago. I should like to express my gratitude to Professor Harris for guiding the dissertation upon which this study is based, for selflessly continuing to advise me as I revised the work for publication, and for her many other efforts on my behalf. From beginning to end of this project she has shown unwavering enthusiasm for my topic, and her many astute insights have improved my work.

I am also fortunate to have worked with the late Howard Mayer Brown at the University of Chicago, who with Professor Harris served as an official reader of my dissertation. To acknowledge that Professor Brown's criticisms helped to clarify and sharpen my arguments does not begin to do justice to the special role he has played in my life and work. Many others who knew Howard Brown as a colleague or mentor must feel that their relationship with him stood apart from the routine—this is a logical result of the unique blend of qualities that made up the man. I do not expect to meet anyone quite like Howard again in my life, and I am thus all the more proud to have been able to claim him as a friend as well as a teacher. I valued his praise, which was characteristically rendered with wit and irony (and generally not without a mild sardonic barb at some point), more than he was aware. Our consolation for his death, if there can really be any, lies in what he has left us: the example of his scholarship, the quality of which will remain apparent even though methodologies change, and an anecdotal legacy in its way worthy of Dr Johnson himself.

I must acknowledge a number of other scholars whose help has been crucial for my work. My thoughts about Handel have been profoundly influenced through my contact with my friend and colleague C. Steven LaRue, who has read many parts of this book and offered helpful advice. Donald Burrows and Martha Ronish generously provided me with invaluable paper and watermark information before their *Catalogue of Handel's Musical Autographs* was published; no study of Handel's compositional process is possible without the information contained in that volume. To Professor Burrows

I owe additional thanks for information and advice provided both by letter and word of mouth, and for his support and advice during various stages of this book's genesis. John Roberts of the University of California, Berkeley, has played a similarly germinal role in the creation of this study, graciously providing me with information concerning Handel's borrowings, often before his findings were published, and offering useful information and insights pertaining to many other matters. My contact with Anthony Hicks over the years has also influenced my thoughts to no small degree.

Other scholars who deserve thanks for their support and/or advice include Graydon Beeks, Terence Best, Winton Dean, David Gable, Philip Gossett, William Gudger, Peter Lefferts, the late Hans Lenneberg, Lowell Lindgren, Michael McGrade, Anne Robertson, Ellen Rosand, Ruth Smith, Reinhard Strohm, and Mary Van Steenbergh.

I thank Dean Orville Brill, Vice-President Robert Ratzlaff, and Pittsburg State University for a generous subsidy that has helped to cover the costs of musical examples and plates. I owe a debt of gratitude to Murray Steib for his expert music engraving, his intelligent queries that helped to detect many an error, and his patience. I am also grateful for the support of Keith Ward and Gene Vollen, chairs of the Music Department at Pittsburg State, who helped me find time to complete this project.

In 1986 a University of Chicago Overseas fellowship allowed me to consult Handel's autographs in London and Cambridge. I was able to continue work with primary manuscripts in England and Hamburg as a result of an American Handel Society Fellowship in 1989. In the same year a University of Chicago Travelling Fellowship took me to the manuscript librettos of the oratorios in San Marino, California. Although this book was not the primary reason for my trip to England on a Handel Institute Award in the summer of 1998, my discoveries pertaining to Handel's oratorio singers came in time to influence the book. I should like to thank Malcolm Turner, Deputy Music Librarian of the British Library, and Paul Woudhuysen, Keeper of the Department of Manuscripts and Printed Books at the Fitzwilliam Museum, Cambridge, and their assistants for the use of their collections and their permission to reproduce material from their holdings in this book. I also wish to thank Dr Bernhard Stockmann of the Staats- und Universitätsbibliothek, Hamburg, and Leona Schonfeld of the Huntington Library, San Marino, California, and their assistants for their courtesy and helpfulness. I am also grateful to Patricia Herr of the Diözesan-Bibliothek, Münster, for microfiche copies of relevant materials from the Santini collection.

Thanks also to Bruce Phillips and Helen Peres da Costa of Oxford University Press for seeing this work through production.

Two of my students at Pittsburg State University, Eric Haag and Jason Hubbard, offered much-needed help in practical matters during the final stages of the project. For their personal support I must thank Kathy Holmes and the late Zita Cogan.

Above all, I am grateful to my parents Gene and Marceline for their patience and support, without which this book could not have been written.

D.R.H.

Pittsburg, Kansas

CONTENTS

LIST OF ILLUSTRATIONS

LIST OF FIGURES

LIST OF TABLES

LIST OF MUSICAL EXAMPLES

LIST OF ABBREVIATIONS

D-Hs   Germany: Hamburg, Staats- und Universitätsbibliothek

FM   Cambridge, Fitzwilliam Museum

BL   London, British Library

HG   *G. F. Händels Werke: Ausgabe der Deutschen Händelgesellschaft*, ed. Friedrich W. Chrysander (Leipzig and Bergedorf bei Hamburg, 1858–94, 1902)

HHA   *Hallische Händel Ausgabe im Auftrage der Georg Friedrich Händel Gesellschaft* (Kassel, 1955–)

HWV   *Händels Werke Verzeichnis*: Bernd Baselt, *Händel-Handbuch*, i–iii (Kassel: Bärenreiter, 1978, 1984, 1986)

I

Introduction

SCHOLARS interested in compositional process have by now turned their attention to several composers of the eighteenth century. Musicologists have not only explored the compositional methods of prominent figures such as Bach and Mozart; even composers such as Hasse, who are today relatively obscure, have been studied.[1] Yet Handel's compositional process in the most familiar of his works, the oratorios, has (apart from the specific area of borrowing) been by and large neglected, and only very recently have compositional revisions in his operas been evaluated.[2] This fact becomes even more surprising in view of the source situation: virtually all Handel's composing scores are housed in the British Library, his sketches in the Fitzwilliam Museum. This attractive state of affairs contrasts dramatically with Beethoven, whose autographs and sketches are strewn all over Europe.

The availability of sources in itself is neither sufficient justification for a full-blown investigation of compositional procedure nor a defence of the relevance of such a study for a postmodern age. Musicology today enjoys a new richness of approaches unlike anything in its past: issues of feminism, gender, and other elements of social contextualization of music are bringing us fresh ways of understanding music history. Unfortunately, academia sometimes privileges new methodologies for their own sake over new knowledge. There are those who go so far as to argue that sketch studies, in their attempts to come to grips with musical structure, exclude other avenues of research. Philip Bohlman believes that 'by using the analysis of chord progressions to show that a passage in Beethoven has nothing to do with sexuality but everything to do with a set

---

[1] See Robert Marshall, *The Compositional Process of J. S. Bach* (Princeton: Princeton University Press, 1972); Frederick Millner, *The Operas of Johann Adolf Hasse* (Ann Arbor: UMI Research Press, 1979); and Alan Tyson, *Mozart: Studies of the Autograph Scores* (Cambridge: Harvard University Press, 1987).

[2] Two important contributions to the field of Handel's compositional process have appeared during the last decade or so: Paul Brainard, 'Aria and Ritornello: New Aspects of the Comparison Handel/Bach', in Peter Williams (ed.), *Bach, Handel, Scarlatti Tercentenary Essays* (Cambridge: Cambridge University Press, 1985), 21–34; and C. Steven LaRue, *Handel and his Singers: The Creation of the Royal Academy Operas, 1720–28* (Oxford: Clarendon Press, 1995).

of obvious, though still brilliant, compositional decisions, we continue to keep the body out of Western music'.[3]

Yet at the same time that a new generation of musicologists begins to question the validity of sketch studies, French literary critics have become increasingly involved in manuscript studies that analyse earlier versions of texts—what Peter Brooks calls 'genetic criticism'.[4] We thus see the reverse of the typical relationship between the two disciplines: normally what has begun to look 'passé' in literary criticism becomes 'cutting edge' for musicologists. At any rate, it is not surprising that studies of the gestation of works, no matter what the endeavour is called, should not vanish. For the sheer number of issues that it raises and potentially illuminates, the investigation of compositional process (or perhaps we should now rename it 'genetic music criticism') constitutes a particularly bountiful field of enquiry. This is particularly true of a composer like Handel, whose autographs, unlike Bach's or Mozart's, contain numerous corrections and revisions that reveal remarkable transformations in the composer's musical thought. By analysing these changes I seek to identify many of Handel's creative tendencies: among others, his attempts upon revision to achieve a continuous musical surface, his use of 'cut and paste' techniques akin to eighteenth-century *ars combinatoria*, his concern with musical imagery and drama, and the roles of specific singers in the creation of the oratorios. In short, analysis of compositional process involves more than 'just looking at notes': it also has much to say about music's context, social and otherwise. The inherent interest of these issues—which is the ultimate justification for any scholarly endeavour—strikes me as self-evident.

In many ways, the oratorios are ideal subjects for an investigation of Handel's compositional process. Winton Dean has sorted out the numerous versions of the dramatic oratorios made for performances in Handel's lifetime, and has even provided discussion of some striking compositional changes.[5] Studies devoted to analysing musical revisions must be preceded by source studies, and recently, with the valuable work of Donald Burrows and Martha Ronish, which provides detailed information about Handel's paper types, the necessary groundwork for an investigation of Handel's revisions has been laid.[6]

Moreover, the oratorios deserve further study simply by virtue of the fact

---

[3] See Philip Bohlman, 'Musicology as a Political Act,' *Journal of Musicology*, 11 (1993), 411–36 at 424.

[4] See his review of Julia Kristeva's *Time and Sense: Proust and the Experience of Literature* titled 'Proust on the Couch', in New York Times Book Review, 19 May 1996.

[5] Winton Dean, *Handel's Dramatic Oratorios and Masques* (Oxford: Oxford University Press, 1959).

[6] Donald Burrows and Martha Ronish, *A Catalogue of Handel's Musical Autographs* (Oxford: Clarendon Press, 1994).

that they are products of Handel's mature years, when his compositional skill was at its height, and they remain the most popular of his works. Containing a number of different types of pieces and musical forms—choruses, arias, accompanied recitatives, and instrumental pieces—and at the same time exemplifying Handel's concern for drama, the oratorios offer a summary of Handel's entire compositional career.

Because of the wealth of compositional changes that they contain, the works examined here must somehow be limited, but this is not easily done. The oratorios do not divide neatly into groups. One cannot choose a set of 'typical' works, because the differences are so great between individual pieces called oratorios that none can be described as typical. Indeed, scholars even disagree as to which works can be called oratorios. Jens Peter Larsen's 1957 definition of the genre, encompassing a variety of types, included works such as *Alexander's Feast* and *Ode to St Cecilia* as 'non-biblical concert or cantata oratorios'.[7] Winton Dean narrowed the topic by choosing to write about only the dramatic oratorios, but he thereby included some secular works that were apparently not called oratorios by contemporary sources, *Semele* and *Hercules*,[8] and which Howard Smither dismisses from his discussion of Handel's oratorios.[9] The simple fact is that any definition of the genre is open to criticism, and it is quite difficult to identify works as either typical or atypical. All choices thus being to some degree arbitrary, I have chosen works that represent what I think are the two most significant avenues of Handel's creative endeavours in the period 1743–8: secular 'musical drama' and biblical oratorio.

With the composition of *Semele* in June and early July 1743 Handel embarked on a new path. Before *Semele* the dramatic oratorios were on biblical subjects and easily distinguished from operas not only in subject matter and language (English versus Italian), but often in musical content as well— while choruses and a variety of aria forms characterize oratorios, the most common aria form in opera by far is the da capo, and operas contain few elaborate choruses.[10] In *Semele*, however, there are numerous da capo arias, and

---

[7] Jens Peter Larsen, *Handel's Messiah* (New York: Norton, 1972).

[8] Dean, *Handel's Dramatic Oratorios*.

[9] Howard Smither, *A History of the Oratorio*, ii: *The Oratorio in the Baroque Era: Protestant Germany and England* (Chapel Hill: The University of North Carolina Press, 1977). The *London Daily Post* of 10 Feb. 1744 advertised 'SEMELE: After the manner of an Oratorio', and *Hercules* was called 'A Musical Drama' on the title-page of the libretto. Charles Jennens tells us in his annotations to his copy of Mainwaring's biography of Handel that Semele was called 'by fools' an oratorio. See Dean, 'Charles Jennens's Marginalia to Mainwaring's Life of Handel', *Music and Letters*, 53 (1972), 160–4.

[10] Choruses at the ends of operas are generally brief, simple, homophonic pieces for the solo singers. Even when choruses appear more frequently in Handel's operas, they are less complex in design than oratorio choruses.

in general the choruses lack the weight of earlier oratorios.[11] *Semele* is in fact an English opera libretto, written by William Congreve for John Eccles, probably in 1705.[12]

Carole Taylor has advanced a theory to explain Handel's unexpected operatic turn in *Semele*.[13] According to a July 1743 letter of John Christopher Smith, Handel had been offered £1,000 to compose two operas for Lord Middlesex's opera company. He did not accept the offer, but instead composed *Semele*, which Jennens called 'a bawdy opera', quite possibly in competition with Middlesex's company.[14] Certainly the opera party, which was apparently upset by *Semele*, considered the production of *Semele* a competitive act.

Viewed in the light of his later works, however, *Semele* is not merely an interruption in the steady flow of biblical oratorios, but the beginning of a new trend. Certain of its operatic features—mythological subject and frequent da capo arias—can also be found in *Hercules*, composed a year later.[15] Of course Handel continued to compose biblical oratorios as well, such as *Joseph and his Brethren*, at the same time as *Semele* (1743), and with *Hercules* in 1744, *Belshazzar*; but even so, operatic elements—da capo arias, for example—were to become more frequent in later oratorios. Both *Theodora* (1749)—based on a sacred but not a scriptural story—and *Jephtha* (1751), for instance, parallel Italian opera in that they include long stretches filled with da capo arias separated by simple recitative, and without choral participation. Significantly, both have been criticized for these qualities, mirroring twentieth-century criticisms of Baroque opera seria.[16]

---

[11]   This is a tricky matter. Certainly the moralizing choruses in Semele, such as 'Oh terror and astonishment' in Act III, scene 7, constitute a typical type of chorus found in oratorios, as do the act-ending choruses. Many choruses, however, are short and lightweight, and there are long stretches during which no choruses appear.

[12]   Dean (*Handel's Dramatic Oratorios*, 366) gives 1706. According to Calhoun Winton a letter by William Cleland dated 6 Dec. 1705 relates that 'Eccles [has] another [opera] the words by Congreve'. See Calhoun Winton, *John Gay and the London Theatre* (Lexington: The University Press of Kentucky, 1993), 178–9.

[13]   See Carole Taylor, 'Handel's Disengagement from the Italian Opera', in Stanley Sadie and Anthony Hicks (eds.), *Handel Tercentenary Collection* (Ann Arbor: UMI Research Press, 1987), 165–81 at 165.

[14]   Handel's *Alessandro* was arranged by Lampugnani under the title *Rossane* and produced by Middlesex in 1743/4. It is thought that Handel may have agreed to this arrangement to compensate for his refusal to compose new operas for the company. (See Taylor, 'Handel's Disengagement', 172.)

[15]   The Opera of the Nobility was unable to undertake the 1744–5 season at the King's Theatre. That year Handel produced oratorios at the King's Theatre in lieu of the opera company. Hercules was composed for this season, and Handel revived *Semele* in Dec. 1744. (Taylor, 'Handel's Disengagement', 173.) Handel's ultimately unsuccessful efforts to attract the opera company's audience with his secular oratorios might explain why he inserted five Italian arias from his operas with their original Italian texts into the Dec. 1744 revival of *Semele*; it was perhaps an attempt to make the work even more like an opera.

[16]   Dean writes of *Theodora*: 'Act I is long and diffuse. Eight out of ten airs have the full *da capo*, and although the leisurely pace of the action might be pleaded in justification the effect in modern performance is wearisome' (Dean, *Handel's Dramatic Oratorios*, 563). *Jephtha* fares no better: 'As in Act I of *Theodora*, and for the same reason, there are too many mechanical *da capos*; in these two sections [Act II, scenes 1–2 and the 'later stages of Act III'] eight out of fourteen airs and one long duet follow the strict form' (ibid. 597).

This slow transformation of Handelian oratorio, a path full of works that point both ways, may cast light on Handel's true musical interests. Upon leaving Halle and changing the direction of his artistic training, which pointed to a career as a church composer and organist, Handel became an opera composer. After spending the greatest part of his career writing Italian operas, he gave the genre up in 1741. But in his last years it was perhaps in part an abiding interest in opera that transformed his oratorio production.[17] In this sense, Handel remained an operatic composer until the end of his life.

By the time he was composing his last oratorios, however, Handel had already attempted a synthesis of the two genres of large-scale vocal composition characteristic of the period beginning with *Semele*. The first such amalgamation was *Alexander Balus* of 1747, and the second attempt was *Susanna* of 1748, both laying claims to being the most operatic of Handel's biblical oratorios. Thus the period from the composition of *Semele* in 1743 and ending with *Jephtha*, Handel's last original oratorio, in 1751 may be described as a period in which he wrote operatic oratorios and biblical or religious oratorios with continuous influence of the one on the other. Six works from this period representing each important type of endeavour form the basis of this book: *Semele* (1743) and *Hercules* (1744), secular music drama; *Belshazzar* (1744) and *Solomon* (1748), biblical oratorio; and *Susanna* (1748), which represents a synthesis of the two types. Later chapters of the book also include examples from *Jephtha* (1751), another 'operatic' biblical oratorio.[18] (See Table 1.1 for the dates of composition and first performance for these pieces.) Apart from their musical worth, these works embody a network of interesting compositional matters. In addition, I occasionally draw upon other works to clarify the issues raised.

Each performance, particularly each run of an oratorio, presented Handel with changes of cast and audience. These physical differences as well as his own creative spirit made alterations necessary, and every run of performances involved recomposition. In order to delve into Handel's creative endeavours as musician and dramatist this book is limited to discussion of changes made

---

[17] Handel's operatic interests might also have had a pragmatic element in them. In Ch. 10 I suggest that the use of Italian-born singers experienced in Italian opera in England might, *pace* Larsen, have influenced Handel's increased use of the da capo aria in his late oratorios.

[18] Because this study aims to clarify Handel's 'normative' compositional process, it approaches *Jephtha*, whose composition was anything but typical, with due caution. As is well known, Handel began *Jephtha* unusually late in the season, and its composition was interrupted and protracted by his failing sight. (See Dean, *Handel's Dramatic Oratorios*, 617–18 and Donald Burrows, 'Handel's Last Musical Autograph', *Händel-Jahrbuch*, 40/41 (1994/5), 155–68.) Thus the whole concept of 'precomposition' (see Ch. 3), for instance, might take on new meaning in *Jephtha*. In Chs. 7 and 9 to 11, therefore, I have drawn upon only those revisions in *Jephtha* that illustrate particularly well points that would have arisen even without considering that work.

TABLE 1.1. *Dates of composition and first performance*

Work	Period of composition	First performance
Semele	begun 3 June 1743; Act I draft completed 13 June; Act II draft completed 20 June; entire completed 4 July 1743	10 February 1744
Hercules	begun 19 July 1744; Act I draft completed 30 July; Act II draft completed 11 August; Act III draft completed 17 August; entire completed 21 August	5 January 1745
Belshazzar	begun 23 August 1744; Act I completed 3 September; Act II completed 10 September; entire completed 23 October 1744	27 March 1745
Solomon	begun 5 May 1748; Act I draft completed 23 May; orchestrated 26 May; entire completed 13 June 1748	17 March 1749
Susanna	begun 11 July 1748; Act I draft completed 21 July; Act III draft completed 9 August; entire completed 24 August 1748	10 February 1749
Jephtha	begun 21 January 1751; Act I draft completed 2 February; Act II draft to 'How dark, O Lord' reached by 13 February; Act II draft completed 23–7 February; Act III through 'Theme sublime' composed 28 June–15 or 17 July 1751; entire completed (without quintet) 30 August	26 February 1752

before first performance, where alterations for purely practical reasons—such as cast changes—are not the primary type of revisions found.

While devoted to several different aspects of Handel's compositional process, this book is divided into three large parts. The first extends through Chapter 3, and deals with introductory matters such as Handel's music-writing process as well as 'precompositional' concerns as reflected by sketches and drafts. The second part, comprising Chapters 4 to 8, addresses compositional revisions that Handel made primarily for musical reasons (though Chapter 8, which deals with changes of musical form, also begins to examine issues of text-setting and drama). The third section of the book, beginning with Chapter 9, explores the 'extramusical' issues of text, word-setting, and the role of certain singers in the compositional process.

Within this three-part framework a number of specific issues are addressed. In analysing Handel's surviving sketches and borrowings in Chapter 3 I address an inconsistency in the Handel literature that has hardly been realized, much less resolved: was Handel predominantly a spontaneous, 'improvisatory' composer or did he plan his compositions before the event? Although the question cannot be answered definitely, posing it allows us to create new models for Handel's compositional acts.

As one of the first studies devoted to Handel's compositional process as a purely musical phenomenon, Chapters 4 to 8 concentrate primarily on types of revisions that crop up repeatedly in the autographs—an approach influenced by Robert Marshall's major study of Bach's autographs.[19] In part this approach is meant to safeguard against an objection to genetic musical scholarship, expressed with some frequency and not entirely without justification nowadays, on the grounds that the analysis of compositional changes by no means establishes the *raison d'être* of a musical revision—that what the composer hoped to achieve by a revision and what the analyst believes to be important might not be the same. By its nature, the study of compositional process often conflates analysis with 'speculative reconstruction of the composer's intentions'.[20] Although a distinction exists between the scholar's analysis and the composer's intentions, we may hope that in most cases the analysis sheds light on the composer's compositional efforts. Certainly many aspects of the composer's intentions must remain opaque, but analysis is still our best hope for suggesting likely hypotheses about those intentions. Therefore the attempt is at least worth making. It seems to me that recurrent changes, more than unique revisions, pinpoint important compositional concerns likely to be those of the composer, revealing the 'daily' workings of his or her musical mind. Accordingly, Chapters 4 to 7 are devoted, in turn, to issues of thematic repetition and thematic diversity; revisions of harmonic goals and formal proportion (drawn largely from arias with bi-partite B sections); revisions of texture; and revisions that achieve a more seamless musical surface. Together these four chapters present an overall picture of Handel's compositional art: his manipulation of the discrete units that, on a number of levels, comprise his music while at the same time exploring ways to produce a homogeneous, coherent musical texture. Chapter 8 deals with

[19] Robert Marshall, *The Compositional Process of J. S. Bach.*
[20] See David Shulenberg's review of Paul Brainard and Ray Robinson (eds.), *A Bach Tribute: Essays in Honor of William H. Scheide*, in *Notes*, 52 (Sept. 1995), 88.

revisions of musical form and what these revisions tell us about Handel's approach to his librettos. I also examine changes of form as well as aria substitutions that are interrelated over a large span, such as a scene, and their significance—or more precisely, the significance of the relations between these revisions—for the drama, thereby exploring a second dimension of Handel's compositional process.

In Chapter 9 I address one of the most salient features of Handel's works, their heavy use of musical imagery, and the role of this imagery both in composition and in revisions in which music that originally served one text is reused with a new text. Chapter 10 moves to another aspect of Handel's creative endeavour, his special concerns as an impresario and vocal composer who had to counterbalance the issue of musical expression with that of the capability of the singers. In particular, this chapter focuses on transfers of material from one singer to another, and the changes wrought in the transfer. Finally, in Chapter 11 I ponder the ramifications of the previous chapters for our view of Handel's creative process and musical style.

Editorial Procedure

Since this book covers much music that was rejected before first performance and therefore remains unpublished, it is necessary to include a number of musical transcriptions as examples. I have modernized and sometimes even corrected Handel's own musical notation. For instance, Handel generally placed note stems on the right side of note heads even when the notes are above the middle lines of the staves and point downward. He often drew barlines sporadically. He also dotted notes over the barlines rather than using ties. There being no reason to preserve these notational idiosyncrasies, I have followed modern practice in all of these matters.

Additionally and more important, Handel customarily employs clefs that are no longer in common use—tenor, alto, and soprano—for his vocal parts. Chrysander's practice was to use modern treble clef instead of soprano clef.[21] I have chosen to use modern clefs for the vocal parts, largely for the sake of convenience for the reader.

In order to curb the number of musical examples it has not always been possible to reproduce all the published music cited. In many cases I instead refer the reader to the only complete edition of Handel's works, Friedrich

---

[21]   G. F. *Händels Werke: Ausgabe der Deutschen Händelgesellschaft,* ed. Friedrich W. Chrysander (Leipzig and Bergedorf bei Hamburg, 1858–94, 1902). This edition will hereafter be abbreviated *HG*.

Chrysander's Händel-Gesellschaft edition. References to this edition (*HG*) give the volume, the page number, the number of the system (reckoning from the top of the page), and the bar number within that system. Thus the entry *HG* 8: 49, 3/4 indicates the eighth volume of the Händel-Gesellschaft edition, which happens to be *Theodora*, page 49, fourth bar of system 3.

Because some readers might be using other editions, references to the bar number of the piece cited are also included. In the musical examples, the first bar number always indicates the place where the passage occurs in the final setting.

Aria Forms: Terminology

Differences in scholarly use of terminology necessitate a brief review of five-part da capo aria form and modifications of this form frequently encountered in this study. Other arias in Handel's oratorios comprise forms that are more commonly known, such as strophic and through-composed forms, and need not be described here.

The formal plan of the five-part da capo aria includes an A section consisting of two complete statements of the A section text (A1 and A2), the first modulating from tonic to dominant and the second returning to the tonic.[22] These are surrounded by ritornellos: (1) an introductory ritornello in the tonic; (2) a 'middle', 'intervening', or A1 ritornello in the secondary key; and (3) a 'concluding', 'final', or A2 ritornello, which often differs from the introductory ritornello, in the tonic key. In major-key arias the A section generally modulates to the dominant, while in minor-key arias, though there is more variation, the modulation is generally to the relative major (III). The B section, which sets the remaining lines of text, is always shorter than the A section, offers a change of key (and often mode), without ritornellos. Handel frequently—but by no means always—ends the B section in the minor mediant if the A section is in a major key and in the minor dominant if the A section is in a minor key. This is followed by a da capo repeat of the A section. A typical overall plan for the da capo aria can be diagrammed as in Table 1.2.

In Handel's hands the basic da capo scheme is as often as not subject to profound variations in key scheme and form. In fact, arias that follow the five-

---

[22] This form has previously been described in Frederick Millner, *The Operas of Johann Adolf Hasse*; Eric Cross, *The Late Operas of Antonio Vivaldi 1727–1738* (Ann Arbor: UMI Research Press, 1981). For Handel's da capo forms in particular, see Ellen T. Harris, 'Harmonic Patterns in Handel's Operas,' in *Eighteenth-Century Music in Theory and Practice: Essays in Honor of Alfred Mann*, ed. Mary Ann Parker-Hale (Stuyvesant, NY: Pendragon Press, 1994), 77–118.

TABLE 1.2. *The five-part da capo aria*

A section

Opening ritornello	I	i
First vocal section (A1)	I–V	i–III
A1 ritornello	V	III
Second vocal section (A2)	–I	–i
A2 ritornello	I	i

B section

Third vocal section with new text	vi–iii	III–v

Da capo repeat of A section

part da capo model in all parameters are relatively rare in his oratorios. The A1 ritornello is sometimes very short or eliminated altogether. Upon the da capo repeat Handel sometimes either omits the opening ritornello or provides a new one, written after the vocal cadence of the B section, using a dal segno repeat. The A section text may be stated numerous times rather than just twice. These 'modifications' of the standard plan sometimes require decisions about the application of terminology.

In particular, the numerous ways of constructing the A section in Handel's oratorios require some discussion. One must evaluate the importance of tonality, especially cadences, and other elements of formal structure as well as the number of text statements in order to determine how to schematize A sections. For instance, the *Hercules* aria 'Alcides' name in latest story' contains altogether four complete statements of the A section text rather than two. Nonetheless, the A section can be divided into two parts, labelled A1 and A2, on the basis of the strong arrival in the dominant and an extensive A1 ritornello (*HG* 4: 159, bb. 1–7). Thus I would describe the A section of the aria in terms of A1 and A2, each containing two statements of the text.

In other cases, however, the A section may be divided into three parts. 'The Parent Bird' from *Susanna*, a minor-mode aria discussed in Chapter 5, for instance, includes a full statement of the A text modulating to the minor dominant and followed by an abbreviated ritornello in that key (A1); a repeat of the text ending in the subdominant (A2); and a third statement of the text cadencing to the tonic at the end (A3). Each of these statements is discrete enough to invite the labels A1, A2, and A3. While those adamantly committed to the five-part da capo plan might argue that the real 'mid-point' of the aria occurs with the modulation to the minor dominant and that all the material after the A1 ritornello should be called A2, I would argue that such strict adherence to the model distorts the important structural distinction between A2 and A3.

In other cases, such as 'More sweet is that name' in *Semele*, the A section does not divide into parts on the basis of text repeats or ritornellos. There is a cadence to the dominant, so that the A section could be divided into two parts, but this transitory arrival in the dominant is not reinforced in any way.

A number of Handel's aria forms can be related to da capo form. At times Handel's dal segno arias omit the restatement of A1—a form sometimes called a 'half da capo'. An aria that is constructed like the A section of a da capo aria alone is called a cavatina. A written-out da capo has an A section that ends in the tonic, a B section, and a written-out return. A modified da capo follows the same pattern with the significant difference that its A section ends in the dominant or mediant.

2

Writing the Score

INVESTIGATION of Handel's compositional process involves consulting a number of sources. The most important of these include Handel's composing scores in the British Library and the sketches and fragments in the Fitzwilliam, Cambridge. Useful in determining the first performance version of a work—and sometimes interesting from the standpoint of compositional process—are the 'conducting scores' provided by Handel's copyists, which now reside in the Staats- und Universitätsbibliothek in Hamburg.[1] Fortunately, Winton Dean had access to all these materials, and the invaluable source information in his *Handel's Dramatic Oratorios and Masques* provides the basis for this study.[2] With its narrow focus on compositional process, however, this book differs from Dean's broader intentions. The following summary of the sources, therefore, concentrates on those sources most important for understanding the compositional process rather than those used to determine the first performance version of the oratorios. This discussion will emphasize as much as possible the differences from received opinion the sources disclose, beginning with primary autograph sources—excluding sketches, which will be discussed in the next chapter—and concluding with contemporary copies.

Handel's Autograph Scores

Handel's typical procedures in his autographs as illustrated by their physical characteristics have been discussed by others, most notably Dean and Burrows and Ronish, and merely require summary here.[3] It is possible to trace Handel's compositional process back to a point before the composer even entered the picture, to the blank page, for he probably purchased his paper after it had

---

[1] One purely textual set of sources was also consulted: the handwritten copies of the oratorio texts in the Huntington Library, San Marino, California. These are discussed in Ch. 8.

[2] In particular, Dean admirably sorts out Handel's various performance versions of the oratorios. See Dean, *Handel's Dramatic Oratorios*.

[3] See Dean, *Handel's Dramatic Oratorios*, and Burrows and Ronish, *Catalogue*.

been folded and cut, and ruled with stave lines.[4] There are two basic methods of folding and cutting, resulting in two distinct quarto formats, either a horizontal cut and a vertical fold, producing an oblong quarto format, or a vertical cut and a horizontal fold, producing an upright quarto format. Handel most often used paper in the oblong quarto format except in scores requiring large choral and orchestral forces. In *Solomon*, for example, he generally used oblong format for the arias and upright format as well as uncut pages for the double choruses.[5] As a result, it is sometimes difficult to discern whether a given insertion in the autograph of *Solomon* is actually a compositional revision or merely a change of paper type due to changes in orchestral and vocal forces.

After cutting and folding, one half-sheet or folio was placed inside the other, producing a bifolio. This gathering of four is the most common unit found in Handel's autographs, but in the oratorios one also finds other numbers of gatherings, such as six or eight, with some frequency; occasionally a page or so was cut or added to a folio during composition. Often these constructions disclose a compositional revision, but this is not always so, and in certain cases it is difficult to tell. Since Handel was working with bifolios rather than pages, he tended to number each bifolio, so that a number appears once every eight pages. *Semele*, *Hercules*, *Belshazzar*, and *Susanna* are so numbered. As Winton Dean first noted, Handel's bifolio numbers are an aid in retracing his compositional process, because any irregularity in numbering may disclose an insertion, deletion, or substitution in the autograph.[6] In addition to Handel's numbers, a later hand has numbered each of the folios. These later numbers, together with an indication of recto or verso, provide the standard means of reference to an autograph.

Of course, the type of paper that Handel used varied from time to time, and a change in paper (as traced by its watermarks) can be a useful guide to various versions of a work. For this information I have primarily relied on Burrows and Ronish. In addition to these aspects of the Handel paper industry, a picture of Handel's typical music-writing practice emerges from the autographs.

A paradigm[7] of Handel's working methods that is still firmly held today was

---

[4] Burrows, whose work underlies this discussion, postulates that Handel's paper supplier was John Walsh. See Burrows and Ronish, *Catalogue*.

[5] There are altogether four different paper types in *Solomon*, including 12-stave, 16-stave, and 20-stave pages. [6] See Dean, *Handel's Dramatic Oratorios*.

[7] My understanding of the terms paradigm or model has been influenced by writers who distinguish between fact and theoretical models. The literary historian C. S. Lewis describes the distinction thus: 'In every age it will be apparent to accurate thinkers that scientific theories . . . are never statements of fact. That stars appear to move in such and such ways, or that substances behaved thus and thus in the laboratory—these are statements of fact. The astronomical or chemical theory can never be more than provi-

first stated in English by Winton Dean and is commonly invoked whenever Handel's compositional process is sketched:

In the autographs Handel's normal (though not invariable) procedure was to write first a skeleton score, comprising bass line and top part (first violin or voice) only, of a whole act and sometimes of a whole oratorio, adding dates generally at the beginning and end of each act and always at the end of the oratorio. The words of the recitatives would be written out in full, but without music. After this and without appreciable interval, he would go through the score again, filling up the inner parts and recitatives, etc.[8]

The broad parameters of this paradigm have proved useful for understanding the way in which Handel composed oratorios; at the same time, Dean is right to point out that it is not invariable in all its aspects. Handel does not always proceed by a single method—in all compositional matters, in fact, flexibility must be recognized. A more detailed look at the autographs invites additions and modifications to the model. The following discussion, therefore, seeks not to replace the paradigm, but to expand it.

Arias

In many, though not all, cases the traditional view—that in arias Handel first drafted a short score containing basso continuo and the important melodic part, either vocal or, during ritornellos, instrumental—is entirely applicable. The rejected versions of certain unorchestrated arias consist of these parts and no others: the first version of 'Would custom bid' from the autograph of *Susanna* (fos. 21 and 24) provides a convenient example. Many other instances, including cancelled passages within arias that were eventually orchestrated, could be cited. (See e.g. Ex. 5.3(*a*), where Handel cancelled the end of the B section of an aria before orchestrating it.)

Other cases, however, reveal quite a different working method. An unfinished early version of an aria in *Belshazzar* is a case in point (see Pl. 2.1). This fragment, an incomplete setting of 'The leafy honours of the field', was

sional. It will have to be abandoned if a . . . person thinks of a supposal which would "save" the observed phenomena with still fewer assumptions, or if we discover new phenomena which it cannot save at all.' (See C. S. Lewis, *The Discarded Image: An Introduction to Medieval and Renaissance Literature* (Cambridge: Cambridge University Press, 1964), 15–16.) Lewis describes in a pithy way a process detailed by Thomas S. Kuhn in his well-known book *The Structure of Scientific Revolutions* (Chicago: University of Chicago Press, 1970). Kuhn explains how scientific models or 'paradigms' operate—rarely do they fit all the facts. A scientific revolution occurs when new facts emerge or when previously known but 'overlooked' facts become, for whatever reason, significant enough to demand a paradigm that will include them.

[8] Dean, *Handel's Dramatic Oratorios*, 88.

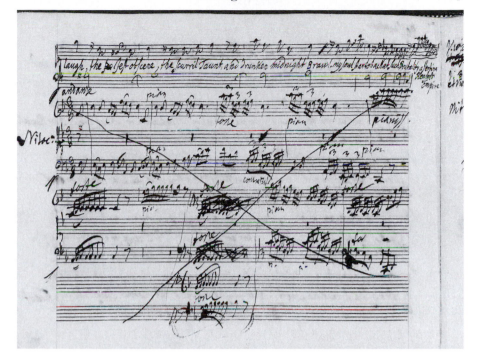

2.1. *Belshazzar*, first draft of 'The leafy honours', BL RM 20.d.10: (*a*) fo. 61ᵛ; (*b*) fo. 66ʳ; (*c*) fo. 66ᵛ

abandoned after the vocal cadence to the dominant.[9] If we assume that Handel intended to compose a full da capo aria, the fragment represents the entire first half of the A section. Now the puzzling fact is that the fragment is completely orchestrated and includes dynamic markings and revisions that one would normally assign to the 'filling up' stage or later, thus defying our

---

[9]   There exist four versions of 'The leafy honours': (1) the 3/8 fragment in the autograph; (2) the complete 3/8 setting in the autograph (published in *HG* 19: 83); (3) a complete 12/8 setting in RM 20.f.12, fos. 39ʳ–42ᵛ; (4) Andante fragment in common time in RM 20.f.12, fo. 43ʳ⁻ᵛ (published in *HG* 46B: 86). The first is the fragment under discussion, the second the complete version of the aria as used in the first performance of the work in 1745. The others have proved difficult to place chronologically. Dean believed that the third, which was inserted into the conducting score, belonged to the 1745 run; it uses the same material as a setting of 'Come, fancy empress of the brain' from *Alceste*, but *Belshazzar* was not revived before the composition of *Alceste* in 1749. (See *Handel's Dramatic Oratorios*, 452–3.) On the basis of the watermark in the conducting score, Hans Dieter Clausen assigned the third setting to the 1751 performance of *Belshazzar*. (See *Händels Direktionspartituren ('Handexemplare')* (Hamburger Beiträge zur Musikwissenschaft, 7; Hamburg: Verlag der Musikalienhandlung Karl Dieter Wagner, 1972), 122–3.) However, a comparison of the autograph of the third setting of 'The leafy honours' with 'Come, fancy empress' shows, by nature of the compositional revisions, that the *Belshazzar* aria must have been composed first, as Dean believed. Recent paper studies suggest that this third setting of 'The leafy honours' was one of the numbers for Nitocris that Handel reset in about 1748, probably for a revival of *Belshazzar* that never came to pass. More than likely, this version was later used in the 1751 performance. The fourth version is a fragment based on 'Gentle Morpheus' in *Alceste*. The first two settings of 'The leafy honours' exclusively involve the 1745 run.

received view of Handel's typical music-writing procedures. This example raises a host of questions. Should the received model simply be abandoned, or merely qualified? Or does the fragment at hand represent an exception that requires explanation—for example, that Handel was working from a pre-existing draft, or that the aria contains unique features that might explain its exceptional treatment? In fact, there are several possible explanations.

1. If 'The leafy honours' represents an anomaly, the exception could be explained if Handel were working from an extensive pre-existent 'draft'. This raises the question of exactly what the term 'draft' means in Handel studies. This will be discussed more extensively in the next chaper. For now, in the musicological literature 'draft' often denotes a precompositional piece that serves as the basis for a new piece. There is little evidence that Handel ever created such drafts *that were intended to serve as precompositional drafts from the beginning.* Certainly almost anything—a completed composition, a rejected work, works by others—might serve Handel as model or raw material for new compositions. But there is little evidence, if any, to suggest that he prepared precompositional drafts before setting a piece down in the autograph score. Some sketches survive (which we will consider below), but these are generally brief, and could hardly explain the relatively developed and 'finished' appearance of 'The leafy honours' fragment. In Handel studies the term draft is more commonly used to refer to a composition that was drafted into the autograph, but not completely orchestrated, and abandoned before or during Handel's 'filling up' stage.

If a surviving precompositional item served as the source for 'The leafy honours', it has not been located. The possibility that this was nonetheless the case cannot be ruled out—there are certainly instances in which Handel copied from pre-existent works—but this hypothesis is not essential to the history of this particular aria.

2. At least one other reason that this aria might have required special treatment when it was written down concerns the particularly important role of the orchestra and of dynamics, which must be understood in the light of Handel's use of musical imagery. The opening text ('The leafy honours of the field') evokes a pastoral setting, which is represented in musical terms by 3/8 metre and occasional pedals, as well as the key of F major. However, the 'furious driving wind', a metaphor for Belshazzar's debauchery, disturbs the pastoral landscape: the forte marking and the register have much to do with the effectiveness of its musical representation. It could well be that the important role of this element explains why Handel might have wished to record the orchestral material from the beginning, and even to make revisions (such as

adjusting the register of the 'furious, driving wind') before reaching the end of the aria. Indeed, the musical imagery (including the falling triplets for 'in giddy dissipation fly') must belong to an early creative layer of the piece; it is not the sort of writing one later 'fills in'.

3. There can be no doubt that Handel did, indeed, set out many pieces in skeleton score, filling in the orchestral parts after completing the whole. In many of the oratorio autographs he included dates for the completion of specific acts in skeleton draft and the dates of 'filling up'. But this paradigm does not apply throughout Handel's oeuvre, nor necessarily to every item within a given work. Steven LaRue has found that in the Royal Academy operas, as opposed to the oratorios, Handel composed the arias in all parts as he worked, rather than drafting melody and bass line only.[10] The most obvious explanation for this difference is that the arias in the operas are relatively lightly scored in comparison to those in the oratorios. It is reasonable to assume, then, that oratorio arias that were lightly scored could have been written down in all parts from the beginning. Because the first version of 'The leafy honours' is scored for voice, bass, and *violini unisoni* it would not have been odd or even unusual if Handel had written down all these parts from the beginning of the aria. When the scoring was heavier, as in 'Would custom bid', he followed the practice described by Dean, sketching the basso continuo and principal melody.

Between these two contrasting music-writing methods remains a wide margin in which several different procedures, variously closer to one pole or the other, can be seen. It is clear from the autographs that the amount left for 'filling up' in arias varied from case to case. This must be borne in mind when we wish to establish the chronology of a given revision.

Because of subtle differences in handwriting and ink, it is possible to reconstruct the skeleton draft of 'Where e'er you walk' in *Semele*, which apparently required filling in. By and large these distinctions cannot be seen on microfilm, but the original manuscript discloses a somewhat duller ink for the first layer and darker ink for filling in. Handel began by notating the one-bar ritornello in violin and bass, thereafter turning to voice and bass until the internal ritornello, where he again wrote violin and bass. Thereafter he wrote voice and bass until the concluding ritornello, where he notated both violin parts and bass. It is clear from the cancelled original conclusion of the B section on fo. 70[r] that here he wrote out voice and continuo first. Except for the closing ritornello of the A section, then, the aria follows the traditional paradigm quite closely.[11]

[10]   See ch. 2 of LaRue, *Handel and his Singers*.

[11]   Similarly, in 'See the dreadful sisters rise' in *Hercules*, fo. 114[r], Handel provided everything for the first bar, thereafter leaving only the viola part to be added later.

The first setting of 'Golden Columns' in *Solomon* presents a puzzle. The opening ritornello of this aria appears on fo. 117 of the autograph, the concluding ritornello on fo. 126^r; a central bifolio containing the 'middle' of the aria exists in the Fitzwilliam.[12] For most of the aria Handel drafted a skeleton score including basso continuo and principal melody, either in the voice or the violin (see Ex. 9.7(*b*)). The first page of the aria on fo. 117^r, however, is completely orchestrated (see Ex. 9.7(*a*)). There are two possibilities: Handel may have rejected the aria during the orchestration period, after filling in the first page. Or he may have begun the aria by scoring the first page, to set all the parts in motion, as it were, as a reminder of how he intended them to continue. In this particular case the handwriting, somewhat larger for the outer parts, might support the first paradigm, but it is difficult to be certain.

Iole's 'My father, ah!' in *Hercules* is also worth mentioning in this regard. At the beginning of the second half of this aria ('Peaceful rest', etc.), transcribed in Ex. 9.2, Handel abandoned his first thoughts for the six-bar beginning

2.2. *Susanna*, 'Who fears the Lord', BL RM 20.f.8, fo. 18^r

---

[12] This version of the aria is treated extensively in Ch. 9.

before continuing in the score. Since the abandoned passage ends with an incomplete bar, it is clear that he had been orchestrating these bars, at least from the beginning of 'Peaceful rest'. Thus, as far as we can see, this piece fits the second paradigm I have proposed, where no filling in was later required.

Occasionally in the arias we find a composing method we shall see again in choruses. In the bass aria 'Who fears the Lord' in *Susanna*, for example, some of the cancellations reveal that Handel composed the vocal bass and continuo and the first violin part first (Pl. 2.2). But in one place in the second system he composed the vocal part only. The voice is bass, but it is interesting that he gives us the vocal bass rather than continuo. I would not conclude from this example that of the two bass parts here and in similar passages in arias and choruses Handel typically wrote the bass voice before writing the continuo, though at times this might have been the case. On fos. 106 and 107 of the chorus 'With thy own ardours' in *Susanna*, he clearly composed the basso continuo first, for this is the only voice written in certain excised passages. Thus it is impossible to state which of the two bass parts Handel typically wrote down first.

Recitatives

The traditional paradigm obtains in all the recitatives I have seen. Numerous instances exist where Handel has written down the words and clefs without providing the music. He left the recitatives unset because they could be filled in with little trouble later and he wanted to get on with the composition. Examples have so often been cited in the Handel literature that to do so here would be superfluous; suffice it to point out one important ramification of this process for Handel's compositional practice. The fact that he waited until orchestration to provide music for these recitatives nicely fits Ellen T. Harris's arguments for the significance of the relation of recitative cadence to B sections of the arias that follow them—Handel waited until after the arias were composed, apparently, to decide on the tonality of the recitatives.[13] This practice also left him free to change the key of a movement, if necessary, without having to alter the previous recitative.

Choruses

The traditional paradigm particularly requires expansion when it is applied to choruses, where the frequent changes of texture and musical material did not

---

[13] Harris, 'Harmonic Patterns in Handel's Operas'.

allow Handel simply to write out melody and bass. At least one factor remains constant, however—his autographs offer abundant testimony to the importance of the bass line in the choruses.

In all likelihood Handel wrote down the basso continuo first of all, pausing often (every few bars or beats) to add other parts, as we see from cancelled passages in 'Impartial Heaven' from *Susanna*.[14] On fos. 105[v] and 106[r], in a rejected passage of four and a half bars, which occurs at *HG* 1: 180, 1/1, Handel wrote down only the contrapuntal voice parts and the basso, but at the end of the passage only the basso with figures appears. Similarly, on fo. 107[r] (*HG* 1: 181, 1/3) a three-bar passage of the instrumental bass part appears alone. It is difficult to find any cancelled passage in choruses where the bass is not present, but none of the choruses examined contains cancelled passages where only the melody is written.

Long ago Edward Dent noted Handel's proclivity to work from the bass up.[15] Gerald Abraham discussed Dent's observation in relation to pieces where Handel began with a familiar bass pattern and composed a new piece over it.[16] More recently, Patrick Rogers has argued that Handel most often added continuo figures while writing the short score or while filling up.[17] All these observations neatly fit the evidence of the autographs: when notating the choruses in skeleton score Handel wrote down the bass part first of all, stopping every few bars to add additional parts.[18] Handel's tendency to 'think upward' from the bass represents one of the thoroughly Baroque aspects of his compositional method. In fact, one of his contemporaries, Friedrich Niedt, claimed that the thorough-bass was literally 'the whole foundation of music'.[19]

Handel's practice of composing choruses upward from the bass might help explain a somewhat puzzling revision in the closing ritornello of the chorus 'Sing, o ye heav'ns' in *Belshazzar*, which originally included a diatonic

---

[14] Another possibility, of course, is that he first provided the continuo part for an entire movement, then went back and wrote the upper parts that formed part of the skeleton score. If this were a common method, however, there is surprisingly little evidence of it.

[15] Edward Dent, 'The Operas', in Gerald Abraham (ed.), *Handel: A Symposium* (Oxford: Oxford University Press, 1954), 25. Dent was discussing a truncated aria in *Amadigi*, 'Susurrate, onde vezzose'. After singing 'io manco, io moro', Amadigi goes into a trance and the aria is concluded by continuo alone. While fascinating in a number of respects, this particular case does not strike me as the best illustration of Dent's point, but the point itself is well taken.

[16] Gerald Abraham, 'Some Points of Style', in *Handel: A Symposium*, 269–70.

[17] Patrick J. Rogers, *Continuo Realization in Handel's Vocal Music* (Ann Arbor: UMI Research Press, 1989), 24.

[18] As we shall see in the next chapter, however, in the earlier stage of 'precomposition' Handel tends to sketch melodic ideas. Writing down the basso continuo represents a stage of formal creation.

[19] Friederich Erhardt Niedt, *The Musical Guide*, trans. Pamela L. Poulin and Irmgard Taylor (Oxford: Clarendon Press, 1989), 74–5. See also Elaine Sisman, *Haydn and the Classical Variation* (Cambridge, Mass.: Harvard University Press, 1993), 49.

2.3. *Belshazzar*, 'Sing o ye heav'ns', BL RM 20.d.10, fo. 52ʳ

descending tetrachord in the bass later crossed out by Handel (Pl. 2.3). If played with the string parts this bass line produces glaring parallel fifths between the A minor and G minor chords. It is likely, however, that the bass line was never intended as an accompaniment to the violins; rather, the former replaced the latter. Originally Handel might well have had a different closing in mind, of which he wrote the bass first. Upon deciding against this first version, he cancelled the bass line and then wrote the violin parts. His ultimate decision to feature an unaccompanied ritornello mitigates the sense of closure at the end, which was not great even in the first version with its conclusion on the dominant. With the revised ritornello the chorus seems even more to dissolve into an inconclusive unaccompanied duet for violins, creating a greater sense of continuity between this choral introduction and the fugue that follows it.

Handel's deep orientation towards the bass is well illustrated by a rare instance of his 'shorthand' in *Solomon*. He significantly altered the form of the chorus that begins Part II, 'From the censor', through simple means. At bar 86 he decided upon a repeat of the vocal entrance (bb. 11–23; *HG* 26: 113, b. 1 to 116, b. 1). Towards this end he inserted fo. 49, on which he wrote out only the basso continuo for bars 87–98 (*HG* 26: 132, b. 1 to 134, b. 4), with instructions for the copyists to take the other parts from bars 11–23. Interestingly, he did not take down a melodic part, which would have served equally well.

During the vocal sections (as opposed to the purely orchestral sections) of choruses Handel generally provided both the continuo and vocal bass with text. The two bass parts commonly were identical. The text-setting may have been roughly worked out before he began composition and refined at this early stage of writing the autograph score.

A vast variety of working methods obtain in choruses, as Chrysander was aware; in his introduction to the facsimile of *Jephtha*, in fact, he points to a number of different procedures for drafting choruses.[20] Although the impressive variety of compositional techniques that appear in the choruses makes it impossible to speak of a single working method, certain characteristic patterns can be linked to specific compositional techniques or musical textures. I should like to propose three predominant choral paradigms.

1. In homophonic passages where the chorus has chordal declamation and an elaborate melodic accompaniment—the 'wonderful, counselor' passage from 'For unto us a child is born', with accompanimental sixteenth notes in the violins over a declamatory chorus, being perhaps the most famous example of this familiar Handelian technique—Handel typically composed in short score the continuo bass (with or without figures), the vocal bass with text, and the active melodic accompaniment in violin (or whatever the predominant melodic instrument was), leaving the composition of the upper vocal parts, simply a matter of realizing the thorough-bass, to the filling up stage. In these cases the soprano voice does not usually carry an important melody, and thus did not need to be recorded at this creative stage.

Clear examples of this procedure occur in the autograph of the Dettingen Anthem (BL Add. MS 30308, fo. 6[v]—see Pl. 2.4), where the bass supports a rising series of first-inversion chords. Where this pattern changes, Handel includes all four voices, not wishing to forget the precise pitches he has in mind for these passages. Numerous other examples can be found, as in *Susanna*, fos. 83[v] ('O Joacim') and 75[v] ('Let justice reign'). Chrysander noted one such passage in 'When his loud voice' from *Jephtha*.[21] In the chorus 'How

---

[20] *Das Autograph des Oratorium 'Jephtha' von G. F. Händel*, ed. Friedrich Chrysander (Leipzig and Bergedorf bei Hamburg: Deutschen Händel-Gesellschaft, 1885).

[21] 'erst von S. 85 an bleiben grössere Räume für die Ausfüllung; Seite 86 notirte er von den Singstimmen nur noch Bass und Oberstimme' ('on page 85, for the first time [in this chorus], there is more room left for "filling in"; on page 86 he notated, of the vocal parts, only the bass and upper voice'); ibid., p. iii.

2.4. *Dettingen Anthem*, BL Add. MS 30308, fo. 6ᵛ

engaging, how endearing' from *Semele* the basses and the violin melody came
first, as excisions made before orchestration reveal. In 'Jealousy, infernal pest'
in *Hercules* Handel followed this same procedure on fo. 59ᵛ, but here the vocal
bass differs from the continuo bass. The abandoned first draft of 'Avert these
omens' from *Semele* (a fragment) included continuo, bass voice with text, violin, and the unusual timpani roll.

2. When the soprano carries a more important melody than in these declamatory passages, however, Handel includes it as part of the short score. In other
words, when a significant melody, whether vocal or instrumental, occurs in the
treble, he begins by writing down treble and bass. In 'To him your grateful
notes' in *Hercules*, the handwriting indicates that Handel began by writing out
all parts for the first four bars. Thereafter he wrote the instrumental and vocal
bass parts and the soprano parts, leaving the rest to be filled in later, except at
the first vocal entrance, where he also wrote all vocal parts with bass and first
violin. A shorter passage reveals this same shift of melodic interest to different
parts in 'O Joacim' in *Susanna*, fos. 82ᵛ, 83ʳ (*HG* 1: 149, 1/4). In the first few
bars of this five-bar passage, he wrote down the bass voice, basso, and soprano.
Later, for an orchestral interlude, he wrote the lower parts and violin.

This brings up the matter of orchestral passages. Ritornellos in choruses
reveal the same practice as do ritornellos in arias: Handel provided basso continuo and the melodic line. This occurs for a medial ritornello for 'How long,
o Lord' in *Susanna*, fo. 8ᵛ (Ex. 8.3) and the opening ritornello of 'Righteous
Daniel', fo. 108ᵛ (Ex. 3.2(*b*)).

3. In fugal choruses, or contrapuntal passages within choruses, on the other
hand, Handel notated the continuo bass with figures and all vocal parts and
the text, leaving the orchestral parts for filling up. The fact that a number of
contrapuntal sketches survive may suggest that he had often worked out
much of the counterpoint before drafting choruses. This hypothesis must
remain conjectural, of course, for not enough sketches survive, and Handel,
by all reports, was a master of improvised counterpoint. At any rate, filling up
contrapuntal passages could be done quickly, particularly when the instruments simply double the vocal parts.

This is the case, for example, in 'Impartial Heaven' and 'Righteous Daniel'
from *Susanna*, where voices and continuo only are notated in a number of
rejected passages. In the first of these, fos. 100ᵛ–101ᵛ (*HG* 1: 173, 2/2), Handel
cancelled a passage originally meant to serve as a second exposition before
orchestrating the piece. He wrote down voices and basso continuo only, except
for one down-beat chord in the strings (also on fo. 106ᵛ). The same method
was used on fos. 111–12 of 'Righteous Daniel'. There are several further examples in *Belshazzar*: in 'And ev'ry step' Handel wrote down the vocal parts first

2.5. *Susanna*, 'And to thy faith', BL RM 20.f.8, fo. 86ᵛ

(fos. 81, 82; see Ex. 6.2); in 'All Empires upon God depend' the vocal parts and continuo are ever present, and the violin part is included when it adds to the contrapuntal fabric (fo. 33ʳ⁻ᵛ)—Handel even includes two bars of the second violin part in one spot, with one-note cues in the oboes, apparently to remind himself when he returned to the piece to orchestrate it that the oboes would double the violins in this passage (fo. 33ᵛ). In fact, Chrysander's examples from *Jephtha*, in which Handel notated the bass and voices only before filling up, are fugal ('When his loud voice in Thunder spoke', fos. 88–97).

   A particularly interesting example in *Susanna* may provide insight into an even earlier stage of Handel's composition of fugal passages. In the fugue 'And to thy faith' on fos. 86ᵛ–87ʳ he began, as usual, by supplying the basso continuo, and above it he has written the subject as it passes from alto to bass and to soprano. The countersubject is provided only once, with the first statement of the subject (Pl. 2.5). Given Handel's typical practice of providing all vocal parts in contrapuntal passages, it seems likely that he rejected this passage not only before orchestration, but before he proceeded beyond this point; that is, before the short score was fully prepared. Even when writing down fugues, then, Handel sometimes used a 'layering technique'—as this case illustrates.

All these methods and others can often be found within the boundaries of a single chorus, owing to Handel's penchant for contrasting texture. Thus in 'Let justice reign' in *Susanna*, he cancelled on fo. 74^v a lengthy passage comprising a sort of second exposition (transcribed in Ex. 6.3). Typically, he provided the basso continuo and the vocal parts for this contrapuntal passage, leaving the orchestral parts for later, through its cadence on fo. 75^r, bar 4. At this point he planned an orchestral interlude, and notated its basso continuo and two contrapuntal violin parts only. Thereafter the chorus was apparently to have a chordal passage; he has provided the basso continuo and bass voice with text only. On fo. 75^v these last events are repeated: for six bars we have the two imitative violin parts and basso continuo, then four bars of only the bass parts. This chorus is thus a compendium of Handel's most typical methods.

Of course, other processes besides these described obtain in Handel's choruses. Sometimes he wrote down almost everything in the skeleton score, leaving little for filling up. Moreover, the number of parts provided for the skeleton draft can change from place to place in a chorus. Again, we must be careful not to restrict Handel to his normative processes alone.

Overtures and orchestral pieces

A noteworthy characteristic of the orchestral pieces in the oratorios, within the large domain of Handel's compositional process on the whole, is their peripatetic nature. Handel apparently conceived of oratorio as first and foremost a vocal genre. Thus he wrote 'Solomon An Oratorio' on the first page of the chorus 'Your harps and cymbals sound', and the overture was apparently added later. The famous Symphony in Act III of *Solomon* was inserted into the autograph, and its paper type leads one to associate it with *Joshua*. The Sinfonia for the entrance of Persian wisemen in *Belshazzar* is cued into the score, but the sinfonia itself was apparently (and typically) not added until later. The Sinfonia for Act II of *Semele* is added to the *Semele* wordbook, and the overture is written partly on paper not otherwise found in the score.[22]

Because there are few instrumental pieces in the oratorios it is difficult to

---

[22] Since this sinfonia is today found, inexplicably, in the autograph of *Riccardo Primo*, we cannot say whether it was an insertion, but this seems likely.

contrive an authoritative and comprehensive paradigm of the music-writing process, but the little evidence that exists demonstrates a working procedure akin to that for choruses and arias. The original overture for *Susanna* can largely be recreated by combining what remains in the British Library with the Fitzwilliam draft. In the homophonic slow introduction, both at the beginning and when it recurs after the fugue, Handel has written melody and bass. For the contrapuntal fast section, however, more is provided. The bass is always present and in some passages he provides all parts. Generally, however, only enough is given to maintain the contrapuntal framework.

Considering these points, the traditional paradigm may be restated as follows: in the oratorio autographs Handel typically composed first a short score. Arias were composed according to two different methods. If large forces were required, he began by writing the basso continuo, with or without figures, and principal melodic part in voice or, during ritornellos and orchestral interludes, first violin. In more sparsely accompanied arias (admittedly a minority in the oratorios), however, he wrote out all the parts from the very beginning.

In choruses (and probably in orchestral pieces as well) the texture determines the working method. In fugal passages Handel generally wrote first the vocal parts and the basso. In homophonic passages, he sometimes provided melody and bass only, but in chordal passages where the sopranos do not carry an important melody he provided the continuo and first violin part (if it is of sufficient interest), leaving the vocal parts above the bass to be 'realized' from the continuo during orchestration. Generally some of the orchestral parts were provided in certain passages—in both arias and choruses the amount of filling in to be done could vary enormously.

At a later point, after finishing an act or oratorio, Handel would go through the score orchestrating it fully. However, he had clearly thought out the orchestration before writing the short score, for appropriate instrumental designations were provided at the beginning of every stave. The music of recitatives, whose texts and appropriate clefs alone were provided in short score, was written during the orchestration or filling-in period. In many cases, though certainly not all, the overture and other instrumental pieces were added (though not necessarily composed) last.

Secondary Sources: Conducting Scores

By far the most significant of the sources not in Handel's own hand are the conducting scores contained in the Staats- und Universitätsbibliothek, Hamburg. These were copied from the autograph by Handel's copyists, in this period mainly by Smith, S1, and S5, before first performance. These copies were used as the principal source from which the orchestral and vocal parts were copied, and presumably the complete conducting score was used by Handel in rehearsal and in performance of the works. The scores often contain revisions in Handel's hand, and sometimes these are not included in the autograph. Hans Dieter Clausen has written a guide to these sources.[23]

The conducting scores contain a number of passages that were covered over by other sheets and partial sheets. Upon direct examination, one can sometimes see under and through these sheets, allowing a reconstruction of rejected passages. Such investigation shows that a surprisingly large number of changes were made in the autograph after the conducting score was copied. For instance, in *Belshazzar* the arias 'O Sacred Oracles' and 'Lament not thus' were apparently both copied into the conducting score as full da capo arias, which Handel later shortened. This is apparent because passages belonging only to the full da capo forms of the arias are visible underneath the added sheets on pages 9 and 48–9. Winton Dean suggests that the revision of these two arias are referred to in the letter Handel wrote to Charles Jennens on 2 October 1744, in which Handel mentions that he has curtailed much of the music because of the length of the libretto.[24] Since Handel finished Act I on 3 September, Act II on 10 September, and Act III on 23 October, the conducting score for Acts I and II was most likely at least in preparation at the time he received the Act III text from Jennens. This was probably typical: Smith regularly began to copy performing scores while Handel was still composing. Thus the time elapsed between completion of individual acts or the entire autograph and the copying of the conducting score was usually short. Because conducting scores were also used for revivals, however, they often give a confusing text.

Small-scale revisions that are shared between the two scores can be revealing. For instance, Handel excised a short passage from 'No longer, fate, relentless frown' in *Hercules* for a purely musical reason, and this brief passage also had to be removed from the conducting score (see Ex. 4.2). This is but one of several examples. The fact that Handel was willing to go to the trouble to make such a minor musical change even though it involved correcting more than one score reveals the importance of such revisions to him. He was not a haphazard and careless composer or adapter, but an artist who clearly took care in revising. If Handel found revision of details worth making, then they deserve far closer scrutiny than they have hitherto received.

---

[23] Clausen, *Händels Direktionspartituren*. Also see Clausen's chapter in Terence Best (ed.), *Handel Collections and their History* (Oxford: Clarendon Press, 1993), 10–28.

[24] This letter is quoted in Otto Erich Deutsch, *Handel: A Documentary Biography* (London: Adam and Charles Black, 1955; repr. New York: Da Capo, 1974), 595. Also see below, Ch. 8.

3

The Process of Creation: Forethought and Spontaneity

HANDEL'S 'precompositional' autograph materials include three basic kinds of items: sketches, drafts, and fragments. The bulk of his sketches and rejected drafts, along with detached sections from other autographs and Handel's hand-written copies of works by other composers, reside now in the Fitzwilliam Museum, Cambridge.[1] To these we can add the drafts and fragments sometimes found in the British Library autographs.[2] Throughout this book the term sketch refers to musical ideas, generally brief, that Handel more than likely jotted down before setting out to compose a piece in score, though some sketching may have taken place during the process of composing. A draft, on the other hand, is a piece that was laid out in score in a more 'public' manner: after all, drafts were ultimately to be viewed by copyists, whereas sketches served the composer alone. Drafts apparently originally formed part of (or at least were originally destined for) the autograph composing score, but were rejected and in many cases replaced by new settings. Most often drafts were never fully orchestrated, but the score layout makes it clear that Handel intended to do so.

The term fragment sometimes bears more than one meaning, but I apply it exclusively to drafts that Handel himself did not complete. There are a number of drafts that only survive in part, but for our purposes these are not true fragments. Of course, in such cases it is not always possible to tell whether a draft was completed, a fact which will be pointed out when examples arise. (The relevant sketches, drafts, and fragments for the five oratorios examined here are listed in Table 3.1.)

Handel's sketches—this chapter's primary concern—survive merely by chance. His method of sketching distinguishes him from Bach, the greatest number of whose sketches seem to be memory aids written at the bottom of

---

[1] MSS 251–64. A description of this material is included in the preamble of Burrows and Ronish, *A Catalogue of Handel's Musical Autographs*, pp. xx–xxii.

[2] There are also, of course, fragments among the Fitzwilliam materials, but those of importance for this book's purposes form part of the autograph scores.

TABLE 3.1. *Sketches, drafts, and fragments*

Oratorio	Sources	Pieces
SKETCHES		
Hercules	FM MUS MS 262, p. 12	Chorus, 'And pitying heav'n' Aria, 'Ah, think what ills'
Belshazzar	FM MUS MS 259, pp. 37–8	Overture, allegro Aria, 'Alternate hopes'
Solomon	FM MUS MS 259, pp. 67–73	Air, 'When the sun o'er yonder hills' 'Thrice bless'd be the king' 'Pious king' 'Praise the Lord' 'From the east unto the west' 'Swell the full chorus'
DRAFTS		
Semele	FM MUS MS 259, p. 79	Arioso, 'Somnus awake', first version
Hercules	FM MUS MS 263, p. 79	Aria, 'Banish love from thy breast'[a]
Solomon	FM MUS MS 259, pp. 71–3	Aria, 'Golden Columns', earlier setting Aria, 'How green our fertile pastures look'
Susanna	FM MUS MS 259, pp. 75–80	Duet, 'When thou art nigh' Aria, 'The Parent Bird'
	FM MUS MS 262, pp. 47–50	Overture, earlier version
FRAGMENTS		
Semele	BL RM 20.f.7	Chorus 'Avert these omens'
Hercules	BL RM 20.e.8	Duet 'Joys of freedom'
Belshazzar	BL RM 20.d.10	Aria 'The leafy honours'

[a] This page is something of a puzzle. It is clear exactly where it would appear in the autograph, but it is not complete, and there is nothing on the page's reverse side, even though the page has been heavily revised. Conceivably there was originally another page forming a bifolio, part of which has been excised. Alternately, if it was always a single leaf, it is possible that Handel intended it to be pasted over one page of the autograph.

a recto in the composing scores to record the immediate continuation of the music on the next page while the ink dried.[3] Handel's sketches, conversely, were written on separate sheets. While a certain number of sketches were possibly memory aids, others show Handel in the process of creating material to be used in the autograph. There is no evidence, however, that he made

[3] Robert Marshall, 'The Sketches', *The Music of Johann Sebastian Bach* (New York: Schirmer Books, 1989), 111. Handel never made 'continuation sketches' of this sort. In Bach's composing scores there are also a certain number of sketches that represent earlier versions of thematic ideas, but according to Marshall, 'the sketches and drafts testify overwhelmingly . . . that Bach's initial melodic ideas were normally completely formed by the time he set them to paper' (117).

sketchbooks. The paper types and layout of the sketches instead suggest that he randomly used empty staves on rejected drafts or other scrap pages and sometimes blank sheets: the pages concerned were often contemporary with his composing scores, but occasionally he picked up folios that were years older. There is little, in short, to suggest that Handel's sketching process was either methodical or extensive.

It has been assumed that there were originally many more sketches, but we cannot know how many.[4] A relatively high number of sketches have survived for certain works, such as *Solomon*. Combined with the wealth of borrowings from Telemann, documented by John Roberts,[5] the borrowings from Steffani and Porta,[6] as well as self-borrowings, these provide us with a wealth of precompositional material to serve as a basis for a study of Handel's compositional process in that work. In fact, it is questionable in the case of *Solomon* whether there were ever any more sketches, a need for which would presumably have been limited by Handel's possession of the Telemann scores from which he borrowed.[7] As to their function in Handel's compositional process, very little distinction can be drawn between certain types of sketches and borrowings; indeed, some sketches *are* borrowings.[8]

These materials—sketches, fragments, and drafts—are obviously not an end in themselves, but merely a means through which we can approach a fascinating issue: exactly how did Handel go about composing? Addressing this question more than forty years ago, Gerald Abraham compared Handel's propensity to work from a borrowed 'datum' to improvisation, a theory that arises from two observations. First, a number of historical documents attest that Handel was a superlative master of spontaneous improvisation on the organ and harpsichord. In addition to Mattheson's report, quoted by Abraham, that

    [4] See Dean, *Handel's Dramatic Oratorios*, 87.
    [5] John Roberts, 'Handel's Borrowings from Telemann: An Inventory', *Göttinger Händel-Beiträge*, 1 (1984), 147–71.
    [6] These are listed in Dean, *Handel's Dramatic Oratorios*, 646. See also Roberts (ed.), *Handel Sources: Material for the Study of Handel's Borrowings*, 9 vols. (New York, Garland Publishing, 1986–8). The question of why Handel borrowed has been raised in many publications. Recent works on this matter include George Buelow's 'The Case for Handel's Borrowings: The Judgement of Three Centuries' and John Roberts's 'Why did Handel Borrow?', both in Stanley Sadie and Anthony Hicks (eds.), *Handel Tercentenary Collection* (Ann Arbor: UMI Research Press, 1987), and John Winemiller, 'Handel's Borrowing and Swift's Bee: Handel's "Curious" Practice and the Theory of Transformative Imitation' (Ph.D. diss., University of Chicago, 1994). None of the authors would claim to know the definitive answer to this question, and it is not my intention in this book to try to resolve it. I am concerned with the borrowings only as materials with which Handel worked—in other words, their role in the compositional process.
    [7] See Roberts, 'Handel's Borrowings from Telemann', 148.
    [8] For instance, two of the Fitzwilliam volumes (MUS MS 260, pp. 51–2 and MUS MS 263, pp. 75–6) contain pages on which Handel copied excerpts from Habermann's masses that were used in *Jephtha*. See Dean, *Handel's Dramatic Oratorios*, 624 and Burrows and Ronish, *A Catalogue of Handel's Musical Autographs*, 241–3, 253–8.

Handel was a great composer of fugues, especially *ex tempore*, one could cite Thomas Morell's account of the composition of a chorus in *Judas Maccabeus*:

'Well', says he [Handel], 'and how are you to go on?' 'Why, we are to suppose an engagement, and that the Israelites have conquered, and so begin with a chorus as
Fallen is the Foe
or, something like it.' 'No, I will have this', and began working it, as it is, upon the Harpsichord. 'Well, go on.' 'I will bring you more tomorrow.' 'No, something now',
'So fall thy Foes, O Lord'
'that will do', and immediately carried on the composition as we have it in that admirable chorus. . .[9]

Second, in Abraham's day a majority of Handel's known borrowings were incipits; the composer often seemed to take merely the ritornello or opening head-motif and from it compose an entire movement. According to Abraham, this is related to improvisation, where one begins with a borrowed subject. Thus Handel's approach to composition could be described as improvisatory.

A rigorous critique of Abraham's theory might begin by attempting to delineate the knotty issues raised by the term 'improvisatory'. There are surely differences, first of all, between the eighteenth-century usage of the term (as a matter of practice with no value judgement assigned to it), Abraham's understanding of Baroque improvisation (informed, but no doubt coloured by a need to save Handel for the vestiges of what might be called 'the cult of originality'—the Romantic view that a work must be entirely original in order to be a work of genius), and our own understanding of improvisation.

In the eighteenth century on the whole, composition and improvisation went hand in hand, a relationship contemporary theorists realized. Johann Mattheson, for instance, clearly perceives the relationship between composing and improvising (albeit on a mundane level) when he writes in his editor's preface to the 1721 edition of Friedrich Niedt's *Musikalische Handleitung*, part 2: 'it is my belief that the present guide can actually be of much more service to *unimaginative composers and organists deficient in improvising* than to those who only wish to embellish the thorough-bass with some elegance'.[10] Furthermore, Baroque genres such as variations, partitas, chaconnes, and many others have been called stylized written versions of old performance practices.[11] In short, composition and improvisation were inseparable during

---

[9] Hodgkin MSS, published by the Historical Manuscripts Commission, perhaps written in 1769. See Dean, *Handel's Dramatic Oratorios*, 461.

[10] Niedt, *The Musical Guide*, 67.

[11] Hans-Peter Schmitz, *Die Kunst der Verzierung*, 25. This point of view is discussed in Elaine Sisman, 'Haydn's Variations' (Ph.D. diss., Princeton University, 1978), 36.

the Baroque age. Therefore Abraham's attempt to relate Handel's borrowing practice to improvisation rings true to the spirit of the age and, on the level of analogy, it succeeds in placing his compositional process within the compositional practices of his day.

The difficulty arises in the particular manner in which Abraham describes Handel's working method:

> The point that Handel often borrowed or repeated mere introductions . . . appears to throw light on a peculiar aspect of his creative processes. . . . There is ample evidence that Handel frequently began to compose by playing the harpsichord, starting from the first favourite cliché that came under his fingers—whether his own, someone else's, or common property of the age, he probably neither knew nor cared—and allowing it to grow into something that was usually in the end absolutely his and his alone.[12]

Behind this description, whether or not Abraham intended to propagate it, lies the notion that Handel began composition with an opening ritornello and proceeded in a linear manner to the end of the piece—a model which, both consciously and unconsciously, has played a dominant role in our understanding of Baroque composition. In this chapter I pursue the limitations of this theory of 'linear' composition as a model for Handel's compositional process, offering alternative ways of viewing his process of composing from its earliest stages (the precompositional sketches) to the finished score. Accordingly the first section covers the relative chronology of the composition of the ritornello and the vocal body of arias and choruses, a chronology controlled by structural aspects of the music. The second section deals with the implications of linear vs. non-linear models for Handel's borrowings, while the third section explores non-linear aspects of fugal composition.

If the first three parts of the chapter deal with Abraham's 'text', the last section addresses his 'subtext'. To my mind Abraham's improvisatory model of Handel's borrowing attempts to preserve the status of the composer for an audience whose understanding of the nature of genius includes complete originality as a requisite element. Handel's 'questionable' practice of borrowing could now be seen as a function of one of the most potent manifestations of compositional genius: 'spontaneous' improvisation. But in accomplishing this transformation of the borrowing 'problem' Abraham raises a momentous question: to what extent can Handel's compositional process be described as 'spontaneous' (the view I believe that Abraham meant to propagate); and to what degree did he plan a work or aspects of a work before the 'event' of

---

[12] Abraham, 'Some Points of Style', 266.

composition? Such questions are perhaps ultimately impossible to answer. The relationship between planning and inspiration is apt to be a fluid one, changing from piece to piece, or even from moment to moment during the act of composition, and we cannot expect the state of the autographs to detail all, or even most, of Handel's mental processes. But certain questions are worth asking for the sake of the light they shed upon important issues. By pursuing the unanswerable, Part IV uncovers two models that explain certain aspects of Handel's compositional process.

The Ritornello Problem

In response to the basic question 'how did Handel compose?' one might suggest that at times he apparently began at the beginning—at least this is what the autograph materials, if interpreted naively, might imply. The written record of the composition of 'Ah, think what ills' from *Hercules*, for instance, starts with sketches of two versions of the ritornello (Ex. 3.1, sketches A and B).[13] The second (sketch B) replaces the head-motif of the first (sketch A), alters somewhat the second and third ritornello elements (marked in the example) while maintaining them in essence, and provides new cadential bars featuring sixteenth notes. The final version (*HG* 4: 114) extends the head-motif (which went through two slightly different versions in the autograph score) and adds a new musical idea just after it, curtails the ritornello by eliminating its third element, and excises the sixteenth notes from the cadential material.[14]

By the time Handel penned 'Ah, think what ills' in the autograph score, then, he had worked out—at least in a rough form—the opening ritornello, though he was to make further slight changes. We cannot, of course, know just how far ahead into the aria he had thought at this point. Indeed, we cannot be absolutely certain that the creation of the ritornello was the first compositional event. As Laurence Dreyfus points out, 'composition—or, for that matter, analysis or criticism—cannot rely on a verifiable starting point'.[15] But if we adopt Abraham's view, we might see this aria as an example of Handel's

---

[13] Handel's first sketch leaves one ambiguous matter to the interpreter: in Ex. 3.1(*a*) it is unclear whether the last bar is intended as a substitute for the antepenultimate bar (bracketed), or if both bars should be present, as transcribed.

[14] It should be noted, however, that the head-motif from the closing ritornello is closer to Sketch B than is the opening ritornello. We need not conclude, however that Sketch B was intended solely for the final ritornello, although this view would not contradict the paradigm of Handel's compositional process I shall advance in this chapter.

[15] Laurence Dreyfus, *Bach and the Patterns of Invention* (Cambridge: Harvard University Press, 1996), 101.

Ex. 3.1. (*a*) Sketches for 'Ah! think what ills' in *Hercules*, FM MUS MS 262, p. 12: opening ritornello, first version.

propensity to work from a 'datum', indicating an improvisatory approach to composition. The fact that the ritornello of 'Ah! think what ills' is not a borrowing, as far as we know, is less important than the fact that, as a sketch, it is precompositional and thus potentially a datum for improvisation.

The vocal sections of the aria, however, hardly represent an improvisation

EX. 3.1. (*b*) Sketches for 'Ah! think what ills' in *Hercules*, FM MUS MS 262, p. 12: opening ritornello, second version.

upon material from the ritornello. Admittedly the jagged vocal line in bars 23–5 relates to bars 7–8 of the ritornello, as do the chromatic lines throughout the aria. But the vocal line is in fact largely distinct from the ritornello melody.[16]

Such a distinction between the ritornello and the vocal sections is often found in arias with borrowed ritornelli. A famous example occurs in 'Hush ye pretty warbling quire' in *Acis and Galatea*, whose ritornello derives from an aria in Keiser's *Octavia*, 'Wallet nicht zu laut'.[17] Handel uses the ritornello to represent birdsong, while the contrasting vocal section of the aria presents Galatea's attempt to silence the birds. Now Abraham views certain instances of departure from ritornello material as evidence of improvisation:

---

[16] The bass line of bar 1 appears underneath a sustained C at the vocal entrance. This is a short-breathed and simple example of the technique of writing a new melody over a pre-existent bass, which Abraham views as related to improvisation. But the passages involved are very brief.

[17] John Roberts, 'Handel's Borrowings from Keiser', *Göttinger Händel-Beiträge*, 2 (1986), 51–76.

the melody itself is abandoned and not heard again, but the basic idea of the quietly throbbing repeated chords goes on and seems to generate a fresh melody, indeed a whole entirely fresh movement. Far from being exceptional, that is an exceedingly common procedure with Handel. . . . it is clear that a large proportion of his published work originated in private improvisation . . .[18]

Yet surely such a model does not explain cases in which the ritornello and vocal materials have virtually nothing to do with each other. In the examples we have seen, the borrowings do not represent data for improvisation so much as data against which other material is juxtaposed.

In certain cases the ritornello and the vocal sections derive from different sources. The opening ritornello of the chorus 'Righteous Daniel', cut from *Susanna* before first performance, is indebted to a theme which appears in a number of previous works,[19] including the Chaconne from the C minor Suite for two clavecins (*HWV* 446) of *c*.1703/6; 'Cara pianta' in *Apollo e Dafne* (*c*.1708); the first movement of the Sonata in G minor (*HWV* 404) of *c*.1718/20; and in *Alcina* ('Dall'orror di notte cieca') of 1735. The *Susanna* chorus follows *Apollo e Dafne* and the sonata more closely than the other pieces. (The *Apollo* and *Susanna* ritornellos are transcribed in Ex. 3.2(*a*) and (*b*)). In the autograph of *Susanna* Handel takes down the pre-existent idea almost literally, melody and bass only, as a ritornello. Thereafter the chorus develops along different lines. The first four bars of the vocal entrance, a passage that recurs throughout the chorus, indeed derive from the theme (Ex. 3.2(*c*)). However, the theme in its original form never appears after the opening ritornello, which is among the passages Handel decided to cut before orchestration. This seems at first to be precisely the sort of borrowing as 'datum' that Abraham was talking about. In the case of 'Righteous Daniel' it could even be argued that the fact that the chorus turned out to have little to do with the original datum was Handel's reason for cancelling the ritornello.

In spite of its appeal, however, Abraham's theory does not apply so easily to 'Righteous Daniel' when other facts about the piece are considered. Much of this work derives not from the incipit, but from other pieces: 'Cangia i gemiti' from the duet 'Langue, geme' and 'Thou hast prevented him' from the Coronation Anthem 'The King shall rejoice'.[20] Thus the borrowed ritornello served as a source only for the first twenty-eight measures of the piece. The role of 'improvisation', then, is far more limited than we originally imagined.

---

[18] Abraham, 'Some Points of Style', 266.
[19] The relationship of 'Righteous Daniel' to this set of borrowings has not previously been acknowledged.
[20] I am grateful to John Roberts for graciously sharing his discovery of these borrowings with me.

This example neatly illustrates how Abraham's idea has become dated and must be revised. Abraham founded his argument on the fact that Handel generally borrowed material to serve as an incipit, such as a ritornello.

EX. 3.2. (*a*) *Apollo e Dafne*, opening ritornello of 'Cara pianta'; (*b*) *Susanna*, original opening ritornello of 'Righteous Daniel', BL RM 20.f.8, fo. 108ᵛ; (*c*) 'Righteous Daniel', vocal entrance

Ex. 3.2. *(cont.)*

Senza Ripieni

Ex. 3.2. (*cont.*)

This is certainly a common type of borrowing (still perhaps the most heavily documented borrowing procedure), but recent research—primarily the work of John Roberts[21]—has identified other typical borrowing habits of Handel. These include the use of pre-existent material as internal matter and the use of two or more borrowed passages in different positions in a new work.

Abraham's theory, then, illuminates only a circumscribed gamut of works. It does not explain arias in which the ritornello and the vocal body of the aria or chorus each have their own entirely distinct material. The use of contrasting

---

[21] See the bibliography under 'Roberts, John'.

material for the ritornello vs. the vocal body is an aspect of the structure of the aria that was more than likely planned in advance; the creation of entirely different material for the vocal sections of the aria, therefore, hardly constitutes 'improvisation upon a theme' in the same way that spontaneous composition of a fugue does. This is particularly apparent when the vocal body of the aria is borrowed from a different source than the ritornello, as is by and large true of 'Righteous Daniel'. Neither does Abraham's model help us when the ritornello and vocal body share the same material, as the following discussion will disclose.

A model that underlies Abraham's description of Handel improvising from a borrowed incipit—the assumption that Handel composed in a 'linear' manner, from beginning to end of a piece—has enjoyed a broad sweep of influence upon Handel scholarship. This idea of 'linear' composition to some degree girds Paul Brainard's excellent study of ritornello and aria construction in Handel and Bach, for instance.[22] If one tries to extract from Brainard's individual analyses a general overview of Handel's method of composition, however, one finds two very different *modi operandi*. Although these models appear to contradict each other, in one case Brainard applies both to the same aria, 'Consider, fond shepherd' from *Acis and Galatea*. Significantly, this aria differs from the pieces we have examined thus far in that its vocal sections share material with the ritornello.

On the one hand, several of Brainard's remarks seemingly imply that Handel had thought through some of the body of the aria before composing the opening ritornello:

The introduction of 'Consider, fond shepherd' thus falls into one of the largest and most characteristic classes of Handelian ritornellos, in that it constitutes a kind of synopsis of prominent musical/textual events from (especially) the opening and closing portions of the A vocal section.[23]

Similarly, he later describes the ritornello as 'a résumé before the event'.[24]

On the other hand, however, Brainard seems to suggest (like Abraham) that Handel actually began composition with nothing in mind except the ritornello as a datum:

there seems to be a general readiness on Handel's part to let the later restatements of his ritornello be (as it were) filtered through the musical events of the intervening vocal section(s), producing subtle modifications . . . Handel's improvisatory approach to such matters may also be seen, as Gerald Abraham and others have pointed out, in

---

[22] See Brainard, 'Aria and Ritornello'.
[23] Ibid. 24.   [24] Ibid. 26.

his much-discussed expropriation of material from his own and others' compositions. Of obvious relevance to our topic is the well-known fact that in an aria Handel's *direct* borrowing is often limited to the ritornello, following which the remainder of the source-composition is either ignored or so extensively rewritten as to constitute a new work.[25]

Brainard thus seems to embrace the view that Handel composed linearly, from beginning to end of an aria. This is the paradigm that he presumably adopts when he describes an excision between bars 28 and 29 of the same aria, 'Consider, fond shepherd,' which he believes to result from Handel's discovery, during the composition of the A vocal section, that the text does not fit the passage he destined for it.

Thus Brainard's discussion does not adopt a consistent paradigm or model of Handel's compositional process; indeed, it is difficult to know whether he means to describe the actual compositional process, or the aria itself as heard.[26] Is the ritornello a sampling of important melodies that arise again in the course of the aria (therefore composed with text-setting already in mind), or is it a datum from which Handel spontaneously improvised? It would be unfair to insist that Brainard cannot have it both ways, for in different cases either scenario might be true. More troubling is the fact that Brainard applies both models to the same aria without addressing the resulting inconsistency.

The effect of a ritornello having changed after filtering through the aria (as in 'Consider, fond shepherd') might not in all cases result from linear and improvisatory composition, but may rather constitute a revision that serves to correct an oversight on the composer's part. In arias where the ritornello and the voice share exactly the same material, Handel often (although not always) considered text-setting, and therefore the body of the aria, *before* he composed the ritornello. Brainard's description of the ritornello as a 'résumé before the event' thus reflects one of Handel's methods of composition.[27] This is certainly the sensible way of going about it: a composer faced with the task of writing a da capo aria of this sort (that is, with literal or nearly literal 'melodic preview') for a specific text does not start with merely a ritornello as datum; the text often serves as the datum. Even exclusively orchestral material, never

---

[25] Ibid. 31.

[26] Recently Brainard has more carefully explored the issue of the 'quoting' vs. the 'non-quoting' ritornello in Bach's arias. See Brainard, 'The "Non-Quoting" Ritornello in Bach's Arias', in *A Bach Tribute: Essays in Honor of William H. Scheide* (Kassel: Bärenreiter, 1993), 27–44.

[27] Handel was not the only composer to compose in this manner. There is at least one instance in the works of Mozart. The ritornelli for the two arias from *Der Schauspieldirektor* do not appear in Mozart's autograph score, but they are included in what is probably the first copy of the score in the Bayerische Staatsbibliothek, Munich, written either for or shortly after the Schonbrunn première of the work (see Stefan Kunze, 'Mozarts *Schauspieldirektor*', *Mozart Jahrbuch* 1962/3, 156). Presumably Mozart planned to have ritornelli from the beginning, but wrote them only after he had composed the body of each aria.

sung by voices, sometimes grew from consideration of the text—its *Affekt* if not its setting. For instance, both the undulating sixteenth notes and the Telemann borrowing from 'Kein Vogel kann' in the ritornello of 'May no rash intruder', both of which appear only in the orchestra, were clearly inspired by the text; the first is linked to 'their slumbers *prolong*', the second is imitation of the nightingales. These couplings of text and music must have been apparent to Handel from the beginning, and therefore consideration of the contents of the body of the chorus preceded the creation of the ritornello. This must to a degree have been the case even with 'Ah, think what ills' (Ex. 3.1 above) where the chromatic sequences in the ritornello are ultimately associated with the text 'endless pain'; it is highly probable that the text inspired the chromaticism. Thus even the fact of a pre-existing ritornello does not always mean that the text was not Handel's first concern.

It is true that the use of a limited number of poetic forms in the wordbooks sometimes made it possible for Handel to fit old music to a new text, and there is ample evidence that in revision he frequently did so—a process discussed in Chapter 9. Nonetheless, empirical evidence for his 'retroactive approach' to ritornello composition, to use Brainard's own useful phrase, can also be found among the sketches. For instance, Handel began 'Alternate hopes and fears' from *Belshazzar* by sketching the head-motif with the text underneath (see Ex. 3.3). In both versions of the completed aria (presented as versions A and B in Chrysander's score) this head-motif, though altered from the sketch, is preceded by an eighteen-bar ritornello, previewing the aria's material.[28]

Perhaps the clearest evidence for the retroactive composition of a ritornello comes from *Solomon*. The Fitzwilliam sketches for 'When the sun o'er yonder hills' offer a rare opportunity to follow the genesis of a Handel aria from its earliest traceable stages to the final version.[29] These sketches allow us to recreate Handel's compositional procedure (Pl. 3.1, transcribed in Ex. 3.4). He began on the first two systems of the manuscript page by composing a setting of the entire text of the aria—text, vocal line, and bass only—in common time and tonally closed. This sketch not only corresponds closely to the first vocal statement in the finished aria (*HG* 26: 143, 2/3, bb. 18–40), but, as we shall see, also constitutes the primary musical material from which much

---

[28] To 20th-c. Americans, it looks as though the word 'alternate' is badly set, with stress on the second syllable, but this is clearly what Handel intended. In the second setting the accent on the second syllable is maintained. Handel's setting matches Johnson's *Dictionary* (and modern British pronunciation), where the second syllable of 'alternate' is similarly stressed. The word 'alternately' is set this way in 'But hark! the heav'nly sphere turns round' in *Semele*, bb. 21–2 (*HG* 7: 141, 2/3–3/1).

[29] FM MUS MS 259, p. 67.

EX. 3.3. Sketch for 'Alternate hopes' in *Belshazzar*, FM MUS MS 259, p. 38

Al- ter-nate hopes   and   fears

3.1. Sketches for 'When the sun' in *Solomon*, FM MUS MS 259, p. 67

of the aria grew (Ex. 3.4(*a*)) Then, on the third system of the page, he revised the first phrase, reworking it both melodically and harmonically, this time not bothering to include the text (Ex. 3.4(*b*) B).

At this point, apparently, Handel decided that the metre should be changed from duple to triple, and he added to the middle of the third system of the manuscript page a triple-time version of the revised first phrase (Ex. 3.4(*c*)).

At a later time, Handel composed the music that will occur with the third statement of the text in the aria (Ex. 3.4(*d*); final setting, bb. 58 ff. = HG 26: 144, 3/7–145, 1/3). The fact that sketch D appears at the end of the third system and

Ex. 3.4. Four sketches for 'When the sun' in *Solomon*, FM MUS MS 259, p. 67

(a)

g: i⁶₄   V   VI   iv⁶ ii⁶   V   i⁶   i   iv   V   i

in the empty space that remained on the second system probably means that Handel had already written the sketches for 'Thrice bless'd' on the fourth system. This suggests that he began composing these airs by looking at the text and sketching musical ideas for more than one piece at a time.[30]

---

[30] Sketch D still must have been prepared before Handel had begun his autograph score of 'When the sun', since the ritornello will draw upon it before it appears in the aria. See below.

EX. 3.4. (*cont.*)

(b)

(c)

(d)

By the time he actually sat down to compose the aria, apparently, Handel
had thus worked out most of his essential thematic material in its texted form.
And at least one major revision—a shift of metre from common time to triple
time—had taken place.[31]

Particularly important in understanding the way in which Handel expands

---

[31] Such metrical changes or variations are discussed in treatises of Handel's day. In the second and
third chapters of part II of his *Musikalische Handlung* of 1721, dedicated to variations of the thorough-bass,

the sketches into an entire aria are the harmonic changes that make this structural expansion possible. Apart from the first two bars, to which I shall return
later, sketch A corresponds closely to the vocal opening of the final setting
until the final phrase (though inessential harmonies in the sketch are at times
removed from the final score in order to accommodate the shift from duple
to triple metre). In their final phrases (sketch A, bb. 13–17; score, bb. 32–40
= *HG* 26: 143, 4/3–144, 1/4), however, the two versions diverge dramatically, especially in regard to tonality and harmonic use. In sketch A, this
phrase contains a typical, diatonic harmonic progression involving common
cadential chords, the tonic, subdominant, supertonic, submediant, and dominant (marked in Ex. 3.4).

In the finished aria Handel began expanding the sketch by repeating the
cadence to the minor dominant (that appears in sketch A, b. 13 and final
score, b. 30) rather than returning to the tonic (which is delayed until bb.
55–6 = *HG* 26: 144, 3/4–5). In doing this he chose not to maintain the bland
harmonies of this original phrase. Instead, the new version is richer, containing modal shifts achieved by chromatic alteration of pitches, and deceptive
resolutions, before the final cadence in 37–40.[32]

In spite of the new tonal content, other musical features suggest that the
last phrase of the finished aria is clearly an expansion of the last phrase of the
sketch. Both versions contain a three-note idea beginning with a dotted quarter note (this first appears with the second statement of the text 'he shall ever'
in Ex. 3.4), which is presented sequentially in stepwise ascent.[33] In the finished aria, the sequence is expanded by one additional statement (*HG* 26: 143,
4/3–144, 1/1). A process of expansion is applied to the cadence as well. Certainly the cadential formulas are similar (Ex. 3.4(*a*), bb. 16–17 and final setting, bb. 37–8), but in the final version the cadence is doubled: a deceptive
cadence is followed by an authentic cadence.

Handel's additive method of composing this aria thus far resembles the
composing process discussed by Joseph Riepel in his *Anfangsgründe zur*

Niedt demonstrates how a given thorough-bass may be recast in various metres (*The Musical Guide*, 75–8,
88–93). Johann Mattheson, who edited the 1721 edition of the second part of Niedt's treatise, discusses
recasting the metre of melodies in his *Vollkommene Capellmeister*. Other examples of Handel's own metrical changes can be found in C. Steven LaRue, 'Metric Reorganization as an Aspect of Handel's Compositional Process', *Journal of Musicology*, 8 (1990), 477–90.

[32] Beginning with the final beat of bar 31, the chord progression in D minor is: V^7 of III / III i /
Major IV ii^7 / V^6 / Major IV^6 / V^6, etc.

[33] It is not a strict sequence in either passage, of course. At the end of sketch A, the second statement
of this three-note idea is varied; the original conjunct motion is abandoned, and it becomes a triad of vii.
In the final version of the third statement the original three-note idea is altered to two pitches, and thus
this 'motif' undergoes rhythmic transformations throughout the sequence. Apparently the sequence, particularly the rising stepwise melodic line that it produces, is more important than the motif itself.

musikalischen Setzkunst and later enriched by Heinrich Christoph Koch in *Versuch einer Anleitung zur Composition*.[34] Though scholars have attempted to demonstrate manifestations of Riepel's theories in the music of the late eighteenth century, Riepel was far closer to Handel's time, and an affinity exists between Riepel's and Handel's approaches to composition:

> Riepel, drawing largely on the compositional practice before 1750, arrives at a generally symmetrical expansion, tending to treat each phrase equally . . . Riepel explains that a piece may be made longer by repetitions (Wiederholungen) of all or part of a phrase, through expansion (Ausdähnung) by adding new notes and measures, especially to a contrasting harmonic progression, by insertion (Einschiebsel) of phrases or smaller units between or within phrases, and by the doubling of cadences (Verdoppelung der Cadenzen).[35]

In essence Riepel's expansion techniques apply closely to Handel's expansion of the sketches for 'When the sun'. Between the last phrases of sketch A and the corresponding phrase in the finished version, for example, Handel expanded the sequence by restating the motif (Koch describes this as a specific type of repetition involving a new pitch level). Here (and at the end of the ritornello), Handel 'doubled the cadences' of the sketches by adding a deceptive cadence before the tonic. And in the next chapter we shall see several examples of Einschiebsel—'insertion of phrases or smaller units within or between phrases'. No doubt many of these techniques are relevant to improvisation as well as composition, although the actual process of expanding the sketches does not fit our conventional notion of 'improvisation'. At some levels, then, it is difficult to draw a meaningful distinction between the two concepts.

The various versions of the first phrase of 'When the sun' as represented in the sketches raise interesting questions about the intended structure. While the first phrase ends in B flat (III in G minor) in both versions, in sketch A the first two bars are clearly in G minor, and the second two bars go directly to B flat. Sketch B is more discursive, inflecting F major and C minor on the path to B flat, and departing from G minor much sooner. Sketch C (eliminating for the moment the question of whether Handel intended a ritornello) weakens the tonic even further by eliminating the half note G in the bass: but, of course, this may be a mere side-effect of the metrical change rather than a goal of the revision. It is impossible to know whether, when Handel

---

[34] Joseph Riepel, *Anfangsgründe zur musikalischen Setzkunst*, 5 vols. (Regensburg, Frankfurt, and Augsburg, 1752–68); Heinrich Christoph Koch, *Versuch einer Anleitung zur Composition*, 3 vols. (Leipzig, 1782–93).

[35] Elaine Sisman, 'Small and Expanded Forms: Koch's Model and Haydn's Music', *Musical Quarterly*, 68 (1982), 444–75 at 449.

first wrote down sketch A, he intended to compose an introductory ritornello. Certain facts might seem to suggest that he did not. Many of the common-time arias in *Solomon* begin, like sketch A, with a half note in the bass and the voice commencing on the third beat, without a ritornello.[36] Furthermore, if the beginning of sketch A were preceded by the ritornello as it exists in the finished aria, the emphasis on G minor at the vocal entrance would be unnecessary. It is conceivable, then, that Handel corrected the first four bars (in sketch B), which constitute the vocal entrance and its harmonization, because he had decided to compose a ritornello that ended strongly in the tonic.

On the other hand, because these sketches do not yet reflect the larger harmonic structure of the aria, there is no strong reason to suggest that Handel did not plan an introductory ritornello from the beginning.[37] In an aria in which the ritornello follows the vocal line so precisely, it only stands to reason that Handel would first have conceived of the melodies as they were to set the text, leaving the ritornello for later.[38] Remarkably, he eventually formed the ritornello by the simplest method possible, by joining sketches C and D, both expanding the cadence at the end of sketch D and transforming it for its new instrumental idiom. Though he may have planned the appearance of sketches C and D as a ritornello from the start, they were clearly first conceived as settings of the text in the aria proper, not the ritornello *per se*. As we have seen, each sketch receives its own clef, and the two passages appear to have been written at different times. Moreover, sketch D matches its occurrence in the vocal portion of the aria rather than the varied form of the ritornello. In short, this aria provides a supreme example of Handel's retroactive approach to ritornello composition.

It is clear, then, that we cannot always simply assume that Handel generally began in a strict sense with the composition of the ritornello and proceeded to the end of the piece. The ritornello was often conceived after material for the vocal body of the aria was decided upon. In all probability,

---

[36] For example, 'Your harps and cymbals sound' (the voice begins on the fourth rather than the third beat), 'From the censor', 'Words are weak' (here instead of a half note there is a quarter note followed by a rest in the bass), 'Can I see', 'See the tall palm', 'Ev'ry sight these eyes behold', and 'Now a diff'rent measure try'. Unlike these common-time arias, which generally start with a full measure, the triple-time arias in this oratorio often begin with an anacrusis on the third beat of an incomplete bar.

[37] In this case the reason for the change from sketch A to sketch B would not be related to a decision to create a ritornello. The revision might have been wrought for melodic reasons: in sketch A bars 2–3 of the opening melody recur in bars 10–11, and Handel may have wished to eliminate this thematic redundancy.

[38] Ironically, he later subjected 'When the sun' to an altogether different compositional procedure, adapting it to the text 'Virtue, truth and innocence' in preparation for a 1751 performance of *Esther* (see Burrows, 'Handel's Last Musical Autograph', 156–7). The compositional history of 'When the sun' thus neatly illustrates Handel's multiple creative practices.

Handel began by creating or collecting main ideas, particularly melodic ideas, with the requisite *Affekt* and often with the text-setting in view. (This does not mean, of course, that a given borrowing always had to match the text for which it was destined. He could easily bring about changes.) In some cases these ideas were sketched—melodies alone or with texts and/or harmonic accompaniment, in other cases borrowed, and sometimes both (Handel sometimes jotted down borrowings), with the text-setting already in mind. He might change his original ideas in the course of composing an aria, often themes were developed in some way or altered as he composed, and some-times previously unplanned thematic ideas were introduced in the course of composition. But the degree to which this occurred should not be over-stated. While the process of writing the aria in the autograph admittedly left a wide margin for spontaneous creation—especially in non-thematic realms—there was also a substantial degree of compositional forethought, especially in regard to thematic or expositional material. 'When the sun' well illustrates this picture of Handel's composing process.

If we view Handel's music as improvisatory in some sense—even in terms of formal structure—we must also understand what 'improvisatory' does not mean. When he composed, Handel did not simply begin with a ritornello and progressively, bar by bar, 'improvise' a piece. The composition of the ritornello was often not the first of his creative acts. Brainard aptly describes Handel's compositional method when he calls the ritornello a 'sampling' or 'résumé before the event'. Furthermore, both the sketches and borrowings imply compositional forethought, and the revisions indicate thoughtfulness and care, in contrast to Abraham's view of Handel's composition as 'slap-dash'. As it applies to Handel, improvisatory cannot mean entirely spontan-eous.

Linear versus Non-linear Compositional Models

One corollary of the paradigm of linear composition (not necessarily held by Abraham) relates to borrowings: namely, the belief that Handel did not think of using a borrowed passage until he arrived at the point in a given work at which it first appears. As long as we limit ourselves to consideration of bor-rowings of the incipit type, such is obviously the case, but borrowings that first occur later in a piece (hereafter called internal borrowings) constitute an entire-ly different phenomenon. Some scholars maintain that Handel stored musical passages in his memory: that borrowings which occur within the course of a composition rather than at its beginning emerged when he inadvertently, as it were, composed similar passages.[39] While in some instances borrowings undoubtedly emerged during the course of composition, there are numerous cases in which they did not. Very often even 'internal' borrowings served the same precompositional function as a sketch, as the following example will demonstrate.

John Roberts lists two borrowings in Handel's aria 'Bless'd the day' from Telemann's 'Singet Gott', one of which concerns us here.[40] Bars 15–18 of 'Bless'd the day' derive from bars 1–4 of 'Singet Gott' (Ex. 3.5). These opening bars of 'Singet Gott' also bear a strong resemblance to bars 9–16 of Pantaleon Hebenstreit's 'Amor, amor reizt zum Springen' in Keiser's *Octavia*, which Handel had borrowed in 'Faccia ritorno l'antica pace' in *Ottone* of 1722 (Ex. 3.6).[41] This raises the possibility that Handel borrowed the passage from *Octavia* rather than Telemann. However, the similarities between the passages in 'Singet Gott' and 'Bless'd the day' as well as the existence of other passages shared by the two arias suggest that Telemann was Handel's immediate source.[42]

In revising bars 1–4 of 'Singet Gott' for use in bars 15–18 of 'Bless'd the day' Handel changed the key from D major to A major. His harmonic setting is also not quite the same, though the passage's overall movement from tonic to dominant is maintained. Melodically there are few differences, the most significant being the added returning notes in the last half of the second bar. Since the Telemann material does not appear until bar 15, one can classify this as an internal rather than an incipit borrowing.

It is not merely an internal borrowing, however; there is no question that the vocal entrance in Handel derives from the Telemann material. Handel makes his opening more stable than Telemann's by ending on I rather than V—in effect transforming the Telemann melody into a period with antecedent and consequent phrases[43]—but the similarities in melody, rhythm,

---

[39]   The notion of borrowings being stored in long-term memory is held, if I understand him, by Ellwood Derr; but it is not clear to me whether Derr believes that Handel called upon these borrowings before or during composition of a movement. In any case, the notion that Handel's borrowings typically emerged as he composed is prominent today. It is true that some of the borrowings may well have come about in this way, but once again, we must allow for multiple compositional processes.

[40]   Roberts, 'Handel's Borrowings from Telemann'. The example from Telemann is taken from Georg Philipp Telemann, *Musikalische Werke* (Kassel and Basle: Bärenreiter, 1950–), v, ed. Gustav Fock, 450–2.   [41]   This borrowing was recently discovered by Roberts.

[42]   This example raises particularly interesting issues about the borrowing practices of Handel's contemporaries. Did Telemann take the passage from *Octavia*, or from *Ottone*, or is the passage simply one of the period's clichés?

[43]   The process of allowing an internal borrowing to shape the beginning of a composition, which I describe in 'Bless'd the day', may have occurred when Handel composed 'Faccia ritorno' in 1722, and it is not impossible that this chorus influenced the composition of the opening bars of 'Bless'd the day' a quarter of a century later. I do not wish to overstate the case, however. While it is true that the first phrases of

EX. 3.5. (a) Telemann, 'Singet Gott', bb. 1–4; (b) Handel, *Solomon*, 'Bless'd the day'

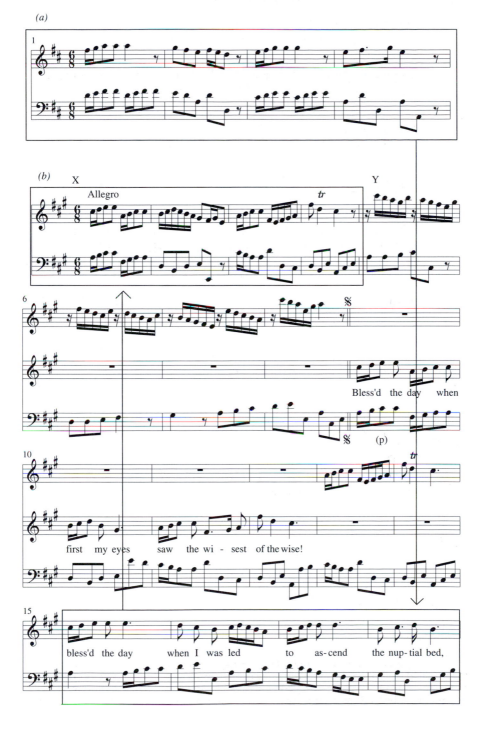

Ex. 3.6. (a) Pantaleon, 'Amor, amor' in Keiser, *Octavia*.

the *Ottone* chorus draw upon the borrowed material for their rhythmic contour, and to some extent upon the beginning of Pantaleon's aria (b. 1 of Handel seems to derive from b. 2 of Pantaleon), the degree to which the opening is derived from the internal borrowed passage is far greater in 'Bless'd the day' than in 'Faccia ritorno' (compare Exs. 3.5 and 3.6).

Ex. 3.6. (*b*) Handel, *Ottone*, 'Faccia ritorno'

and phrase structure are too striking to be coincidental. Koch might classify the relationship between these materials as 'varied repetition' in spite of the harmonic change. And the ritornello head-motif simply constitutes a somewhat more elaborate, instrumental version of the opening vocal phrase, which occurs in bars 9–10.

When the Telemann material arrives in bar 15, it sounds like a melody derived from the opening tune, and it leads to an establishment and prolongation of the dominant as well as an excursion through various keys, before the return of the tonic in bar 52. Nevertheless, the possibility that Handel began by composing the ritornello and that the borrowing issued forth from his memory at bar 15 seems a touch far-fetched; it is far easier to believe that the borrowing provided a sort of sketch for the aria. Particularly in a case such as *Harmonischer Gottes-Dienst* and *Solomon*, where a high number of borrowings from one source are concentrated in a single work, it seems likely that

Ex. 3.6. (*b*) (*cont.*)

Ex. 3.6. (*c*) Handel, *Ottone*, 'Faccia ritorno' opening

the borrowings were largely conscious and that the new piece derived from them. In other words, the retroactive model of Handel's compositional process described above probably reflects the order in which these units were created.

The degree of indebtedness to Telemann in 'Bless'd the day' will be assessed differently according to what we consider. Handel does indeed derive other material from the Telemann unit. Interestingly, Telemann by and large does not; apart from repeats of the first four bars, most of the other musical material of his aria seems largely unrelated to the first phrase of the ritornello (except for some toying around with the ritornello head-motif). Handel's aria seems more highly integrated in terms of motif than the original; therefore it does not resemble Telemann's aria taken as a whole. In this regard, Handel is not interested in his source as a formal model but as provider of melodic 'cells'. The way the aria was constructed out of the cell and material derived from it follows Riepel's and Koch's descriptions. While Handel makes use of a datum, the manner in which he does so cannot be described as impro-visatory.

In some cases the distinction between sketch and borrowing breaks down entirely. 'Swell the full chorus' from *Solomon*, which involves a sketch rather than a borrowing (or, at least, a sketch not currently recognized as a borrow-ing), also illustrates Handel's techniques of expansion on a previously con-ceived melody.[44] A sketch for this chorus, which comprises an unaccompan-ied musical period, constitutes its 'main theme' (see Ex. 3.7).

According to my own maxim, when Handel jotted down this melody he should have had the first two lines of text for the chorus in mind, if not physically before him. In fact, however, the evidence is contradictory. The antecedent phrase (bb. 1–3) of the sketch indeed represents Handel's vocal conception of the theme rather than his instrumental conception of it, or so the autograph would seem to suggest.[45] These two notes appear as the dra-matic opening vocal utterance 'Swell! Swell!'—not in the opening orchestral ritornello (Ex. 3.8). Handel must have felt that these sustained pitches would have been less effective in instrumental guise. Certainly their unannounced appearance at the vocal entrance is powerfully dramatic, an effect which would have been lost if these two notes had appeared at the beginning of the

---

[44] FM MUS MS 259, p. 74. Winton Dean was the first to identify this sketch. See Dean, *Handel's Dramatic Oratorios*, 534.

[45] The time signature of the sketch is 6/8, but the sketch itself is notated in 6/4, as is the chorus; although 3/4 is indicated as the time signature, barlines appear every six beats. Handel must have changed his mind about the metre before he wrote the first note. This is not a drastic metrical revision, since a bar of 6/8 is essentially two bars of triple metre, but the 3/4 metre is truer to the heavily accented, pompous style of the music.

EX. 3.7. Sketch for 'Swell the full chorus' in *Solomon*, FM MUS MS 259, p. 74

EX. 3.8. 'Swell the full chorus' in *Solomon*, BL RM20.h.4: (*a*) ritornello, fo. 79ᵛ; (*b*) closing ritornello, fo. 81ᵛ

ritornello. Furthermore, their omission results in a symmetrical phrase structure of 2 + 2 bars for the orchestral introduction.

The consequent phrase of the sketch, however, raises interesting questions about the relationship of words to music during the chorus's earliest stages. Handel first began the consequent phrase (bars 5–6 of the sketch) like the first phrase of the sketch, with two dotted half notes. This, of course, is not true to the text, which requires more notes for its many-syllabled second line: 'Record him, ye bards, as the pride of our days.' While the two dotted half notes appear in the original ritornello (Ex. 3.8(*a*), bb. 5–6), they are transformed when the chorus sings the consequent phrase (*HG* 26: 201, 1/2); the principal notes are preserved on the first and third beats of the bar, separated

Ex. 3.8. (*cont.*)

by lower returning notes, all in a steady quarter-note rhythm. The consequent phrase of the sketch is therefore just the opposite of the antecedent
phrase; it seems to have been composed with the ritornello, rather than the
vocal utterance, in mind.

This example recalls Brainard's discussion of 'Consider, fond shepherd' in
which Handel altered a passage when he discovered that it would not fit the
text for which it was destined. Apparently, then, he did not always work out

every detail of the text-setting until faced with the task, even though he must have had it generally in mind. It is conceivable, however, that the melodic sketch for 'Swell the full chorus' is itself a borrowing. Handel may have jotted down a tune by another composer, later changing and manipulating it as his text and creative impulses required, which would explain why the original tune does not fit the text perfectly.[46]

Again, through an array of expansion techniques similar to those we saw in 'When the sun', Handel developed this theme into the substantial A section of 'Swell the full chorus'. There seem to be three primary methods of expansion here, which are often combined: repetition (of an entire phrase or, more frequently, part of a phrase), variation, and substitution. To understand precisely how Handel utilized these techniques here, we must consult the original version of 'Swell the full chorus' as it appears in the autograph. In the following, I reconstruct the original by referring to my musical examples and to Chrysander's edition, when it reproduces the original.

We have already discussed Handel's original orchestral introduction. After it, the opening vocal exclamation is answered by a varied restatement in the orchestra (*HG* 26: 200, 1/1–2). Next, the antecedent phrase from the orchestral ritornello is extended in bars 5–7 (*HG* 26: 200, 2/2 to 201, 1/1) by several varied repetitions, the last an orchestral echo. By repeating the half-cadence I–V several times and thereby emphasizing the end of the antecedent phrase, this passage matches one of Koch's principal expansion techniques, the multiplication of closing formulae and cadences ('der Vielfältigung der Absatzformeln und Cadenzen')—as Sisman points out, an enrichment of Riepel's doubled cadences.[47]

The consequent phrase (*HG* 26: 201, 1/2–3) is again stated in its entirety, and immediately repeated in varied guise (*HG* 26: 201, 1/4 to 2/1). The next bar begins a large-scale textual repeat, beginning with a restatement of the first two bars of the chorus, now accompanied by increased rhythmic activity in the orchestra. The restatement of the antecedent phrase that follows is shorter than its appearance in bars 3–6, but bars 16–19 (*HG* 26: 202, 1/3 to 2/3) are greatly expanded from bar 7. Rather than presenting the consequent phrase, Handel inserts new material in the subdominant—thereby providing contrasting music. This is followed in bars 20–1 of the piece (*HG* 26: 202, 2/4 to 203, 1/1) by a restatement of the antecedent. The consequent phrase and its extension in bars 22–5 exactly duplicate its earlier appearance (8–11). Handel originally rounded

---

[46]   This point cannot be proved at present, however. The melody is not found in the major source from which Handel borrowed for *Solomon*, Telemann's *Harmonischer Gottes-Dienst*, and it is certainly possible that the melody is Handel's own.   [47] Sisman, 'Small and Expanded Forms', 454.

off the A section with a concluding ritornello consisting of the antecedent phrase followed by a new version of the consequent phrase, which was repeated (Ex. 3.8(*b*)). Much of this original version was cut—only the repeat of the consequent phrase is printed in Chrysander.

We need not proceed further in the piece, though we shall return to it in Chapter 8 to see how it was revised. Both 'Swell the full chorus' and 'Bless'd the day' provide illustrations of Handel building entire musical sections out of a single phrase, a process described by Koch.[48] The fact that one begins with a borrowed datum and the other with (presumably) an original sketch as datum seems to have had little impact upon the processes of expansion. These examples have illustrated two points: first, that little distinction can be drawn between the respective compositional functions of borrowings and sketches in Handel's compositional process (as I suggested at the outset); and second, that 'internal borrowings' do not always involve a radically different compositional approach than 'incipit borrowings': both types of borrowings may constitute precompositional data.

Non-linear Aspects of Fugal Writing

An avenue of Baroque composition that required non-linear precomposition of primary thematic material while allowing a free approach to form was the fugue. A group of sketches exist for a fugal chorus from *Hercules*, again allowing us a detailed recreation of Handel's compositional method. Alfred Mann's discussion of Handel's fugal practice formed part of his study of Handel's composition lessons for Princess Anne, published in a supplementary volume to the *HHA*. In the course of his discussion, Mann identified for the first time some sketches relating to the choral fugue 'And pitying heav'n' from *Hercules* (*HG* 4: 38–45) on page 12 of FM MUS MS 262 (Ex. 3.9). He writes of this material: 'In the upper portion of the manuscript . . . appears the draft for a triple fugue exposition—the only example of triple counterpoint contained in the collection.' A comparison of this 'draft' with 'And pitying heav'n', however, reveals that this material does not constitute a draft for a fugue exposition, but three separate sketches for distinct 'expositional moments' of 'And pitying heav'n'. It is clear that Handel did not intend these passages to form a whole, for the three sketches are separated by long lines running through the entire system. Of course he could have formed a fugal exposition from his sketches, but he chose instead to let each serve as an expositional moment within a choral movement.

---

[48] Sisman, 'Small and Expanded Forms', 449.

Ex. 3.9. Sketches for 'And pitying heav'n' in *Hercules*, FM MUS MS 262, p. 12

The sketches, scored for soprano, alto, tenor, and bass, present different permutations of the fugue subject and countersubjects. Apparently Handel worked out his invertible counterpoint before attempting to compose the chorus in autograph score.[49] Even at this stage, minor revisions took place. For example, in the first two sketches Handel removed the leap of a fourth

---

[49] Both the consistency of the handwriting and the fact that these subjects consistently appear in a slightly different version in the score than in the sketch suggest that the sketches were written down before rather than during composition of the chorus.

EX. 3.10. 'And pitying heav'n' in *Hercules*, BL RM 20.e.8, fo. 19^v

(original not shown in the examples) in the second bar of the first counter-subject, changing three eighth notes to a dotted quarter. By the third sketch he had incorporated the new version of the countersubject.

Again, the sketches reflect in a rough way the form of the piece in regard to thematic presentation, but not in regard to harmonic structure. As we shall see, the use of this material in the chorus follows the order of the three sketches. Before proceeding, however, the unusual form of the entire chorus must be understood.

The chorus begins with a triple-metre largo in C minor ('Oh filial piety'), and it is rounded off by an abbreviated return of this material at its end. Between these is a contrapuntal movement, in common time and E flat major ('Immortal fame attends thee'), or rather two movements. The fugue 'And pitying heav'n', beginning on page 38, is musically attached to the preceding chorus, but it sounds like the beginning of a new movement. In fact, the thematic and textual links between 'Immortal fame' and 'And pitying heav'n' are so intimate that the two pieces are inextricably (and delightfully) intertwined.

When Handel wrote the fugue subject for bass in the autograph, he first considered a slight alteration, introducing an anticipation at the cadence (Ex. 3.10). This idea was rejected immediately. The fugue first appears accompanied only by continuo, and the soprano statement that follows immediately transposes the subject to the dominant (B flat). With the third statement of the subject, in E flat again, Handel first introduces the countersubjects. This presentation follows his first sketch with certain changes. First of all, the dispensation is alto, tenor, and bass rather than soprano, alto, and bass, but the pitches used and the permutations are exactly the same as the sketch. Secondly, the second countersubject, always the most flexible of the subjects here, is altered, partly as a response to the text.[50]

There are two other noteworthy characteristics that help to establish continuity and coherence in the chorus. With the third statement of the subject comes an appearance in the soprano voice of the motif and text from the previous section of the chorus. Moreover, the first countersubject is closely

---

[50] There is more than a single change involved here: Handel first attempted a textual repeat, but this was soon altered to the version of the countersubject we now have, which is an extended and ornamented version of the sketch.

related to the subject of this previous section, and also bears its text ('immortal fame').

The links to the preceding chorus are not confined to the countersubject, however. The first short episode of the piece (bb. 13–15) recalls material from the preceding chorus, and this material will reappear later on; Handel thus weaves together the new fugue with the old in an impressive new movement.

The fourth statement of the subject occurs in bar 16, and this one follows Handel's second sketch, transposed to the dominant and with an extended second countersubject. Sketch 3 was the basis for bars 21 ff., but here a number of tonal adjustments are made near the end. This is followed by an appearance of the subject in the bass, with only the first countersubject (tenor). A long episode based on the first countersubject then ensues, followed by a reappearance of music from the earlier chorus. A stretto is followed in bar 52 by a recurrence of sketch 2, and music from the earlier chorus leads finally to a climactic homophonic statement of the subject.

It is not surprising that Handel first worked out the combinatorial possibilities of subjects—the most difficult moments of triple counterpoint. In order to compose a polythematic fugue it is necessary first to work out the permutations of subjects. Arguing along these lines, Christoph Wolff has conjectured that Johann Sebastian Bach must have composed or at least sketched the combination of subjects that was to occur in the quadruple fugue of *The Art of Fugue*.[51] This order of events—the creation of the primary thematic material in order of appearance in the chorus, but without yet putting them in the keys in which they would appear—links this sketch to that for 'When the sun'.[52] In other words, the composition of a fugue is related to composition of certain ritornello arias with melodic preview in that certain aspects of the body of the work must be worked out before composition begins. In both cases a strictly linear model of composition cannot explain the composer's creative processes.

The Need for Contrasting Compositional Models

It is important not to overlook an obvious but revealing fact about Handel's precompositional autograph materials: a high percentage of his sketches consist of important melodic ideas that are often brief—sometimes merely two to four bars of melody; many of his melodic borrowings (including a number of

---

[51] See Wolff, 'Bach's Last Fugue: Unfinished?', in *Bach: Essays on his Life and Music* (Cambridge, Massachusetts: Harvard University Press, 1991), 259.

[52] Moreover, certain aspects of the fugue were worked out 'before' composition simply by virtue of the fact that Handel had composed the movement that precedes the fugue.

those identified by John Roberts) also often consist of short two- to four-bar resemblances that are nonetheless significant enough to merit pointing out. Moreover, there are many shared features in the use of such borrowings and sketches—a fact that this discussion has heretofore taken for granted. Their very existence would seem to indicate that Handel began composing by collecting or creating melodic ideas—a common practice in tonal composition. The fact that he prepared sketches of this sort but did not intentionally write out long drafts might suggest that the actual formal creation of a piece, once the main melodic ideas were decided upon, could be done more or less 'automatically'. This explains why Handel could, at least some of the time, compose directly into the final autograph score.[53]

To put it differently, Richard Strauss observed that 'the melodic ideas which provide the substance of a composition seldom consist of more than two to four bars, the remainder is elaboration, working out, compositional technique'.[54] Ironically, this statement seems more true for Handel than for Strauss. The existence of sketches and borrowings (which are quite often two to four bars in length) may suggest that for Handel the creation of the melodic (or contrapuntal) ideas that provide the substance of a piece was not an effortless task. Once it was accomplished, he tended to retain these ideas even when pieces were extensively recomposed. The elaboration or working out, including the harmonic creation of forms, on the other hand, could occur relatively spontaneously and was frequently subject to change. One of the obvious reasons for this is that the conventions of Handel's time, when the musical techniques such as pre-existant modulation plans for A sections of da capo arias or binary forms, sequential repetition, and methods of melodic combination (any of which might necessitate alteration or variation—but not necessarily a wholesale rejection—of original melodic ideas) allowed Handel, once his primary thematic material was found, to compose automatically.[55]

Many of the pieces examined above—'When the sun', 'And pitying heav'n', and 'Swell the full chorus'—support this view, suggesting, remarkably, that the roles of forethought and spontaneity to some extent belonged to different domains of the act of musical composition for Handel. In all three cases, the most variable relation from sketches to finished arias or choruses seems to be the harmonic realm as it affects the formal structure, while the

---

[53] This is a slippery matter, since we cannot know how often he might have used extensive drafts that have not survived. However, the autograph versions of 'Joys of freedom' (Exx. 3.11–15), discussed below, seem to be an instance of more or less direct composition into the score.

[54] Carl Dahlhaus, *Between Romanticism and Modernism*, trans. Mary Whittall (Berkeley: University of California Press, 1980), 40.

[55] See Marshall, *The Compositional Process of J. S. Bach*, 239.

thematic material constitutes a relatively stable element. This relates to what we know at present of Handel's borrowing practice, where he is more likely to borrow a melody, often reharmonizing it, rather than a harmonic progression. This example suggests that the structural realm as determined by harmony was, in certain cases at least, one of the most spontaneous realms of composition for the composer.

Handel sometimes changed his mind about the 'working out' of musical ideas as he composed. At times such changes of inner structure were significant enough to alter outer form.[56] We can thus suggest one tentative model for Handel's normative process in which melodies are worked out before the fact and musical forms result from 'spontaneous' processes—precompositional melodic creation with spontaneous formal creation.

The final section both illustrates and qualifies this point by turning to two pieces for which there exists an unusually large amount of compositional material. The fact that we are dealing with fragments in these two cases ensures that the changes were made during composition rather than after completion of an entire piece.

The interplay of compositional forethought and spontaneity can be seen at its apex in a series of fragments for the duet 'Joys of freedom' in *Hercules*. All four versions of this work derive from an Italian chamber duet, *Beato in ver* (*HWV* 181), a single-movement work written in October 1742, two years before *Hercules*.[57] Analysing the wealth of material created and sifted for a single piece illustrates both the abundance of Handel's imagination and his difficulty in this particular instance in deciding how the piece should continue.

Scored for soprano, alto, and continuo, *Beato in ver* is a da capo structure that follows Handel's most typical harmonic plan, its A section ending in the tonic (A major), its B section ending in the minor mediant (C sharp minor).[58] Like many of Handel's arias, the A section departs from conventional five-part da capo form in several ways. There is no opening ritornello, for example, and the A section does not divide into two halves either harmonically or

---

[56] The terminological confusion surrounding the word 'form' is discussed in Mark Evan Bonds, *Wordless Rhetoric: Musical Form and the Metaphor of the Oration* (Cambridge, Mass.: Harvard University Press, 1991). As Bonds points out, two of the meanings of the word 'form' are diametrically opposed: ' "form" is commonly used to denote those features a given work shares with a large number of others, yet it is also often understood as the unique structure of a particular work' (Introduction, p. i). This confusion is sometimes avoided by using 'outer form' to denote the former and 'inner form' to denote the latter. Although 'outer form' is universally understood, 'inner form' is more mysterious, sometimes bearing meanings that are most compatible with 19th-c. music. In these pages I have adopted the term 'outer form' in its most common meaning. I use 'inner structure' to refer to smaller-scale aspects of form, such as phrase structure, key areas, and so forth—all of which play a role in the creation of outer form, but can be distinguished from it.   [57] John Roberts discovered this borrowing.

[58] Ellen T. Harris has identified the typical harmonic patterns in 'Harmonic Patterns in Handel's Operas'.

Ex. 3.11. 'Joys of freedom', opening ritornello in *Hercules*

in terms of textual repetition. In fact, the A-section text is stated four times rather than twice, and there is no strongly articulated cadence to mark the A section's mid-point.

All versions of 'Joys of freedom' from *Hercules* draw upon melodic, harmonic, and even contrapuntal aspects of *Beato in ver*, but not the form, scoring, or key of the model. Since the extensive opening ritornello of 'Joys of freedom' contains most of the thematic material for the duet, our analysis must begin with labels of its major melodic ideas: *a* (1–4), *b* (5–12), *c* (12–20), *d* (20–5).[59] (See Ex. 3.11.) The first two melodic ideas (*a* and *b*) are apparently original in 'Joys of freedom', but *c* and *d* derive from *Beato in ver*, though

[59] My analysis of this piece follows an unabashedly 'linear' path. This seems to me the most direct manner of describing the course of composition. I assume that there are both linear and non-linear aspects of Handel's approach: the creation of new material for the *Hercules* duet probably took the text into account; the material borrowed from *Beato in ver* must have seemed appropriate for its new context in terms of *Affekt*, and where the original music did not fit the new text it could be altered. Even if Handel's approach were purely linear, however, it would not contradict my earlier stance in this chapter. I do not intend to argue that Handel always composed in a non-linear way, but that there are instances when the linear model is not appropriate. There are also cases in which my own arguments for the primacy of the text do not apply; as noted earlier, the use of a limited number of poetic forms allowed Handel to fit a new text to old music. In addition to Chapter 9, see my discussion of the retexting of original music from 'And to that pitch' in *Semele* for 'Zaphnath Egypt's fate foresaw' in *Joseph and his Brethren* in Hurley, 'The Summer of 1743: Some Handelian Self-Borrowings', *Göttinger Händel-Beiträge*, 4 (1991), 174–93; and John Walter Hill, 'Handel's Retexting as a Test of his Conception of Connections between Music, Text, and Drama', *Göttinger Händel-Beiträge*, 3 (1989), 284–92.

their order of appearance has been changed: *d* was the first thematic event in *Beato in ver* (bb. 1–4) and *c* first appeared eight bars later (bb. 12–16).

In 'Joys of freedom' Dejanira's first vocal statement not only harmonically redirects the thematic ideas, which now move from tonic to dominant, but Handel also changes the order from that of the ritornello to *a, b, d, c*. Having reached the dominant at this point, *d* serves as a medial ritornello in the new key. The next vocal section, featuring Iole with a new text, repeats the new ordering (*a b d c*), followed by counterpoint on *d* for both voices (95–109)—their first moment of interaction in the duet. This last passage corresponds roughly to *Beato in ver* (HG 32: 138, bb. 16–23), although there are harmonic differences: the Italian duet concluded in the dominant (E) before moving through the subdominant (D) and modulating to other keys, whereas 'Joys of freedom' concludes in the tonic (F) before moving to the subdominant (B flat). Even though the oratorio duet and its Italian model differ formally, therefore, Handel nonetheless returned to the original for melodic and contrapuntal material at a major structural point.

All the versions of the *Hercules* duet share these first 110 bars, but beyond this point we must examine independently Handel's various solutions for the continuation of the new duet. It is fascinating that his difficulty with the composition apparently began at this point. In terms of tonal organization, by bar 102 'Joys of freedom' has unfolded as a completely typical da capo A section, lacking only a concluding ritornello: the first statement of the text, as noted, reaches the dominant in bar 56 (HG 4: 178, b. 6), followed by an abbreviated ritornello in the dominant key; the second statement of the text has reached a strong close on the tonic in bar 102. But, in spite of the structure so far, Handel apparently did not intend to cast the duet in da capo form at any stage. Having given each half of the 'A section' to the solo voices in turn, he did not wish the piece to conclude before providing an opportunity for the voices to sing together in an extended passage. Having had an A1 and an A2 in the solo sections (with the actual 'duet' beginning at the end of A2, when the voices finally sing together at bar 95), the duet now needed a concluding section or sections—at least an 'A3', as it were—for which there is no prescribed formal plan. There were several compositional options, and Handel tried different structural schemes before he reached his final solution. Before doing so, a few words are needed about the physical evidence in the autographs for these different versions.

In the original autograph version (BL RM 20.e.8) fo. 89^r followed fo. 86^v, the intervening folios in the autograph being a later insertion. In other words, the first version of the duet follows Chrysander's edition up to bar 111 (HG 4:

180, 2/1). Thereafter comes Ex. 3.12. Handel did not complete this version of the duet. The second version of 'Joys of freedom' exists crossed out on fo. 87$^{r–v}$ (Ex. 3.13.) This version, too, was not completed. The third version, beginning on the bottom system of fo. 87^v and continuing on fo. 88^r, is identical with

Ex. 3.12. First version of 'Joys of freedom' in *Hercules*, BL RM 20.e.8, fo. 89$^{r–v}$

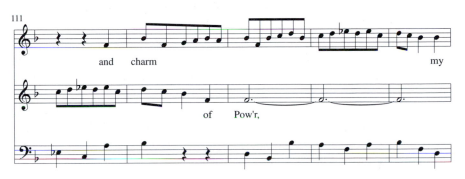

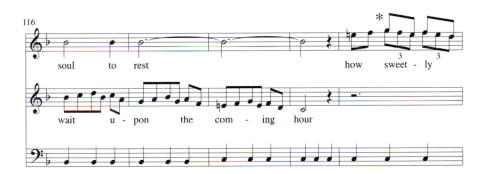

* Triplets later changed to eighth note

Ex. 3.12. (*cont.*)

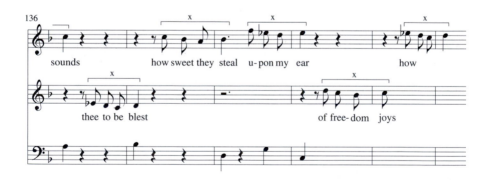

Chrysander's score to bar 141; Ex. 3.14 begins at bar 134 (*HG* 4: 181, 1/6). Again, Handel abandoned this version before completing it. The fourth version on fo. 88ᵛ is the first performance version as we have it in *HG* (Ex. 3.15).

In the first version Handel continued with imitation on thematic figure *a* for the two voices in the subdominant, B flat major (see Ex. 3.12). This is followed by a variation of *b* (based on bb. 37–40, themselves a variation of bb. 9–12), which is restated and ornamented over a C pedal (see Ex. 3.12, bb. 116–23). Finally, there are two ideas derived from *Beato in ver.* The first is imitation on *c* (Ex. 3.12, bb. 123–33), which corresponds to

Ex. 3.13. Second version of 'Joys of freedom' in *Hercules*, BL RM 20.e.8, fo. 87[r–v]

Ex. 3.13. (*cont.*)

several places in *Beato in ver.*[60] In 'Joys of freedom' this material occurs over an F pedal which moves to B flat and E flat. Second, the fragment ends with eight harmonically unstable bars whose tonal direction is unclear. Fittingly, the prominent melodic motif in these bars (marked 'x'

60   See especially bb. 56–64 and 68–72 (*HG* 32: 139–40).

on Ex. 3.12 at its first occurrence, bb. 134–5) comes from an unstable part of the B section of *Beato in ver*. Handel abandoned this first version of 'Joys of freedom' at this point. It might be significant that the vocal line of motif x makes nonsense of the text—possibly one of the reasons he abandoned this first attempt. His revision goes far beyond what was necessary to correct this problem, however; there may therefore have been larger reasons for the new version.

EX. 3.14. Third version of 'Joys of freedom' in *Hercules*, BL RM 20.e.8, fos. 87ᵛ–88ʳ

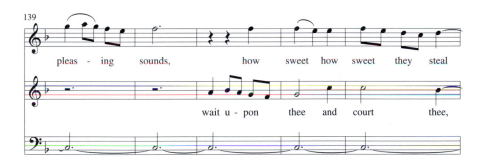

Having reached the tonic already in bar 102, Handel must have wished to achieve sufficient harmonic interest in the new section to justify extending the composition beyond a point at which, in a cavatina, or after the A section repeat in a da capo aria, the piece might have ended. One possibility was to allow the next portion of the duet to take on some of the character of a B section, hence Handel's use of material from the B section of *Beato in ver*. Lest the length of the piece become unwieldy, however, it had to be composed in such a way that it could end convincingly in the tonic without sounding tonally redundant—not a concern in B sections, which end in contrasting keys, and are completed by the return of the A section. Why Handel's first solution proved unsatisfactory in these regards might become clearer after we have examined his next attempt.

The second version follows the first one in many particulars (see Ex. 3.13). The first six bars are almost identical (up to b. 116), except that the imitative entrance of the top voice occurs a bar later. In bar 117, however, Handel makes a tonal shift, presenting *a* in F where the first version had featured material derived from the end of *b* in B flat. In bars 121–5 he employs the beginning of *b* rather than its end. The melodic unit *c* appears over an F pedal, somewhat as in the first version (Ex. 3.13, bb. 124–31). Rather than introducing x, however, Handel next moves to the dominant key and presents *c* over a C pedal leading to a cadence (*d*) in C major, which is echoed by the orchestra.

A comparison of the first two versions clearly shows new thought about the tonal structure of this section. The dominant, which appeared as a long pedal (but not as a key area) moving to the tonic early in the first version, is reserved until its appearance as a key near the end of the second version. The solution offered by the second version, however, emphasizes the dominant perhaps too strongly. Like the end of A1 earlier in the duet, the cadence to the dominant key area is followed by a three-bar ritornello in the new key. In order to conclude the piece Handel would have had to write a new section—in effect, an A4—to return to the tonic and balance the modulation to the dominant. He rejected this plan as well. Coming after A1/A2, this second version was not only formally and harmonically redundant, mirroring exactly the progression to the dominant in A1, but the requisite statement returning to the tonic would perhaps have made too lengthy a composition.

The third version again retains much of the earlier part of the second version (up to b. 134). Thereafter it offers new material over a dominant pedal (see Ex. 3.14). This thematic idea is not really 'new' in the larger context of the duet, however; it derives from bars 29–30. This leads to imitation on *c* (beginning with a brief reference to *b*) at first over the tonic, then spun out

EX. 3.15. Final version of 'Joys of freedom' in *Hercules*, BL RM 20.e.8., fo. 88ᵛ

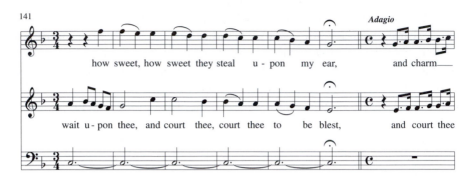

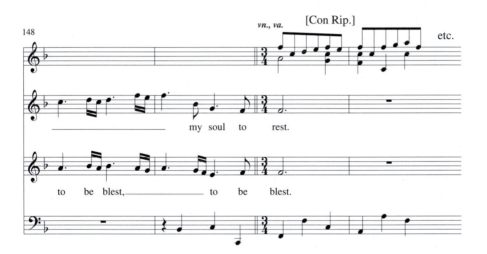

over another dominant pedal. After a strong cadence to the tonic in bars 155–6, the head-motif of *c* gives way to x, which appears over yet another C pedal, again moving towards the tonic at the end. Yet the text-setting at this point in the piece is no better than in the first version. In addition to this problem, Handel might have had concerns about overall structure.

Certainly the dominant is strongly felt in this third version but, with only a passing reference in bar 150, it is never established as a key area as it was in the second version; instead the dominant serves to emphasize the tonic key. Yet after he establishes the tonic in bars 147 and 156, Handel moves back to an area of prolonged dominant harmony (or at least, as in the latter, an area of dominant-weighted harmony). The cadence to the tonic near the end of the draft (bb. 167–8) is therefore one among the many within this section.

In the more pithy final version (Ex. 3.15) the sweet-sounding thirds and sixths ('how sweet they steal upon my ear'; bb. 142–6) are altered from the preceding version, followed by a common-time adagio cadence (147–50), and ending finally with a varied return of the ritornello. This final version is directed towards a strong return to the tonic near the end, withholding emphasis of the tonic within A3 until this point. The remarkable changes— the fermata that arrests the rhythmic momentum with the change to a common-time adagio and an abandonment of the previous melodic material— provide dramatic emphasis for the return of the tonic key. Handel's final solution provides a striking close indeed.

The autograph of this duet, then, shows an array of formal options that Handel actually considered as he developed the movement. On the whole the contrasts in tonality and structure among the various versions are particularly striking, whereas the basic melodic material, in spite of its reordering and the differences in its development, remains essentially the same—until the 'written-out cadenza' at bars 147–9 of the final version. 'Joys of freedom' provides a fascinating illustration of how compositional choice in a section whose modulation plan was not predetermined by convention resulted in significant formal changes as Handel composed. The compositional history of this duet, even more than 'When the sun' and 'And pitying heav'n', supports the view that melodic or thematic content tends to be a planned and reasonably fixed aspect of composition for Handel, but details of harmonic direction as a determinant of formal structure—in this case even the outer form—were not worked out in advance, thus representing a more intuitive aspect of Handel's creativity.

The notion that form as determined by harmonic structure may represent a relatively 'improvisatory' or spontaneous aspect of Handel's compositional process might come as a shock. According to traditional wisdom, the Baroque was the age of stereotyped, even rigid, musical forms, as manifested in its most celebrated genre, the Italian opera seria, whose primary component is the da capo aria. However, many of Handel's Italian operas and especially his oratorios frequently exhibit more freedom in the use of musical forms than is generally imagined. Even the da capo form allowed for a certain amount of structural freedom. (These issues will be taken up in Ch. 8.) Above all, in those cases in which the musical form was not dictated by the text, Handel could forge his musical material as he saw fit. He often chose common patterns, but at times created forms apparently unique.

On the other hand, the text often determined such stereotyped outer forms

as the da capo aria. Handel sometimes chose a different form than that dictated by the text, and he sometimes required changes of text from his librettists. Nonetheless, the choice of outer form, like melodic sketching, must
often have been a precompositional act, and in many cases Handel maintained
this precompositional formal choice even if he made other revisions. In other
words, no sooner do we present a model than we must qualify it. Even if
Handel seems often to have decided on his primary melodic material before
he began to compose a given piece in the autograph score, on many occa-
sions his original melodic material proved unsuitable and he changed it, introducing new material, during composition. There exist cases in which thematic material was significantly reworked, or rejected and replaced. At the
same time, there are many cases in which internal alterations do not affect
outer form. For an illustration we must turn to 'The leafy honours' from *Belshazzar*.

The previous chapter disclosed that the first version of this aria survives as
an unfinished fragment in the autograph manuscript of *Belshazzar* (see Pl.
2.1). One of the most salient ways in which Handel's second setting differs
from the first, incomplete, one is the richer scoring—he adds a part to be
shared by third violin and viola—but the new orchestration does not fully
explain other fundamental musical changes. It seems at first that a reasonable
hypothesis, beyond the scoring, for the composer's abandonment of his first
version of 'The leafy honours' at the arrival of the dominant, marking the end
of the first half of the A section, might be that he was dissatisfied with his
approach to the dominant. But this turns out not to be the case. Indeed, the
new setting maintains almost exactly the features of the last part of the first
version: the C major section that begins with the text 'in giddy dissipation fly'
with its giddy triplets, its lengthy melisma, and its cadence to the dominant.
In spite of very slight changes near the end,[61] both the tonal plan and the form
of the fragment are retained in the second version, unlike the case of 'Joys of
freedom' that we have just examined.

For the most part, Handel's revisions focus rather on earlier parts of the
aria, beginning with elaboration and expansion of the opening ritornello.
This process of expansion involves in part the appropriation of borrowed passages, identified by John Roberts, from the aria 'Va col canto lusingando'

---

[61]   These revisions focus on the idea that appears six bars before the end of the fragment; in the second setting (bb. 62–3) Handel repeats one bar that prolongs the secondary dominant, making the resolution to the dominant key more emphatic, and decorates the bass with triplets, allowing it to share in the
motivic makeup of the aria. The resulting two-bar passage is also added (in a less elaborate form) to the
opening ritornello in the second setting (bb. 25–6), as discussed in the course of this chapter.

from *Clori, Tirsi e Fileno* (*HWV* 96) of 1707.[62] The treatment of the material in the new setting, however, differs from that of the source, and it is this treatment that demands our scrutiny, beginning with the opening ritornello.

On a broad scale, the changes in the new setting serve to tighten the relationship between the ritornello and the vocal A section of the aria—a common type of compositional revision in Handel's autographs that has been discussed by Brainard.[63] The idea added in bars 19–20 of the second setting of the ritornello, for instance, serves to preview the return of this material in bars 62–3, 87, 89, and 101–2. This passage appeared near the end of the fragment (b. 54), but it was not featured in the ritornello of the first setting. This revision well illustrates the 'retroactive' effect of the body of the aria upon the ritornello.[64]

Perhaps more important for our purposes, however, are the local ramifications of the changes within the ritornello itself. On this immediate level, the alterations seem to have two main musical goals: to provide more melodic and rhythmic drive; and, related to this, to reduce the regularity of phrase structure, which had involved predictable patterns of repetition in the first draft of the orchestral opening. (See Ex. 3.16.) Originally the phrase structure of the ritornello was:

$$8 \text{ bars } (4 + 4) + 4(2 + 2) + 8(2 + 2 + 2 + 2) + 6(4 + 2)$$

Within these predominantly regular phrase groupings, bars 1–4 were immediately repeated in bars 5–8 (with an octave transposition in the bass); bars 9–10 (derived from 'Va col canto', bb. 61–2) were duplicated in 11–12 (lowering the bass line an octave); bars 13–14 and 17–18 were repeated an octave

[62]   *HHA* 5/3: 161–8, provides the first printed edition of this work; Chrysander printed only a fragment in *HG* 52B. Roberts had identified certain borrowings from 'Va col canto' within A1 of the new setting, some of which are also found in the first setting; these will be pointed out as they arise. The most substantial borrowings noted by Roberts occur in the second setting beyond the point where the fragment ends, which raises the possibility that the new borrowings in A1 plant seeds for a continuation that relies more greatly on the cantata aria, but this is difficult to prove. It is not entirely clear that the borrowings in the later parts of the new setting would not have been included in the old version if Handel had continued; for the most part they do not rely on new material within A1 of the second setting that was not also present in the fragment. In any case, the new version is audibly different from the old, which Handel surely intended. I thank John Roberts for privately communicating his discovery of the borrowings, and his interpretation of their significance, while this chapter was being prepared.

[63]   Brainard, 'Aria and Ritornello', 24–30.

[64]   A more subtle long-range connection might have influenced Handel's revision of the triplet/dotted crotchet pattern at bars 11–16. The original ritornello had featured the two-bar idea that will appear within the vocal A section of the second setting at 114–23. Although he did not reach this point before abandoning the fragment, the presence of this material in the ritornello might indicate that he had planned this passage in A2 even in the first version, although this is impossible to demonstrate. In any case, the new version makes the relationship between the two passages even closer, for the transposition up a third in 13–16 recurs in 120–3.

Ex. 3.16. Comparison of two versions of 'The leafy honours' ritornello in *Belshazzar*

lower in 15–16 and 19–20, respectively. Only the final six bars are irregular and unpredictable.

The changes to the ritornello that we find in the new version do much to mitigate the pervasive regularity of phrase structure and predictable repetition found in the first version. The opening eight bars are expanded to eighteen. The passage consisting of triplets followed by a dotted crotchet that was stated in bar 9–10 of the original is lowered by a third; after repeating it, Handel adds another statement at the original pitch level, expanding the original four-bar passage to six bars. After the material later used to depict the 'furious driving wind' has been stated and restated at various pitch levels, he adds two bars ultimately derived from 'Va col canto', bars 8–9 (second version, bb. 19–20). The resulting phrase structure is less predictable than in the original:

$$\text{10 bars } (4 + 4 + 2) + 6(4 + 2) + 8(2 + 2 + 2 + 2) + 8(2 + 4 + 2)$$

The new version also involves some reworkings of melodic material, as examination of the opening melody of the ritornello in Ex. 3.16 discloses. The original consisted of a four-bar phrase that had repeated exactly, apart from the change of anacrusis from C to F. In the final version Handel retains the first two bars, but rewrites the last two bars (in a manner that follows 'Va col canto', 2–3), so that the melodic goal at bar 4 is A rather than C. When the opening four-bar phrase is repeated, he uses thirty-second notes rather than triplets, which increases the rhythmic drive. Next, he adds two new bars, which complete the melodic ascent to C. The rhythmic variation of bar 3 in bars 7–10, combined with the melodic ascent, is perhaps mimetic in nature, suggesting an increasing flurry of wind. Together with the transposition of material at bar 11 of the second setting, these changes reduce the melodic emphasis on the note C, which occurred every two to three bars in the original. The melody of the new version is accordingly somewhat more directional and less static in its component parts than the first, although the prolongation of C is (more subtly) maintained. Whether or not the new setting represents an 'improvement' upon the original, its expressive aim has changed: Handel has moved away from the predictable pastoral repose of the fragment to the increased irregularity of the second setting.

The changes between the two settings are of course not limited to the orchestral introduction. While Handel naturally rewrites passages in the vocal body of the aria that restate material from the ritornello (such as the vocal statement of the head-motif) so that corresponding passages match, he also sometimes transforms music that is unrelated to the ritornello. The new setting of 'before the furious driving wind', for instance, discloses another fundamental change of melodic material. (See Ex. 3.17.) Whereas in the first version the accompaniment figure depicting the wind enters right away, in the final version it is reserved until after the voice has stated the line of text once—probably an indication of Handel's concern that the text should be heard in performance before its musical depiction begins. The melody of the new version, though it retains much of the pitch content of the original (in the first three bars of Ex. 3.17), has more character of its own; unlike the draft, it is not merely a counter-melody to the 'wind' motif.[65] This is particularly noticeable in the second half of the passage, where the tail of the melody is repeated against the 'wind' motif in the accompaniment, as opposed to the arpeggiated melody of the original.[66]

The fragments for 'Joys of freedom' and 'The leafy honours' embody two distinct types of fragments that are found among Handel's compositional material. The 'Joys of freedom' fragments illustrate that he sometimes abandoned a composition because he was unsure of its continuation, but quite satisfied with how the piece had progressed up to a certain point. The early version of the 'The leafy honours', on the other hand, was apparently abandoned at least in part because the piece as written required changes, whether for the sake of the immediate context or to lay ground for the continuation, or both. Similarly, the compositional model exemplified by 'The leafy honours' is in a sense the opposite of that of 'Joys of freedom'; for in the former Handel alters original melodic material, but (as far as can be seen) not the form. It is tempting, therefore, to suggest a second model for Handel's compositional method in addition to the one outlined on p. 66: changeable melodic material with predetermined and 'fixed' formal creation. Admittedly 'The leafy honours' illustrates this model only to an extent, for most of the original melodic ideas are retained in the setting; changes in details of the inner structure, however, do not seem to change the outer form. Although these two models cover any number of examples, there are many cases that lie between them, or beyond both, thus requiring different formulations. Some pieces share passages in which the bass line is the unchanging element.[67] In other cases the changes are so extreme

---

[65] Roberts notes that bars 41–4 of the new setting bear a closer resemblance to 'Va col canto', bars 24–30 than did the corresponding bars in the first setting. In my view, the middle of this passage (bb. 42–3) resembles bars 35–7 of the fragment more closely than the cantata aria. The descending line from C to E♮ in 43–4 might represent a simplification of 'Va col canto', bars 29–30. However, the treatment of the tail-motif that follows (described above) is by no means controlled by the source.

[66] Handel's revision also provides a different approach to the passage in the dominant (a setting of the text 'in giddy dissipation'). In the old version, the second half of the passage begins in the dominant (C major), and the use of B♮ creates a tonicization of C before the 'giddy dissipation' passage. In the second version of the aria, on the other hand, the use of the pitch B♭ suggests the dominant seventh chord of F major: we expect to return to F until the tonality is 'diverted' when the C major 'giddy dissipation' passage appears.

[67] Gerald Abraham discusses this phenomenon in the Harpsichord Sonata No. 32 and the Trio Sonata, Op. 2, no. 1. See Abraham, 'Some Points of Style', 270. Composing a new melody over a pre-existent bass line was, of course, an extremely common technique in the Baroque.

EX. 3.17. Original and revised settings of 'The leafy honours' in *Belshazzar*

that we must speak of unrelated settings (such as the two versions of 'Will the sun forget to streak' from *Solomon*).[68]

The study of Handel's compositional process constantly forces us to play devil's advocate with our paradigms. Handel utilized an enormous variety of techniques and formal designs. It would be surprising indeed if a single model could explain his entire output. As we have seen, Abraham's theory of improvisatory linear composition does not: the ritornello can be derived from the vocal body of the aria at least as often as it can be a starting point or datum. In sum, Handel's process of composition stands as a reminder of the nature of paradigms: they never explain all cases and must be recognized as tendencies rather than rules; strict adherence to any single model will inevitably mislead us.

[68] See Dean, *Handel's Dramatic Oratorios*, 531–2.

4

The Quest for Melodic Diversity

IN the process of revising his scores Handel faced certain problems time and again. Examining such recurring revisions enables us to identify stylistic issues that regularly concerned the composer. In this chapter I identify two kinds of revisions in Handel's composing scores that are ultimately interrelated: (1) revisions that curtail excessive thematic repetition; and (2) revisions that manipulate the order of melodic events. Both types of corrections underlie Handel's interest in achieving thematic diversity.

Control of repetition and/or restatement is surely one of the most basic characteristics of a great composer's mastery of musical structure. Handel's best music attains precisely the right balance between repetition and diversity, but in many cases this delicate equilibrium was achieved only after revision. Sometimes original autograph versions of arias were simply too repetitive, particularly in regard to restatements of important motifs or themes. In order to 'tighten up' such pieces, to mitigate the tedium caused by excessive repetition, Handel revised his music by eliminating unnecessary restatements.

A straightforward example of this procedure can be seen in 'Thrice bless'd that wise, discerning king' in *Solomon*; the autograph contains a passage towards the end of the A section that was later removed by Handel (see Ex. 4.1).[1] This three-bar segment constitutes a brief orchestral interlude, which repeats the material immediately preceding it in bars 68–71, where it is presented by voice and continuo. Such orchestral echoes of vocal material are, of course, quite common in Handel's arias. In 'Thrice bless'd', however, this same musical material also occurs in the concluding ritornello of the piece.[2] Thus the original autograph version contained three statements of virtually identical material in a short span, and these occurred near the end of the aria,

---

[1] I shall not discuss the material in 'Thrice bless'd' that Handel derived from Telemann because it has little bearing on my argument here. (See Roberts, 'Handel's Borrowings from Telemann'.)

[2] In the original version at bar 66 there was a passage that also contained this theme (see Ex. 7.10). However, its bass line is incomplete, which suggests that Handel eliminated it before composing the remainder of the aria.

EX. 4.1. Deleted passage from 'Thrice bless'd that wise, discerning king' in *Solomon*, BL RM 20.h.4, fos. 56ᵛ–57ʳ

creating special thematic and harmonic problems. By the end of the A section the thematic material in question has already been stated several times and hardly needs to be restated here three times, especially as the repeated passages are all in the tonic. The reason for Handel's revision is clear. By eliminating the orchestral interlude, he took the simplest solution; the vocal material of bars 68–71 has a textual as well as a musical function and the concluding ritornello is, by definition, of structural significance. The intervening orchestral interlude, however, which serves simply as a sort of rhetorical pause, was rather long, and some time after drafting the first version, Handel trimmed it.

'Thrice bless'd' exemplifies a kind of revision commonly found in the arias of Handel's late oratorios. Such corrections often occur near the ends of arias, as in the example above, or at the ends of self-contained sections of arias. Among the numerous further instances of similar revisions in Handel's autographs is a case found in 'No longer, fate, relentless frown' in *Hercules*, which provides a more involved example than 'Thrice bless'd' of how Handel revised his music to correct excessive thematic repetition within the tonic key.

Except for doubling the statements of text, the A section of this aria follows a standard five-part da capo plan. An opening ritornello in the tonic F minor is followed by A1, which consists of two statements of the first two lines of text, modulating to the minor dominant C minor (10–26) and then an abbreviated return of the ritornello in C minor (26–30). A2, again consisting of two statements of the first two lines of text, modulates back to the tonic (30–43); and a concluding ritornello in the tonic key (43–51) ends the A section.

Ex. 4.2. Deleted passage from 'No longer, fate, relentless frown' in *Hercules*, BL RM 20.e.8, fo. 7ʳ

Ex. 4.2. (*cont.*)

In the original autograph version, A2 ended differently than in the final version (Ex. 4.2). At bar 43 there began a texted restatement of the striking unison motif—more fancifully, the 'relentless fate' motif—which had first appeared in bars 6–8, and this was followed by a written-out vocal cadenza marked 'adagio'. In the original version of the aria, therefore, the end of A2 more closely paralleled the end of A1, which also consisted of a return of this motif followed by a cadence, but no cadenza (bb. 22–6 = HG 4: 12, 2/4–3/1). In both A1 and A2, this material was followed by an orchestral ritornello in which the fate motif is repeated (bb. 26–30 and 47–51 = HG 4: 12, 3/3–7 and 13, 2/6–3/4), so that multiple statements of the motif occurred in close proximity. Handel eventually chose to remove one statement of the motif and the cadential phrase following it from A2.

Handel's decision to revise the end of A2 rather than the end of A1 seems to support the interpretation of his motivation offered above. The musical motif is heard enough during the course of the piece that even two statements of it at the end of A2 are unwarranted. Further, and more significantly perhaps, the change at the end of the A section is probably largely the result of harmonic considerations. The affinity between the end of A1 and the end of A2 regards only thematic material, not harmony: tonally the two passages are entirely different. The passage at the end of A1 bears the important tonal function of completing the modulation to the minor dominant key because it is preceded by a cadence to A flat, the relative major (a more typical medial cadence for arias in minor keys), in bars 20–1. The fate motif and cadential phrase are then preceded by the dominant seventh of C minor, and the cadence to C minor in bar 26 is confirmed by the following ritornello. If the entire second phrase were cut as it is in A2, therefore, we would have the very odd situation of the final vocal phrase of A1 and the internal ritornello cadencing to different keys. The original end of A2 (Ex. 4.2), however, was tonally redundant—once again, a typical feature of concluding sections— since it is surrounded by passages that, like it, cadence to the tonic. This latter passage was thus expendable, both harmonically and thematically, and Handel chose to remove it. These two pieces and others like them serve to demonstrate that Handel sometimes had a tendency towards 'thematic garrulousness' in his first versions of arias, a tendency that revision successfully overcame.

The related treatment of borrowings from Telemann in two arias from *Solomon*, 'Bless'd the day' and 'Beneath the vine', is somewhat more complicated. In the last chapter I discussed Handel's borrowings from Telemann's 'Singet Gott' in 'Bless'd the day'. The relationship of 'Bless'd the day' to the examples discussed above can be seen in a correction at the end of the aria. (See Example 4.3.) The A section's orchestral postlude, in its original form, was longer than the opening ritornello of the aria. As Ex. 3.5 shows, the introductory ritornello comprises two parts: (1) four bars (*x*), which are further divisible into antecedent and consequent phrases (2 + 2); and (2) four concluding bars (*y*). The first draft of the concluding ritornello (Ex. 4.3) included passages *x* (= *a* in Ex. 4.3) and *y* (= *c* in Ex. 4.3) in their entirety, and these were separated by *b*, the Telemann borrowing.

Considered in isolation, this version of the final ritornello is elegantly constructed and, to my ear, appealing. *a*, *b*, and *c* each consist of four bars, and both *a* and *b* can be further divided into two phrases of two bars each. *c* can also be divided into two halves (although less decidedly); its first two bars are identical in terms of rhythm and melodic contour, which change somewhat at the third bar. The symmetrical phrase structure and other similarities of construction among the four-bar components, particularly *a* and *b*, might have resulted in too much segmentation, were it not for the way the units are combined. *a*, the first unit, moves from the dominant at the end of its first phrase to the tonic at the end of its second. Too much closure is avoided by ending with an imperfect authentic cadence (3 over I), and a link to *b* is created by its beginning with the third over the tonic. *b* (the Telemann unit) takes the opposite harmonic path from unit *a*; it is still in the tonic after its first phrase, and the second phrase ends in the dominant (2 over V), creating a link with unit *c*. The final passage *c* moves to the relative minor and back to the tonic (1 over I). Handel offers variety from the opening ritornello by this new combination of materials.

EX. 4.3. Deleted passage from 'Bless'd the day' in *Solomon*, BL RM 20.h.4, fo. 27ᵛ

Large-scale considerations, however, apparently prompted him to revise this postlude. The fact that *b*, the Telemann unit, had just been stated by the voice a few bars before may have been a motivating factor to delete *b* from the closing ritornello. Handel also cut the two bars preceding *b*, which constituted the consequent phrase of *a*. Unit *a* also did not need to be presented again in its entirety. After the cut, the final four bars of the ritornello serve as a consequent to the first two bars of passage *a*. Thus the revision not only eliminates repetition, but also creates a less symmetrical phrase structure.

The aria 'Beneath the vine' in *Solomon* is in some ways quite similar to 'Bless'd the day'. It contains three borrowings from Telemann's 'Wandelt in der Liebe', only two of which need concern us here.[3] The opening ritornello of 'Wandelt in der Liebe' falls into groups of two- and four-bar units. Handel used two of these cells verbatim in his A section: (1) bars 7–9 of Handel's work are taken from bars 9–12 of Telemann (Ex. 4.4); and (2) bars 14–15 of Handel derive from Telemann, 5–8 (Ex. 4.5). From the point of view of revision, the first of these borrowings is the most interesting. It is quite clear from the autograph that Handel thought of borrowing the idea in bars 7–9 only after composing most of the A section. That is, in the first version this two-bar unit from Telemann (hereafter called *x*) did not occur until bar 59 (Chrysander), within the orchestral ritornello that ends the A section of 'Beneath the vine'.

Certain details of Handel's autograph might shed light upon this passage. There seem to be several layers of changes. First he ended with an unaccompanied vocal cadence (rests are visible in the first violin part) at the end of the top system of the page. At this point he may have paused before continuing in the score. When he returned to it, he chose not to begin the concluding ritornello—with which the vocal cadence is elided—in the little space remaining at the end of the top system, but instead in the blank system that followed. He thus removed from the top system the final note of the vocal cadence in voice and bass as well as the syllable '-sure' and moved them to the beginning of the second system. He then continued his composition.[4] The significance of these facts is that if Handel took a period of respite before composing the concluding ritornello, he may have forgotten that the new borrowing *x* in the ritornello had not appeared before in his piece. Or he may have decided upon introducing the new melodic idea after 'sleeping on it', as it were. These possibilities, of course, remain purely speculative.

---

[3] Roberts, 'Handel's Borrowings from Telemann'. 'Wandelt in der Liebe' can be found in Telemann, *Musikalische Werke*, iii. 133–4.

[4] Later, when *x* was inserted in the top system and the unaccompanied vocal cadence rejected, there was room in the top system to write the cadence again, now accompanied. This explanation, at least, best fits the appearance of the autograph.

EX. 4.4. Comparison of (*a*) Telemann, 'Wandelt in der Liebe', bb. 9–12 and (*b*) Handel, *Solomon*, 'Beneath the vine', bb. 7–9

EX. 4.5. Comparison of (*a*) Telemann, 'Wandelt in der Liebe', bb. 5–8 and (*b*) Handel, *Solomon*, 'Beneath the vine', bb. 14–15

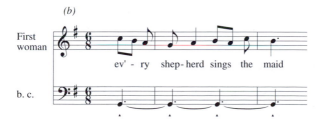

The original form of this concluding ritornello is transcribed in Ex. 4.6. After completing it, Handel decided to go back and distribute x throughout his A section. First he inserted x into the opening ritornello by writing it on the empty staves at the bottom of fo. 84^v and indicating its position in the score with the mark 'NB' (Ex. 4.7(a)). He altered the last melodic note preceding this passage from B to a slide up to D, thus introducing the characteristic rhythmic motif of x: ♫♪. He then inserted x into two further points near the

Ex. 4.6. Original closing ritornello of 'Beneath the vine' in *Solomon*, BL RM 20.h.4, fo. 86^{r-v}

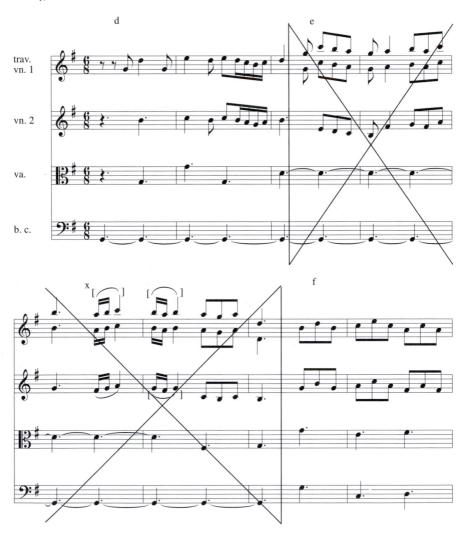

Ex. 4.6. (*cont.*)

A section's end (Ex. 4.7(*b*)). It is squeezed into the lower right margin of fo. 85ᵛ (*HG*, b. 47), where he slightly altered the harmonic setting to fit its new context (this alteration is not shown in Ex. 4.7(*b*)). Finally, again replacing the pedal with alternating dominant and tonic harmonies, he inserted *x* into the top system on fo. 86ʳ (b. 53 ff.), where *x* displaces a repetition of the text 'in a rustic measure' set to a repeat of the vocal cadence.

At this point—or perhaps just before making these last insertions—Handel decided to trim the concluding ritornello—removing the one passage that had contained *x* in the original version! This revision serves as another example of the elimination of excessive thematic repetition similar to, but somewhat more complicated than, those in the two arias discussed earlier; for if he had not cancelled these bars, there would have been three statements of *x* in the tonic within seventeen bars at the end of the A section. He chose to omit the last of these three presentations of *x*, apparently because in the other two passages the inclusion of this unit adds a much needed element of diversity: the use of *x* as an orchestral interlude at bar 57 ff. (Ex. 4.7(*b*), bottom) provides a needed rhetorical pause, separating the last two-bar vocal cadence from the two that precede it; and in bar 47 ff. (Ex. 4.7(*b*), top; insertion written out above it), *x* provides new material for a repeat of the penultimate line of A section text, so that textual and musical repeats do not correspond in bars 43–9—a clever and economical way of adding a touch of variety. This last passage was, I suspect, the primary reason that Handel cut *x* and the two-bar cell preceding it (labelled *e*) from the final ritornello; *e* is stated twice in bars 43–7, followed by *x*, and too shortly afterward, the original version of the concluding ritornello followed, maintaining this order of melodic events. Handel wished to reduce the degree of correspondence between the two passages, and the ritornello could most easily spare the material in question.[5] As a result of the cut, the order of melodic events in the final ritornello does not reflect the succession of thematic cells in any preceding part of the aria.

Such melodic reordering is a salient feature of the piece as a whole. For instance, the redistribution of the Telemann cell throughout the aria constitutes a process of rearrangement; each time that x is inserted, its context is changed. The original concluding ritornello can be divided into a series of

EX. 4.7. Insertions in 'Beneath the vine' in *Solomon*: (*a*) bb. 5–12 (BL RM 20.h.4, fo. 84ᵛ); (*b*) bb. 43–59 (fos. 85ᵛ–86ʳ)

    [5] Handel's omission of *e* and *x* from this final ritornello results also in a more balanced phrase structure of 4(2 + 2) + 4(2 + 2) with a tonic cadence every four bars.

Ex. 4.7. (*cont.*)

musical cells (labelled *d* to *g* in Ex. 4.6); thus *x* occurred between phrases *e* and *f* in the original draft of the concluding ritornello. When Handel inserted *x* in the opening ritornello, however, he placed it between phrases *f* and *g*; when he inserted it at bar 47, he placed it after *e* (as in the original closing ritornello) and before *g* (as in the revised opening ritornello); and so forth. This process of rearrangement of melodic cells applies not only to the Telemann unit, but to almost any cell in the piece, so that the aria is permeated by melodic reordering. As a result, the order of events in the opening ritornello is never again duplicated for more than two cells in succession. Melodic rearrangement is the most significant formal feature that distinguishes 'Beneath the vine' from its source; the order of events in Telemann's ritornello is immediately repeated twice by the singer.

In seventeenth- and eighteenth-century writings the kind of melodic reordering found in 'Beneath the vine' was included in the term *ars combinatoria*.

Sébastian de Brossard's *Dictionnaire de musique* of 1703, for instance, contains the following entry: '*Musica Combinatoria*, that part which teaches the manner of combining the sounds; that is, of changing their place and figure in as many manners as possible.'[6] Leonard Ratner points out that *ars combinatoria* includes 'both permutation, in which a given number of objects is rearranged, and combination, in which it is possible to substitute one object for another in a series'.[7] Both were of interest to Handel, but I am concerned here with what Ratner calls permutation and I shall call reordering.[8] Ratner demonstrates it this way: 'Three letters, A B C, may be arranged in six different ways: ABC ACB BCA BAC CAB CBA.' He has shown the importance of *ars combinatoria* principles to composition in the second half of the eighteenth century.[9]

It seems likely that the melodic *ars combinatoria* of the Classical Period derived from the compositional practices of composers in the first half of the century. As Ellwood Derr has noted, *ars combinatoria* techniques are sometimes used in Handel's borrowing practice, where materials from different parts of a single source or from different sources are rearranged in a new composition.[10] George Buelow has pointed out a relevant passage from Mattheson's *Vollkommene Capellmeister*:

For the theme or principal melody [of a composition], which in the science of melody represents what the text or subject is to an orator, certain formulas must be held in reserve, that can be employed in general [musical] discourse. That is to say: the composer, through much experience and attentive listening to good works, must have collected here and there modulations, little turns, clever motives, pleasing figures, conjunct

---

[6] Leonard Ratner, '*Ars Combinatoria*: Chance and Choice in Eighteenth-Century Music', in H. C. Robbins Landon (ed.), *Studies in Eighteenth-Century Music: A Tribute to Karl Geiringer on his Seventieth Birthday* (London: Allen & Unwin, 1970), 343–63 at 346.

[7] Ibid. 345. Ratner's definition of *ars combinatoria* has been accepted by many musicologists. There is some question, however, whether 18th-c. writers applied the term as broadly as many musicologists do today. According to Heinichin, 'no composer could succeed nowadays if he simply sought and thought of his invention in the otherwise useful *Arte combinatoria*, because by means of this art one can vary 4 notes 24 times and 5 notes 120, etc. according to the usual arithmetical progression. Thus, he could derive from 5 notes 120 *inventiones*, of which only 10 would be useful and dissimilar. In this a composer may succeed once; I am sure it does not happen too often, even though he might change the quantity of the notes at will. Because it is impossible to find the tenderness of the soul of music with mere numeric changes of dead notes . . .'. George J. Buelow, *Thorough-Bass Accompaniment according to Johann David Heinichen*, rev. edn. (Ann Arbor: UMI Research Press, 1986), 330. For Heinichen, then, the term *ars combinatoria* refers to the mathematical or mechanical process as well as the process of recombination. Modern authors are not as rigid as Heinichen; nor shall I be in applying the term to Handel's music.

[8] To my mind permutation implies systematic reordering. Handel is interested in the diversity he can achieve through reordering rather than the process of systematic permutation.

[9] Ibid. He includes as late a piece as the 'Alla Tedesca' movement of Beethoven's Op. 130 as a particularly clear example. See also Wye J. Allenbrook on the 'Catalogue aria' in *Don Giovanni* in *Rhythmic Gesture in Mozart* (Chicago: University of Chicago Press, 1983).

[10] Derr, 'Handel's Procedures for Composing with Materials from Telemann's "Harmonischer Gottes-Dienst" in "Solomon" ', *Göttinger Händel-Beiträge*, 1 (1984), 116–46.

and leaping, which, though consisting only of merely detached things, can bring about something general and complete through suitable combination. If, for example, I should have the three following different and separate passages in mind

and out of them I wished to make one elaborate phrase, it could appear something like the following

For though one or another of these motives and turns might have already been used by other masters and might occur to me without thinking of the first composer or knowing who he was, still this combination of the entire phrase achieves a new form and character. Thus it can be considered as a unique invention . . .[11]

Significantly, Mattheson's phrase changes the original order of the cells.

Roberts's discussion of the borrowings from Keiser, where numerous instances occur of a process of rearrangement of materials from different sources, also would seem to relate to *ars combinatoria*.[12] One example of a rearrangement process quite apart from the borrowing issue has also been discussed by Paul Brainard in regard to the aria 'O placido il mare' in *Siroe*, where Handel changes the order of events in the ritornellos.[13] Clearly the essential principles of *ars combinatoria* (as opposed to strict mathematical permutation) were a central part of Handel's compositional method.

Handel's use of reordering when he composes with borrowings, however, remains an inaudible creative process, for obviously the sources and original versions are not heard when the music is performed. But it is clear from 'Beneath the vine' that he also utilized *ars combinatoria* as an audible phenomenon, an important feature of his musical style, the significance of which has not been fully realized. It is rare that Handel's use of *ars combinatoria* techniques is so thorough as in this aria (perhaps here it makes up for the static harmony), but the technique occurs to a lesser degree in a substantial number of his compositions.[14]

[11] Buelow, 'Mattheson's Concept of "Moduli" as a Clue to Handel's Compositional Process', *Göttinger Händel-Beiträge*, 3 (1989), 272–8.

[12] Roberts, 'Handel's Borrowings from Keiser'.

[13] Brainard, 'Aria and Ritornello', 21–3. He discusses reordering involved in revisions of the ritornellos. He is puzzled, however, by the fact that a passage in A1 ultimately does not follow the order of events in the revised ritornello. The reordering might well have been what Handel was trying to achieve.

[14] Compare, for example, the opening and closing ritornellos of 'Total eclipse' from *Samson* or those of 'The world, when day's career is run' from *Hercules*, to choose only two straightforward instances of this common technique.

'Beneath the vine' reveals two important processes that Handel utilized in the course of revising his scores in order to achieve greater melodic variety: his characteristic efforts to eliminate undue repetition as well as the use of melodic recombination. From the standpoint of form, these two phenomena are related. Both processes—*ars combinatoria* and reducing melodic repetition—insure thematic variety within the context of extended formal structures. This aspect of Handel's music reflects his chronological position in the history of musical style. His music is not so old-fashioned as to follow the Baroque model of a single theme that is spun out and varied in the course of a homogeneous movement. Thus Handel's concern with thematic differentiation and distribution is a relatively forward-looking trait. Yet his style can of course be distinguished from later composers who become even more sensitive to the issue of thematic contrast, particularly in regard to sonata form, which relies on thematic (as well as harmonic) contrast and opposition for its lifeblood.

Moreover, Handel's ability to achieve thematic diversity by manipulating the recurrences and the order of melodic events betrays an obvious but important structural characterisic of his music: the autonomous identity of particular ideas. Brainard has described Handel's musical style as heterogeneous, as opposed to Bach's typically homogeneous, spun-out style. This sort of organization does not apply merely to the melodic aspects of Handel's music, but extends across a number of musical elements and structural levels. Just how profoundly this kind of organization affects Handel's methods of composition and revision will be seen in the following chapters.

5

Handel as Harmonious Blacksmith: Changes in Tonal Structure

THE composing scores of Handel's oratorios include a multitude of revisions involving harmonic structure. This chapter will examine certain recurring types of revisions made possible by techniques of harmonic construction that typify Baroque composition. Such revisions demonstrate that, ironically, Handel often changed harmonic structure in order to alter musical realms other than harmony, including such elements of inner form as phrase structure and sectional proportions, as well as text-setting and dramatic impact. Accordingly, the first category of revisions examined comprises large-scale changes of cadential goals; such changes, made for various reasons, influence a wide variety of musical parameters. The second part of the chapter explores adjustments of harmonic balance and formal proportion, while the third examines the creation of new harmonic areas within movements.

Changes of Harmonic Goals

Leonard Ratner has described two eighteenth-century approaches to large-scale tonality, which he calls circular or 'solar' arrangement and contrasting, or 'polar', arrangement.[1] According to Ratner, the solar arrangement, which represents 'a reinforcement of church modes, in which the tonic was a "sun" surrounded by a constellation of closely related keys', was found particularly in fugues, fantasias, and concertos. In it, unity of key is promoted by subordinating related degrees to the tonic, and by occasional returns of the tonic key. The most systematic explanation of this system is given by Joseph Riepel in his *Grundregeln zur Tonordnung insgemein* (Frankfurt and Leipzig, 1755). Riepel maintains that in a major key the dominant, submediant, and mediant are closer to the tonic than are the subdominant, supertonic, and minor tonic,

---

[1] Leonard G. Ratner, *Classic Music: Expression, Form, and Style* (New York: Schirmer, 1980), 48–51.

a system that reflects Handel's practice, by and large.[2] This hierarchy of key relationships does not necessarily affect large-scale planning, however; Riepel includes charts that list all possible permutations of key relationships in a piece. If, in addition to the tonic, just five keys are used, there are 120 possible arrangements.

The polar arrangement, on the other hand, exploits dramatic conflicts between the tonic and dominant, and typifies the Classical period. However, Ratner maintains that even the polar or 'contrasting key' arrangement also obtained within many Baroque arias:

'Polar' arrangement sets the dominant *against* the tonic (in minor key movements, the relative major is the opposing key). This opposition is potentially dramatic, as the dominant takes over from the tonic in the first part of the movement and the tonic eventually reasserts itself in the second part. Baroque dances, with their choreographic, even dramatic content used this plan, as did many baroque arias, matching the shift of meaning in the text to the shift to the dominant.[3]

Baroque composers, then—certainly composers working in the second quarter of the eighteenth century—could draw on both systems of harmonic arrangement. It is true that in Handel's major-key arias, the 'shift of meaning in the text', at least that between the A section and B section, is generally highlighted by a change in mode rather than a shift to the dominant.[4] However, a modulation from tonic to dominant (or, in minor-mode arias, relative major) governs the majority of Handel's A sections. This tonal progression in A sections is not polar in Ratner's sense, for the 'opposition' of the two keys, often marked by contrasting thematic material, that is found in later sonata form is lacking. Yet even if Handel's A sections are not 'polar' in a strict sense, they rely on a functional tonal relationship—the progression of tonic to dominant to tonic—that sets them apart from B sections, where a 'solar' arrangement can be found.

Substantial changes in harmonic direction, particularly alterations of cadential goals, occur most often in modulatory sections of Handel's arias. It is hardly surprising, then, that in da capo arias such changes are frequently found in B sections, for middle sections are generally more widely modulatory and freer in form than A sections. Because they are not (like A sections) governed by a rigid harmonic plan, middle sections offer the composer multiple, and hence changeable, tonal choices. In the following section, I examine three arias in

[2] See Harris, 'Harmonic Patterns in Handel's Operas'.   [3] Ratner, *Classic Music*, 51.
[4] Handel's minor-key arias often cadence to the minor dominant at the end of the B section (see Harris, 'Harmonic Patterns in Handel's Operas'), but in many cases the mode changes to major at the beginning of the B section.

which Handel altered the B section cadence: 'Where'er you walk' from
Semele, 'Daughter of gods' from *Hercules*, and 'Bless'd the day' from *Solomon*.

These pieces share a significant musical feature: in broad terms, the original
version of every B section consisted of two complete statements of the B section text (though 'Bless'd the day' is a slight exception, as we shall see), and
the setting of each statement was directed towards a cadence in a different
tonality. These two passages, which I shall call B1 and B2, are sufficiently independent that either can be removed without adverse consequences to the
structure of the piece as a whole. In all three of the arias discussed here, Handel literally crossed out B2 from the original versions in his autograph score,
thereby removing an entire tonal area. Although he does not actually recom-
pose passages in order to provide new harmonic orientations, the omissions
result in a change of tonality at the end of the B section, an important structural point within the da capo aria, and these corrections may therefore be
described as changes of cadential goals. In spite of the similarities in both structure and revision, however, each aria offers different reasons for the changes.

Jove's famous aria in *Semele* 'Where'er you walk' serves as a particularly
clear example of the surgical correction described above. This aria originally
had six more bars at the end of its B section, which were cancelled before the
aria was orchestrated (see Ex. 5.1). The six deleted bars constitute B2, a varied repetition at different pitch levels of bars 20–6. After omitting this original ending Handel strengthened the cadence to C minor in bar 27 by replacing the continuous eighth notes in the bass line with two half notes, and
the B section thus ends in C minor rather than D minor.

In its original version, then, the aria exemplifies a typical harmonic pattern
of A section cadence to B section cadence, tonic/minor mediant (I/iii), but
the revision results in a far less common pattern for Handel, tonic/minor
supertonic (I/ii). Both patterns occur in Handel's arias, however, and the evidence suggests that while the revision results in a change of the piece's harmonic structure, this was not Handel's primary concern.

Obviously, the revised version is shorter than the original. This observation has important ramifications for Handel's composing process on the
whole, but for the three arias at hand, all of which are shorter in their final
versions, this result is in most cases at best only a partial explanation of the
motivation behind the revision. After all, the second parts of these B sections
are never exact repetitions of the first parts, and little time is gained from the
cuts. Furthermore, the fact that it was possible to excise either of the two parts
of these B sections does not explain the *raison d'être* of the excisions. Normally
Handel did not alter B sections in this form, for da capo arias with such bi-
partite B sections, though they never constitute a majority, are nevertheless

EX. 5.1. 'Where e'er you walk', original ending of B section from *Semele*, BL RM 20.f.7, fo. 70^{r}

Da Capo without repeating the stanzas, to be wrote

quite common in the oratorios of the 1740s. (Table 5.1 lists such arias in the six oratorios under consideration.) He clearly had no objection to such middle-section construction, then. But in the case of 'Where'er you walk' the simple fact that the B section was shortened may be significant.

Handel's desire for a more concise middle section probably relates to his revision of the A section of this aria, which was originally a binary structure with repeats of A1 (bb. 1–7) and A2 (8–19). The cancelled repeat marks in bars 1, 7–8, and 19 are perfectly legible in the autograph. It appears that he intended that the return of the A section without repeats be copied into the score— a task he apparently meant to leave for the copyists who wrote the conducting score. The original instruction at the end of the B section—undoubtedly intended for the copyist—reads: 'da capo without repeating the stanzas, to be wrote'. This original instruction was replaced with a regular 'da capo' after the

TABLE 5.1. *Da capo arias with bi-partite B sections*

Oratorio	Total	Total da capos
Semele 'Your tuneful voice' 'I must with speed amuse her' 'Come Zephyrs, come'[a]	3	14
Hercules 'The smiling hours' 'When beauty sorrow's liv'ry wears' 'As stars, that rise' 'Banish love from thy breast' 'Alcides' name in latest story' 'Let not fame'[b]	6	13
Belshazzar 'The leafy honours' 'Amaz'd to find'	2	5
Solomon 'Beneath the vine'	1	5
Susanna 'Would custom bid' 'The Parent Bird' 'On fair Euphrates' 'Blooming as the face' 'If guiltless blood' ' 'Tis not age's sullen face' 'Gold within the furnace'	7	16
Jephtha 'Virtue my soul shall still embrace' 'Tune the soft melodious lute' 'His mighty arm'	3	11

[a] Rejected aria; four statements of B text.
[b] Three statements of B text, but 2 authentic cadences.

repeat marks in the A section were removed. At a later point the second half of the B section was also cancelled.

After Handel eliminated the repeat marks, he must have felt that the middle section was disproportionately long and should be shortened as well. In the first version the A section was almost three times as long as the B section, 38 bars to 13 bars. After cutting both sections of the piece the ratio is 19 bars to 7 bars, proportionally about the same as the first version, almost 3:1. The elimination of the last bars of the B section was probably the last event in a chain reaction of musical revisions, and the final revision was primarily a result of Handel's concern with formal balance.[5] We shall see other examples of his concern for formal proportions later in this chapter.

Unlike 'Where'er you walk', the original B section of 'Bless'd the day' from *Solomon* (transcribed in Ex. 5.2) was not completely bi-partite, for the text was never stated twice in corresponding phrases. Nonetheless, the original B section can be divided into two halves on the basis of its harmonic structure. There are two authentic cadences, one to C sharp minor in bars 78–9, and a final cadence to B minor.

Once again Handel's revision is as expedient and economical as can be. The cut was made at the first cadence to C sharp minor (bars 78–9). He then strengthened that cadence by first replacing the authentic cadence with a deceptive cadence, and adding a three-bar unaccompanied cadence to C sharp minor. Again, he might have trimmed the B section when he eliminated the redundant thematic repetition at the end of the A section (discussed in Ch. 4). Although this adjustment of both parts of the aria parallels the revision of 'Where'er you walk', Handel's revision of this aria takes an opposite direction harmonically from that of Jove's aria; that is, the original version of 'Bless'd the day' exemplifies a fairly unusual tonal relationship of A section to B section (tonic/supertonic) which is revised to a more common pattern (tonic/mediant).[6]

The revised version of 'Bless'd the day' offers advantages for the singer, whether or not this was the prime reason for the changes. Because the 'dal segno' repeat of the A section omits the opening ritornello, the singer must begin singing the A section as soon as the B section ends; a shorter B section may have been welcome.[7] Moreover, the mediant key at the end of the B

---

[5] It is possible that the last measure of the original B-section ending is outside the singer's range; in his other arias, Jove does not go below E♭. This hardly accounts for the suppression of B2, however. In order to remedy this problem, Handel could simply have transposed the final measure up one octave, which would make it resemble the C minor ending more closely.

[6] Harris ('Harmonic Patterns in Handel's Operas') has demonstrated that the B sections of da capo arias in Handel's operas frequently cadence to the same key as the final cadence of the recitatives that immediately precede the arias. In the cases of 'Where'er you walk' and 'Bless'd the day' the revised B section cadence so matches the preceding recitative cadence. Harris's findings should not lead us to argue that Handel revised the B section cadences of 'Where'er you walk' and 'Bless'd the day' to match the recitatives, however. In most cases he composed recitatives after he wrote the arias that follow them, and it is as likely as not that he did not compose the recitatives that lead to the arias until after the cadential revisions in the B sections had been made.

[7] In Handel's autograph 'dal segno' appears in a smaller hand than 'Da Capo'. This could indicate that the 'dal segno' mark was added later, and that the B minor ending belonged to the da capo form of the aria, with an opening ritornello that allows the singer to get A major back in her ear. This possibility cannot be proved, however, for the evidence of the autograph is by no means straightforward. First, Handel seems to have eliminated earlier dal segno signs at the end of the B section for unknown reasons. Furthermore, at one time he had placed dal segno signs in the aria at bar 53, shortly before the A section ends. These were omitted before the ink dried. Since this is a highly unlikely place for a dal segno repeat to begin, perhaps he simply made a mistake, or perhaps they were written 'in process' before he had decided to end the A section more immediately.

section allows the singer to end on C#, her pitch at the opening of the A section.

Nonetheless, this compositional change has musical and dramatic consequences that go beyond simply paring down a lengthy aria. For instance, the omission affects the phrase structure of the B section. The soprano's phrases in the omitted passage were quite irregular:

$$3(2 + 1) + 2 + 2\frac{1}{2} + 4$$

This passage, with its uneven phrase lengths, originally followed B1, which in contrast consists of rigorously regular two-bar phrases for the voice (altogether seven of them). Unlike the first half of the B section with its long pedal-point, the intensely expressive second half of the B section offers an active bass line with frequent harmonic changes. After the cancellation, therefore, the B section consists solely of two-bar phrases, almost all with the same basic rhythmic pattern, until the final three-bar phrase. Although the revised B section does not seem to me to be a musical improvement upon the original, it is nonetheless a tour de force, managing to maintain a high level of musical interest both melodically and harmonically in spite of its regular phrase structure and recurring rhythms.

In sum, after revision 'Bless'd the day' is more stable in terms of both local large-scale harmonic progressions and more regular in regard to phrase structure. The irregular phrase lengths and even the somewhat unusual harmonic plan of the original version were perhaps inappropriate for a text describing the peaceful joy of marital bliss. After all, the B section text does not contrast with the A text, but rather intensifies or heightens its meaning ('But *completely* bless'd the day . . .'). As a result of the correction, the textual similarities between the two sections is paralleled by musical similarities, for the A section is also, on the whole, marked by symmetrical phrase structure, and contains a straightforward modulation (to the dominant and back).[8]

Rather than underscoring the stability of marriage, the expressive first setting of the B section of 'Bless'd the day' actually invites an ironic interpretation of the text that suggests just the opposite. According to Ruth Smith, religious writings of the time voiced disapproval of Solomon's relations with women. Old Testament commentator Thomas Stackhouse admitted that 'so

---

[8] All other things being equal, this interpretation may seem contradicted by the example of 'Where'er you walk', in which the B section text also complements rather than contrasts with the text for the A section: it simply continues Jove's blessing. But as I have noted, Handel's harmonic revision is the reverse of that of 'Bless'd the day'. The answer is that, in artistic matters, other things are never equal. It should be pointed out, first of all, that the irregular phrase structure rather than the harmonic content of the original B section of 'Bless'd the day' may have been the deciding factor. Second, the B section of 'Where'er you walk' contains melodic material from the A section, a relationship lacking in the *Solomon* aria, and this alone highlights the affinity between the texts.

unbounded was [Solomon's] Lust, that he had seven hundred Wives, and three hundred Concubines . . .'.⁹ As Smith points out, 'in the biblical narrative Solomon's moral and religious decline sets in immediately after the Queen of Sheba's visit, the point at which the libretto tactfully ends, thus avoiding the major blots on the king's character'.¹⁰ Even so, an eighteenth-century audience would certainly have been aware of Solomon's later adultery. The increased expressiveness of the original B section begins at the point when the queen reminisces about Solomon's 'vowing to be only mine, only mine'. The repeat of the last two words is particularly striking, for it brings about the first break in the steady flow of two-bar vocal phrases in the B section (see Ex. 5.2, bb. 81–2). Underscoring this text, of course, runs the danger of reminding the audience that it is not true, endangering the aim of the libretto to present Solomon as virtuous. Indeed, the first setting comes too close for comfort to the 'major blot' upon King Solomon's character. Admittedly Handel's cut does not remove the text entirely, but it significantly de-emphasizes it. The shorter B section is less suggestive and more innocent—more capable, perhaps, of suspending disbelief in Solomon's vow.

The motivation behind Handel's revision of the B section cadence of 'Daughter of gods' in *Hercules* is impossible to grasp with certainty. The cadential bars are both difficult to read in the autograph score and possibly incomplete, but it is at least certain that the twelve omitted bars ended in D minor. The original B section, reconstructed in Ex. 5.3, was clearly in two parts, the first cadencing to E flat in bars 119–20, the second a different setting of the B section text. We cannot be sure what would have happened after the D minor cadence of the B section, but it seems likely, given Handel's typical procedure, that there would have been a pause followed by a full return of the A section, including the ritornello.

Not only is the second version shorter than the first; it is simpler tonally, because the omitted second half of the B section contained some daring melodic and harmonic moves absent from the first half—such as the leap of a tritone from g' to $c\#''$ in bars 124–5 and the V chord in bar 130 (where the seventh in the bass 'resolves', only after a quarter-note rest, by a leap of a seventh). After removing this second part, Handel inserted bars 119–22 (in *HG* 4: 71, 1/4–2/1), which provide the B section with its only melisma. This addition, in some ways reminiscent of the A section, is harmonically straightforward and directed towards E flat major. Like 'Where'er you walk',

⁹ Thomas Stackhouse, *A New History of the Holy Bible from the Beginning of the World to the Establishment of Christianity* (1737), ii. 775, 791; as quoted by Ruth Smith, *Handel's Oratorios and Eighteenth-Century Thought* (Cambridge: Cambridge University Press, 1995), 316.
¹⁰ Ibid.

Ex. 5.3. 'Daughter of gods' in *Hercules*: (*a*) original B section (BL RM 20.e.8, fos. 35^v–36^r); (*b*) final version, dal segno ritornello

Ex. 5.3. (*cont.*)

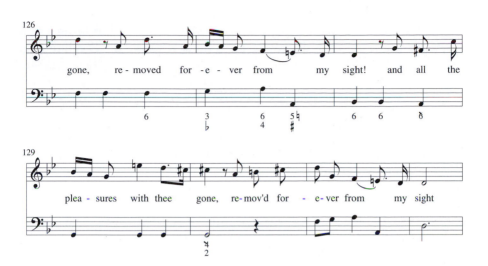

gone, re - moved for -e - ver from my sight! and all the

plea - sures with thee gone, re - mov'd for - e- ver from my sight

(b)

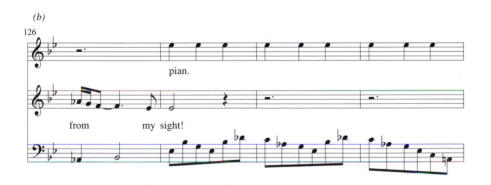

pian.

from my sight!

Dal Segno. %

Dal Segno. %

the first version manifests Handel's most typical relationship of A-section cadence to B-section cadence (I/iii), while the second version is more rare (I/IV), and involves no change of mode between sections A and B.[11]

The key to understanding why Handel altered the aria in this manner may lie in an unusual aspect of the new version. After rejecting the D minor ending, he wrote a 'dal segno' ritornello to replace the opening ritornello—or more specifically, to replace the end of the opening ritornello (bb. 127–32 correspond to bb. 11–18). The musical material of bars 11–12 reappears in 127–9, but at a different pitch level. Whereas the first ritornello has a melodic pedal on F in bars 11–12, the dal segno ritornello uses E flat, which is transformed into the seventh of a chord on F, thus preserving the dominant function that F major had in the opening ritornello (see Ex. 5.3(*b*)). These facts may be significant for two reasons. First, the use of E flat in the dal segno ritornello creates a link with the first ritornello. After bars 11–12, where dominant and tonic chords alternate, the opening ritornello moves to a sustained subdominant chord (13–15), which moves finally to a cadence to the tonic. Second, and more significant, because the dal segno ritornello begins in E flat, the new vocal cadence to E flat allows an elision between the vocal cadence and the beginning of this new ritornello (bb. 126–7). Thus the presence of E flat links the two ritornellos, but its harmonic function differs in each: in the opening ritornello E flat functions as subdominant, whereas in the dal segno ritornello, though it functions locally as a secondary dominant to A flat, it ultimately becomes part of a dominant seventh chord that will resolve to B flat (127–9).

It is impossible to assert with confidence that this final version completely explains the tonal revision of the B section, for we do not know what Handel would have done after the D minor vocal cadence. At the very least, one can assume that the E flat link between the two ritornellos and the elision between the vocal cadence and the dal segno ritornello would not have occurred in the original D minor ending. Handel might, in fact, have chosen an atypical tonal relationship in order to bring about these unusual structural phenomena. Harmonic revision is here related to structural change and continuity, an important topic discussed in Chapter 7.

Changes in Harmonic Balance in B Sections

Even in those arias where the key arrangements are discursive or solar, Handel made revisions which—unlike the insertions and deletions in B sections

---

[11] Two of the three revisions of B sections evidence a change from a more to a less typical harmonic relationship of A-section cadence to B-section cadence, but it would be dangerous to formulate a conclusion about Handel's revisional tendencies from so few examples.

and solar A sections examined above—do not bring about basic alterations of
an aria's tonal content, but rather adjust the degree to which a tonal goal is
emphasized. Such revisions occur here in B sections consisting of two or
more parts. The two arias that exemplify this procedure here happen to contain corrections that affect the first tonal goal of bi-partite B sections rather
than the last.

In Athamas's aria 'Your tuneful voice' from *Semele*, bars 47–51 in *HG* 7:67,
1/2–2/2 were later insertions into the autograph. Originally bar 53 followed
bar 46 (see Ex. 5.4). In this first version there is an authentic cadence to D
major, but the music continues through the cadence to a B minor chord. The
insertion increases the importance of D in two ways. First, there is now a
one-bar rest in the vocal part after the strong cadence in bars 50–1, which is
reinforced by the orchestra in bars 52–3 before it moves to the B minor

EX. 5.4. Original and revised versions of 'Your tuneful voice' in *Semele*, BL RM
20.f.7, fo. 35^r

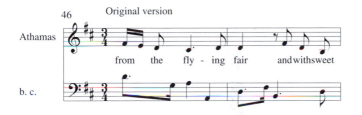

chord, and this strong cadence in bars 50–1 is anticipated by weaker ones: V–I^6 in bars 46–7, V$^6_5$–I in 48. Second, the cadence is strengthened by the new phrase structure, both locally and on a broad scale. The first version cadenced at the end of the third of three two-bar phrases, and another two-bar phrase followed this cadence. The new version of bars 41–51 relieves this regularity:

$$2 \times 2 + 4 + 2$$
$$^\wedge\text{cadence}$$

This general pattern is found at other important cadential points as well; short phrases lead to a long phrase, followed by a short phrase that cadences. In fact, the phrase pattern 2 + 4 + 2 occurs at the most important vocal cadences in the aria, at the end of the A section (bb. 28–37 = *HG* 7: 66, 1/5–3/4) and the end of the B section, bb. 53–61 (*HG* 7: 67, 2/3–3/5):

A section cadence: $3 \times 2 + 4 + 2$
$$^\wedge\text{cadence}$$
B section cadence: $2 + 4 + 2$
$$^\wedge\text{cadence}$$

In all cases the four-bar penultimate phrase sounds incomplete, and demands the resolution of the two-bar cadential phrase.

The weight given to D major in the revised aria is important for both musical and dramatic reasons. The B minor A section of this despondent aria eschews the expected medial cadence to the relative major: D major. The new emphasis on D major makes up for this lack. At this point in the drama Athamas is unaware of Semele's involvement with Jove, but rightly cognizant of the fact that something is wrong with their relationship. The added emphasis on the major mode at this point in his aria reflects Athamas's shift from despair to pleasure as he realizes that his despair has won Semele's pity: 'and with sweet melody compel attention from the flying fair'. The added melisma for 'flying fair' is as much an indication of Athamas's fascination for Semele as it is a mimetic device.

An aria for Athamas from the last act of *Semele*, 'Despair no more shall wound me', shows a revision whose effect is opposite. Handel excised several bars that originally fell between bars 64 and 65 (Ex. 5.5). Most of this passage was directed towards the key in which the B section began, G minor, with G minor cadences of varying strengths in bars 66–7, 70–1, and 72, as well as a cadence to G minor in the bar after this rejected passage (*HG*, b. 65). Thus the original B section was weighted towards G minor, with only the final bars directed towards D minor, the concluding key. Handel's revision

Ex. 5.5. 'Despair no more shall wound me' in *Semele*, BL RM 20.f.7, fo. 110ᵛ

shifts the balance. Now only five of twelve bars prolong G minor, and the weak-beat cadence to G minor in the fifth bar (*HG* 7: 214, 3/2) is further weakened because it initiates a fifths progression. Besides altering the tonal balance, this revision creates a somewhat more continuous harmonic motion. Moreover, melismas on 'joy' and 'surround' are thereby omitted from this already ornate aria. Though the revision thus reduces the emphasis on individual words, it is still conceivable that it reflects a concern with matters of text-setting: a 'circle' of fifths progression seems more appropriate than repeated G minor cadences for the text 'all joy and bliss *surround* me'. After all, Handel rarely missed an opportunity to exercise the art of portraying physical motion in music. The contemporary criticisms aroused by this feature of his compositions will be explored in Chapter 9.

Addition of New Harmonic Areas

The standard modulatory scheme of the A section, when the five-part da capo plan is followed (I–V–I or i–III–i), leaves less room for harmonic alteration than do B sections. Nonetheless, changes in cadential goals can also occur in A sections, especially if they do not follow these conventional tonal paradigms verbatim. For example, the Fitzwilliam contains a fully orchestrated draft for the A section of 'The Parent Bird' in *Susanna* (transcribed in Ex. 5.6). A comparison of the two versions of this aria discloses an opposite (and therefore related) method of revision from that of most of the B sections discussed above, one of large-scale insertion rather than deletion. Though the melody and rhythm were originally somewhat different, the Fitzwilliam draft shares its basic musical material with the final version of 'The Parent Bird', but there are important tonal and structural changes between the two versions.[12] With its two statements of text and fully formed ritornellos, the draft is structurally regular, but tonally atypical, modulating to the subdominant rather than the mediant:

A section:	Rit. 1	A1	Rit. 2	A2	Rit. 3
	i	i–iv	iv	iv–i	i

The final autograph version of the A section has been structurally expanded to contain a central modulation to the ccminor dominant:

---

[12] The Fitzwilliam draft of 'The Parent Bird' is based on the aria 'Quando non son presente' from Handel's Italian cantata 'Da sete ardente afflitto'. The A section of the Italian da capo aria contains two statements of the text, but it avoids an internal cadence; there is no authentic cadence between the vocal entrance and the final vocal cadence to the tonic, A minor.

Ex. 5.6. Original version of 'The Parent Bird' in *Susanna*, FM MUS MS 259, pp. 79–80

Ex. 5.6. (*cont.*)

some rude hand de-spoil her nest, lest some rude hand, lest some rude hand de-spoil her

nest.

The

Pa-rent Bird, in search of food a while de - serts her cal - low brood,

Ex. 5.6. (*cont.*)

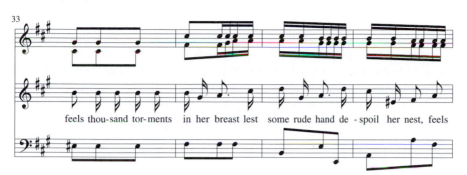

feels thou-sand tor-ments in her breast lest some rude hand de - spoil her nest, feels

thou - sand tor - ments in her breast lest some rude hand de - spoil her

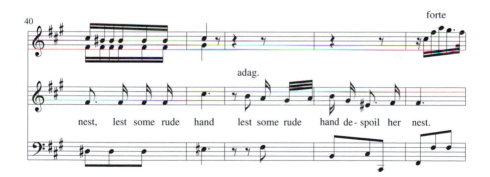

nest, lest some rude hand lest some rude hand de - spoil her nest.

A section:	Rit. 1	A1	Rit. 2	A2	A3	Rit. 3
	i	i–v	v	–iv	iv–i	i

While such a thorough-going overhaul necessitated writing out an entirely new A section (and perhaps the B section as well, though we cannot know for sure), with many changes of detail along the way, a close examination of the two versions shows a strong melodic/harmonic correspondence between the rejected draft (A1 and A2) and A2–A3 of the autograph.[13] In effect, Handel has inserted a new A1 after the first ritornello, ensuring its structural prominence by placing the central ritornello just after it and eliminating the ritornello that initially followed the modulation to the subdominant. Like the B section cuts, this revision can still be described as an alteration of an important structural cadence: he has not altered any harmonic progression, but simply added one more.

The manner in which Handel expanded 'The Parent Bird' was possible because its unusual A section—like the B sections of the three arias discussed in the first part of this section—followed a 'solar' arrangement of keys, which made expansion or deletion simple to bring about. Thus the circular or solar arrangement of keys seems to obtain in all the harmonic revisions discussed in this chapter. Handel does not actually change the order of keys, as in Riepel's table, but he is free to omit or insert new key areas, thus changing the identity of cadences at important structural points within arias. This concept of key relationships is opposed to the more functional, contrasting approach to key areas found in most A sections of da capo arias. Because typical A sections rely primarily on tonic/dominant polarity the introduction or deletion of whole tonal areas would have more serious repercussions upon the coherence of the formal structure.

Handel's revisions involving changes of cadential goals and amplification or diminution of tonal areas sometimes create more regular harmonic patterns, at other times more unusual ones. But often such changes were not made for reasons relating specifically to harmony: rather the tonal structure of sections within da capo arias (particularly B sections) enabled him to make 'harmonic' changes whose primary aims lay in other musical realms. What such revisions show us above all is a composer acutely aware of two issues: first, the purely musical importance of achieving formal balance and proportion; and second, the theatrical capacity of musical structure to convey textual and dramatic meaning.

---

[13] In general, the vocal writing in the final version is more conjunct than the original, which might suggest that the revision was made in part for the ease of the singer (Galli). This could not explain the tonal expansion, however.

6

Texture as Form

DURING the eighteenth century Handel was singled out for his expertise in fugal writing. Mattheson, for one, included in his famous reminiscences the following evaluations of Handel: 'When a certain world-famous man came here to Hamburg for the first time, he knew how to compose nothing but regular fugues . . .'.[1] 'He was strong on the organ: stronger than Kuhnau in fugue and counterpoint, especially *ex tempore*.'[2] Later in the century Charles Burney, in the *Account of the Commemoration of Handel*, eulogized Handel's 'full, masterly and excellent organ-fugues' in which he 'surpassed Frescobaldi, and even Sebastian Bach, and others of his countrymen, the most renowned for abilities in this difficult and elaborate species of composition'.[3]

Although few would agree with Burney's assessment today, we need not rely solely on Handel's contemporaries for high assessments of his contrapuntal ability. Recently Alfred Mann has shown how Handel's profound understanding of fugal techniques is manifested in his composition lessons for Princess Anne. According to Mann, 'Handel deals with all essential aspects of fugue: real and tonal answer, canonic writing, stretto, augmentation and diminution, double counterpoint and melodic inversion'.[4] In short, the fact that Handel wrote fewer 'strict' fugues than Bach seems to have been a practical as well as an aesthetic choice—and not a surprising one for an opera composer—rather than a technical deficiency.[5] The evidence from Handel's autographs, in fact, suggests that he wrote counterpoint with ease.

[1] Johann Mattheson, *Critica Musica*, i, pt. 4, no. 1 (Hamburg, 1723), 243, trans. Deutsch, *Handel: A Documentary Biography*, 146.

[2] Johann Mattheson, *Grundlage einer Ehren-Pforte* (Hamburg, 1740), ed. Schneider (Berlin 1910), 93.

[3] Burney, *An Account of the Musical Performances in Westminster-Abbey, and the Pantheon, May 26th, 27th, 29th; and June the 3d, and 5th, 1784. In Commemoration of Handel* (London, 1785). The statement excited furore when it was published in Germany, particularly from C. P. E. Bach. See Kerry Grant, *Dr. Burney as Critic and Historian of Music* (Ann Arbor: UMI Research Press, 1983), 194–5.

[4] See Mann, *Georg Friedrich Händel: Composition Lessons*, 44.

[5] Janet Levy has pointed out that counterpoint is often given covert value in writings about music, and the absence of counterpoint must be defended, if a composer's position among the 'greatest' is to be maintained. See Levy, 'Covert and Casual Values in Recent Writings About Music', *Journal of Musicology*, 5 (1987), 3–27. In spite of the false values implicit in it, the belief that Handel's neglect of 'true' fugal writing represents a compositional weakness unfortunately persists among those who should know better.

The discussion of Handel's sketches for 'And pitying heav'n' in Chapter 3 disclosed that Handel approached fugal writing just as Bach did, by first setting out various combinations of fugal subjects before beginning to write out the work. In this chapter we shall examine issues of texture that manifest themselves in later stages of the compositional process. The surviving autograph materials allow us to examine Handel's approach to counterpoint in two spheres: (1) changes within bona fide choral fugues; (2) changes involving counterpoint in pieces that are not predominantly fugal.

Changes in Fugal Choruses

Perhaps the most interesting residue from Handel's rethinking of a fugue can be found in the autograph of *Belshazzar*. The fugue 'And every step' underwent at least two interesting changes, and perhaps other untraceable ones. In its first version, the opening statement of the subject, divided between alto and soprano, was accompanied by eighth notes in the bass (Ex. 6.1). The subject itself is somewhat ambiguous tonally, a fact that has ramifications for later revisions in the score. The chromaticism of the head-motif obscures the tonic; because the subject appears after a cadence to E minor, the listener may first assume that the key of the fugue is in that key, and the subject begins by filling in the third between G and E, then between A and F#. Only with the high point of the subject and the ensuing descending scale do we feel that we are in G major, ending on the dominant note, and this ambiguity is an important component of the piece. The harmonized first setting does little to clarify the harmony; certainly it does not emphasize the tonic G major.

Handel rejected this accompanied version for a more typical monophonic first statement of the subject. There are two noteworthy results of the cut. First, the bass, marked 'tasto solo', now doubles the subject, which underscores the word-painting: the doubling emphasizes the chromatically descending quarter notes that depict 'every step' as well as the later scalar passage for 'precipitates the thunder down'. Second, the original accompaniment contains the motif that in the later version becomes one of the countersubjects, labelled *x* in Ex. 6.1. Omitting the accompaniment clarified the function of this motif as a countersubject: in the final setting it first appears with the second statement of the subject.

A later change in this chorus is an extensive cut, which is perhaps best understood if the structure of the whole fugue is taken into account. Here one can speak of a fully formed exposition (bb. 1–23); each statement of the subject is accompanied by drastically different material in the other voices,

EX. 6.1. Original beginning of 'And ev'ry step' in *Belshazzar*, BL RM 20.d.10, fo. 78ᵛ

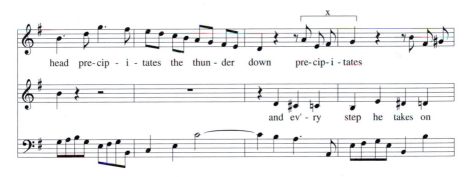

beginning with a striking countersubject and ending with a homophonic set-ting, so that one hears the subject in numerous contexts before the exposition ends. A brief episode leads to a homophonic cadence in A minor (ii), and the next statement of the subject (in the bass, bar 30 ff.) is preceded by appear-ances of the chromatic head-motif of the subject.

A few bars thereafter (b. 37 = *HG* 19: 116, 1/5) comes the deleted passage (Ex. 6.2). In this part of the chorus, Handel features the end of the subject, the scalar descent on 'precipitates the thunder down', in imitation with pedal-points on F# and B before ending in E minor (vi). Following this (picking up again in b. 37) is a modulatory statement of the subject, followed by a stretto on the tail-motif of the subject (not unlike the omitted passage), and finally a homophonic concluding passage.

There are two main results of the cut. First, the amount of material based on the tail-motif is greatly reduced, though this motif remains a significant feature of the piece. The head- and tail-motifs of the subject contrast in every

conceivable way, and alternately featuring one or the other provides enormous contrast. Second, and particularly important, is the harmonic realm.
The piece begins, it seems, in E minor, and ends in G major. As we have

Ex. 6.2. 'And ev'ry step', original bars 37 ff. in *Belshazzar*, BL RM 20.d.10, fos.
81ʳ–82ʳ

Ex. 6.2. (*cont.*)

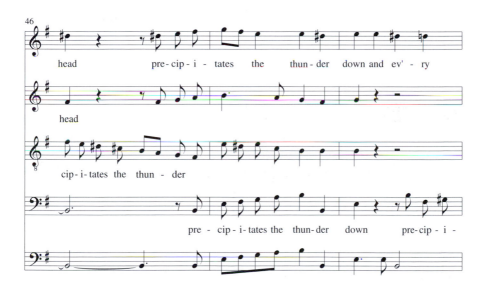

Ex. 6.2. (*cont.*)

seen, so, too, does the fugue's subject (in its tonic statement) begin in E minor and end on the dominant note of G. The thirteen omitted bars are in E minor with a strong cadence in that key, and Handel may have wanted ultimately to obscure E minor as a potential tonic, particularly at this point two-thirds of the way through the piece, where it upsets the harmonic balance by threatening the ultimate tonic function of G major. As it stands in the final version, the cadences of the piece are to A minor and G major.

The fugal chorus 'Let justice reign' from *Susanna* underwent a similar revision. In its present form the fugue is permeated by statements of the subject, making it difficult to determine precisely where, for example, the end of the exposition occurs. Bars 34–48 are the most episodic passages, and bars 49 to 60 or so constitute a second exposition, followed by a homophonic conclusion.

One passage from this chorus was cancelled before or during orchestration (Ex. 6.3). This omitted passage of thirty-six bars (originally between bar 38 and bar 40) provided: (1) three transformed statements of the subject in D minor and A minor, leading to a strong cadence in A minor; (2) a restatement of the ritornello and homophonic passages ('nor youth nor charms', etc.) which return (through F) to B flat major. Handel rejected this passage and replaced it with two bars (38–9).

This revision again raises formal and harmonic issues, since a key area is eliminated from the piece, and the homophonic 'nor youth nor charms' section is reduced and not articulated by ritornellos in the final version. In

EX. 6.3 'Let justice reign' in *Susanna*, BL RM 20.f.8, fo. 74ʳ

Ex. 6.3. (*cont.*)

short, this revision and that of 'and ev'ry step' are similar not only to one another but to a whole class of revisions that one could find in any of Handel's compositions, not one intrinsically tied to fugue. In fact, such revisions that rely on autonomous sections of music that can easily be deleted, compressed, or expanded, or have new sections of music inserted, are essentially like those harmonic revisions discussed in the previous chapter. This

Ex. 6.3. (*cont.*)

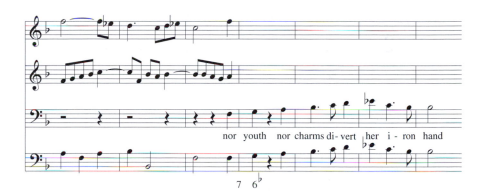

principle of revision, then, cuts across many parameters of Handel's music. Similar revisions, yet more closely related to contrapuntal texture as an important feature in its own right, can be found within choruses of varied textures.

Changes of Texture in Other Choruses

Handel's choruses are profoundly heterogeneous in regard to texture. If full-blown fugal movements are relatively rare in the oratorios, fugatos and contrapuntal passages are an essential aspect of Handelian choral writing. Counterpoint was for Handel one of a number of possible formal constituents, and he sometimes changed his mind about where counterpoint should be introduced in a piece, or even if it should be featured at all.

As noted in Chapter 2, the length of *Belshazzar* in its original version concerned the composer. Among the 'retrenchments' that Handel claimed to have made to the score in his letter of 2 October 1744 to Jennens is the (pencil) deletion of a section of the chorus 'All empires upon God depend'. After the first two bars there originally began a fugue on the text 'as begun by his command'. He cut twenty-six bars, leaving only the homophonic setting of the text that appeared at the end of the fugue.

Similarly, he excised two passages from the chorus 'Praise the Lord' in *Solomon* after the conducting score had been prepared. Both passages begin with a theme that is imitated at the distance of half a bar, and the second omitted passage extends this material into an appearance of a cantus firmus against faster-moving parts. If there were reasons for the removal of these contrapuntal passages besides the possible desire to shorten a long chorus, they remain obscure.

A more interesting change occurs in the famous chorus 'Jealousy, infernal pest', also from *Hercules*. Here Handel has written three distinct themes (including ritornello material) that can be contrapuntally combined. In his first draft, he combined these themes at the end of the first section of the piece, at bar 27 (Ex. 6.4). Before orchestrating the piece, he removed this passage. Since it ended on B, like the passage preceding it, no rewriting was required. This, of course, is typical of Handel's revisions.

The primary importance of the cut relates to form. In the revised version of the chorus the simultaneous appearance of themes is reserved for the return of the first section at the end of the chorus. The contrapuntal artifice therefore becomes a climactic gesture at the end of the piece.

The concluding chorus of *Susanna*, 'A virtuous wife', was entirely homophonic in its original form. Handel made two related insertions at a late stage, adding five bars (28–32) in the margin between fos. 131^v and 132^r, and, by inserting fo. 133, adding bars 59–68. Merely slight changes were necessary in the measures surrounding these insertions. The main function of his insertions was perhaps to ameliorate the previously unrelenting homophony by adding passages that begin with a point of imitation. The counterpoint here serves simply to vary the texture.

Handel's choral style on the whole, then, is remarkable for its flexibility regarding form and texture, encompassing impressive contrapuntal writing and much else. Shifts in thematic material, key, dynamics, and texture in his choruses are often wedded to changes in text. Consequently, Handel's choruses offer a great deal of dramatic and musical contrast to the listener, and present a multitude of formal, including textural, choices to their composer. Handel's revisions involving texture disclose compositional concerns like

Ex. 6.4. 'Jealousy, infernal pest' in *Hercules*, BL RM 20.e.8, fos. 58ᵛ–59ʳ

those found in all his compositions: effective text-setting, tonal balance, formal proportions, and musical contrast.

Together with 'And pitying heav'n', discussed in Chapter 3, these examples take us back to an earlier observation. The kaleidoscope of shifting textures, which lends an improvisatory quality to Handel's choruses, was sometimes a result of careful planning or revision rather than a mere by-product of
his improvisatory approach to composition. We must distinguish between the
composition and the act of composing. The compositions themselves give
the impression of freedom or improvisation, but their creation frequently
involved careful revision, a non-improvisatory aspect of the creative process.

7

The Rough Places Made Plain: Closure vs. Continuity

ON the most basic level, the following discussion is devoted to cadences. Where a cadence is placed, whether it is strong or weak, whether it is emphasized or suppressed, has important ramifications for inner form. Our first task in this chapter is to address the issue of rebarring, a common kind of revision encountered in Handel's oratorios. Such revisions are rarely a simple matter of notation: rebarrings raise significant questions touching not only upon cadence placement, but also upon aspects of metre and thematic construction. In fact, Handel's rebarrings ultimately will lead us to a profound compositional concern of the composer: the need to produce a continuous musical surface.

In the second book of *Der vollkommene Capellmeister* (1739), Johann Mattheson offers practical advice about composing melodies. According to Mattheson, the 'caesura', or the final melodic note of resolution of a cadence or phrase, should occur on the strong beats of the bar—that is, in common time, on beats 1 or 3, but not on beats 2 or 4; in triple time, only on the down-beat:

> The observation of the orderly division of every tactus, namely the so-called *caesura*, gives us the fifth rule of clarity. Such a division always occurs on either the down-beat or up-beat when the measure is even, never on the second and last quarter. But in the uneven pulse this division occurs only on the down-beat; or better said, there is no division at all because the *caesura* is merely at the first note of the segment. It is as much a failure in composition to construct a cadence or an otherwise noticeable pause in the voice contrary to this nature of the meter, as when a Latin poet stresses the end of the poetic foot, and thus lets the *caesura* hang: this may be done only at the end of a verse.[1]

---

[1] Ernest C. Harriss, *Johann Mattheson's Der vollkommene Capellmeister: A Revised Translation with Critical Commentary* (Ann Arbor: UMI Research Press, 1981), 321.

A bit further on he illustrates his point with music:[2]

The following example by an otherwise good master shows how easily one can err here. This also shows simultaneously how easily such failures might be prevented, and really right at the beginning: for otherwise they roll always onward, and grow like snowballs:

Mattheson's advice reflects the practice of competent composers of his time. In fact, these excerpts from *Der vollkommene Capellmeister* explain at least one compositional revision executed by Handel. Mattheson's point about positioning the caesura could be illustrated equally well with the original and revised readings of a passage from the autograph of Handel's *Semele* (Ex. 7.1). In the opening ritornello of the great quartet 'Why dost thou thus untimely grieve' Handel first cadenced to beat 4, possibly by mistake.[3] He revised this at once, before continuing the composition.

My purpose here is not to prove that Handel was familiar with *Der voll-kommene Capellmeister*, though this is certainly possible, but to point out the striking commonality of musical practice between the two men, who, after all, emerged from similar backgrounds and, at least during the early part of their careers, were acquainted with each other's works.[4] Moreover, Mattheson's observations bring to mind a related aspect of Handel's compositional revisions. Although the caesura, as Mattheson states, may properly occur on either beat 1 or 3 of a bar of common time, Handel's practice

---

[2] Harriss, *A Revised Translation with Critical Commentary*, 322.

[3] In the autograph there is a barline before the E in the melody. This makes me think that Handel did not actually intend to cadence to the fourth beat, but had miscounted. There are, of course, other possibilities. Discounting the barline in violin 1, it is possible that the displaced caesura relates to the concept of 'untimely'. Taking the barline into account, it is possible that he intended metrical shifts (like 'Bel piacere'). But miscounting seems to me the most likely explanation.

[4] It is clear from his letter of 24 Feb. 1719 to Mattheson that Handel had read *Das beschützte Orchestre* (1717). See Deutsch, *Handel: A Documentary Biography*, 87–8. Whether or not Handel knew *Der voll-kommene Capellmeister* by 1743 (or ever) I do not know.

EX. 7.1. 'Why dost thou thus untimely grieve' in *Semele*, BL RM 20.f.7, fo. 23ʳ

suggests that, depending on context, it is better placed on one or the other of these positions. Time and time again in the autographs of the late oratorios, particularly in the 'twin' oratorios of 1747 *Solomon* and *Susanna*, Handel seems to have changed his mind about whether to employ a strong, down-beat cadence or a weak cadence to beat 3.

The aria 'Round thy urn' in *Susanna*, whose opening ritornello in its first version appears as Ex. 7.2, provides a classic example of such a revision. It was

Ex. 7.2. 'Round thy urn', first version of opening ritornello in *Susanna*, BL RM
20.f.8, fo. 93^v

apparently just as he reached the ritornello cadence (originally to beat 3) that
Handel decided to rebar his score. Before continuing the composition
beyond this point, he returned to the opening bar, added a half-note rest in
the treble part and a half note in the bass, and then rebarred the ritornello.
This, of course, is the method of moving the caesura endorsed by Mattheson,
executed, in more than one way, 'right at the beginning'. As a result of
Handel's rebarring, the ritornello concludes with a strong cadence.

  This type of revision occurs with impressive frequency. Handel's decision
to rebar the orchestral introduction of Daniel's ''Tis not age's sullen face'

from *Susanna* again seems to have occurred to him just as he approached the cadence. 'Can I see my infant gor'd' in *Solomon* underwent an identical transformation, though here he never wrote out a weak-beat cadence, instead trying to cadence on the strong beat by means of an extension. Dissatisfied with this solution, he went back and rebarred.[5]

Handel's rebarrings are not always confined to such short spans, but may encompass entire musical sections or even whole pieces, as, for example, in the B section of 'Bless'd the day' from *Solomon*.[6] It is difficult to tell from the autograph whether or not Handel had actually reached the last cadence before he decided to rebar, but he was at least in close proximity to this cadence when the decision took place; thus cadence placement may again have played a part in prompting the revision, but there seem to be two other consequences that are even more important. First, shifting the caesuras throughout the B section is certainly an important result of the rebarring; in the altered version the last, stressed syllable of each line, the rhyming syllable, falls on the down-beat of the bar every time. In this way, the rebarred version enhances the structure and rhyme scheme of the poem.

Secondly, at least one non-metrical aspect of the revision deserves mention: in this particular case, the addition of the half bar at the beginning of the B section is itself of some intrinsic interest (*HG* 26: 83, 1/1; the first half-bar was inserted later). The first version, in which the singer had to enter on beat 2 (of six), may have been a touch awkward. The inserted half bar provides a brief 'introduction' to the B section, previewing the vocal entrance with an arpeggio in the upper strings.

Of course, Handel had at his disposal more techniques than Mattheson's addition of a rest (and, as we have seen, glorified variations thereof) to bring about a shift in cadential placement. There are at least four other simple techniques involved—elimination, recomposition, augmentation, and diminution.

An aria in *Semele*, 'I must with speed amuse her', aptly demonstrates recomposition (Ex. 7.3). Here Handel's second version omits part of the text, and changes the original weak cadence to a strong one. The down-beat cadence is retained in the final version, where the text is restored to new music.

The clearest example of augmentation occurs in the first-act duet

---

[5] Together these three arias seem to underscore the improvisatory nature of Handel's composition, for it seems that he had not fully thought through the opening ritornello before setting the piece in score. It is important to keep in mind, however, that he may have been composing the ritornello retroactively, from a vocal body of the aria that had perhaps been worked out in advance.

[6] As I discuss below in Ch. 5, the last half of this B section was eventually cut for harmonic reasons. The rebarring seems to have occurred before this cut was made, however, and, as far as I can tell, the two revisions have little to do with each other.

Ex. 7.3. 'I must with speed amuse her', first and second versions in *Semele*, BL RM 20.f.7, fo. 63ᵛ

'Welcome as the dawn of day' in *Solomon*. The vocal cadence was originally weak (Ex. 7.4; brackets represent my reconstruction of an illegible passage) but in the final version the last notes double their length to make a down-beat cadence, which slows the piece down at the culminating vocal close (*HG* 26: 89, 2/3 ff.). Interestingly, Handel then alters the concluding ritornello not only by providing a new melody but also by utilizing shorter note values near

EX. 7.4. 'Welcome as the dawn of day' in *Solomon*, BL RM 20.h.4, fo. 31ᵛ

Ex. 7.5. 'Tune the soft melodious lute' in *Jephtha*, BL RM 20.e.9, fo. 61ᵛ

the end in order to avoid a second climactic ritard, which would have seemed somewhat overwrought.

In 'Tune the soft melodious lute' we find, quite conveniently, a revision illustrating both elimination and diminution, resulting in a weak cadence (Ex. 7.5). Here the original passage is simply eliminated rather than altered, but as a consequence the weak cadence in the immediately preceding bars serves as the final vocal cadence of the A section. In effect, the cadential note values of the original passage are thus diminished. This is the first time we have seen Handel moving from a strong cadence to a weak one. Although the opposite process occurs more frequently in revisions, such matters must represent a piece-specific concern rather than a general preference. There is nothing wrong with cadences to the third beat, and Handel uses them often, as in the ritornellos of 'I must with speed amuse her'. There are many factors that may relate to which type of cadence is more appropriate, including the nature of the material after the cadence (whether it begins with a pick-up, or on a strong or weak beat).

Another example from *Solomon* at first seems to fit the patterns of rebarring we have observed, but in fact involves other significant compositional issues. The first chorus in that oratorio, 'Your harps and cymbals sound', takes its ritornello with few changes, apart from transposition from C major to B flat major, from the aria 'Vergnügst du dich an Heidenlusten' in Telemann's cantata 'Es ist ein schlechter Ruhm'.[7] Handel's original version of the ritornello can be seen in Ex. 7.6(*a*), bar 7 f. Ellwood Derr has described a revision in which Handel slightly expands Telemann's head-motif and rebars the score (italics mine):

Upon setting out the Telemann material in the strings in the first two pages of the autograph of the chorus, Handel consistently wrote it as it appeared in the cantata. *Apparently before continuing the chorus beyond this point*, he went back to bar 7 and added in the two counts . . . which are common to the usage of this material throughout the chorus. This change then required the cancellation of the existing barlines on these two pages from that point onward and to replace them with new ones two counts later.[8]

Some characteristics of this revision—the addition of a half-bar at the beginning of a ritornello and consequent rebarring—are by now quite familiar to the reader. The alteration, however, is unrelated to cadential placement, but rather involves motivic change. Before fully elucidating this point, I beg to differ with Derr about the revision's chronology.

There is strong manuscript evidence that the revision took place at a much later stage in the composition of the chorus than Derr thought. On fo. 11[r] of the autograph (the final page of the chorus), Handel wrote out the first bar of the ritornello to cue its return at the end of the piece (Pl. 7.1). Here he wrote the original version of the ritornello, which lacks the two inserted beats. It is unlikely that he would have done so if he had decided upon the revised form of the head-motif earlier in the piece. At some later stage, he replaced this version with the new one, which he wrote before this final bar.[9] It seems very likely, then, that the ritornello was not altered until Handel had completely drafted the skeleton score of the chorus.

In the light of this fact, it is interesting to note a second alteration in the

---

[7] See Telemann, *Musikalische Werke*, v. 439. This borrowing is listed in Roberts, 'Handel's Borrowings from Telemann', 167.

[8] Derr, 'Handel's Procedures', 118. The 'added two counts' appear in Ex. 7.6(*b*), bar 7.

[9] In skeleton score, the violin part may well have been empty in many places, apart from where the ritornello was placed.

Ex. 7.6. 'Your harps and cymbals sound' in *Solomon*, BL RM 20.h.4, fo. 5ᵛ: (*a*) original setting; (*b*) revised setting

Ex. 7.6. (*cont.*)

7.1. *Solomon*, final page of 'Your harps and cymbals sound', BL RM 20.h.4, fo. 11ʳ

opening ritornello, which distinguishes this instance of rebarring from those discussed above. By adding two beats (in essence) to bar 15, Handel assures that the cadence is placed in the same metrical position in both the original and revised version (Ex. 7.7), thereby removing the necessity of rebarring the chorus beyond the end of the ritornello.

The non-metrical *raison d'être* of this alteration relates in part to other compositional revisions on the first page of the autograph of the chorus. In its original form, the a cappella unison vocal phrase, ending in a sort of cadence

EX. 7.7. 'Your harps and cymbals sound', original and revised ritornello, BL RM 20.h.4, fo. 5[r-v]

(with the seventh degree resolving to the tonic B flat), is virtually detached from the chorus proper (Ex. 7.6(*a*)). By replacing the last two measures of this phrase with a whole note F, thus replacing the tonic with the dominant, the vocal phrase is rendered more unstable.[10] As a result, the a cappella phrase needs the resolution of the tonic at the beginning of the ritornello; Handel has achieved a far more cogent liaison between the vocal phrase and the chorus proper (Ex.7.6(*b*)).

The function of the ritornello as a 'resolution' of the preceding vocal passage is the key to understanding Handel's alteration of Telemann's ritornello, which, after all, renders it more stable in several ways. First, the insertion at the beginning of the ritornello prolongs the tonic for two beats, thereby providing a more satisfactory resolution for the 'dominant' at the end of the opening vocal phrase. Moreover, by repeating the head-motif, this two-bar addition also gives the whole ritornello a more emphatic character. Finally, Handel's revised ritornello has a more symmetrical (and hence more stable) phrase structure than the original: 2 + 2 + 2 + 4 rather than 1½ + 2 + 2 + 3½.

If 'Your harps and cymbals sound' has ultimately shifted our focus away from rebarrings *per se*, it raises issues of far greater import. In showing how in one case Handel achieved a seamless blend of disparate materials, this example is representative of an urgent compositional concern manifested in a plethora of cases—an issue that the composer faced regularly, on a more or less daily basis.

In retrospect, it is hardly surprising that this should be so. An important, if hitherto unstated, fact emerges from the preceding chapters: in composing and revising music Handel typically manipulates relatively autonomous musical units. As we saw in Chapter 3, the musical material he chooses to borrow from other composers often comprises short, discrete thematic ideas. Frequently his own sketches are similarly brief melodic ideas. As we have seen in Chapters 4 to 6, both primary composition and revision involved rearranging, eliminating and occasionally inserting autonomous units or sections. In short, Handel's music can on a number of levels be divided into relatively independent musical entities ranging from motifs or sub-phrases, each with its own distinct set of characteristics, to complete musical sections.

---

[10] Bar 4 seems to have undergone several stages of revision itself. Handel first set the pitches *b♭* and *a♭* as half notes. Later he crossed out the half-note stems, producing whole notes, and changed the rest indications in the corresponding orchestral parts from four to five bars. This version of the subject is used as a cantus firmus throughout the chorus (tenors bb. 20–5; basses bb. 40–5; sopranos bb. 51–5, etc.). Still later, he decided to change the *b♭* and *a♭* of the a cappella statement of the subject from whole notes back to half notes. In regard to these note durations also, in the final version, the first statement of the 'cantus firmus' does not correspond to its later appearances.

This aspect of Handel's style might be described with the rhetorical term 'paratactic'. Classical grammarians distinguish between two types of prose composition: parataxis and hypotaxis. Elaine Sisman has recently applied these terms to Classical musical forms in a thorough and brilliant way.[11] The rhetorical terms are equally useful on the level of the phrase or sub-phrase as a means of describing aspects of musical style. Parataxis or 'style coupé' refers to a fragmented style of writing. A famous example of this style comes from Pope:

I confess it was want of consideration that made me an author. I writ, because it amused me. I corrected, because it was as pleasant to me to correct as to write. I published, because I was told, I might please such as it was a credit to please.[12]

Hypotaxis, on the other hand, refers to a longer, 'spun-out' style of writing, as in this example from Emily Brontë's *Wuthering Heights*:

While Miss Linton moped about the park and garden, always silent, and almost always in tears; and her brother shut himself up among books that he never opened; wearying, I guessed, with a continual vague expectation that Catherine, repenting her conduct, would come of her own accord to ask pardon, and seek a reconciliation; and *she* fasted pertinaciously, under the idea, probably, that at every meal, Edgar was ready to choke for her absence, and pride alone held him from running to cast himself at her feet; I went about my household duties, convinced that the Grange had but one sensible soul in its walls, and that lodged in my body.

Now just as Handel's musical style is to an extent paratactic, so his revisions characterize the kinds of alterations that are possible for paratactic poetry. According to Barbara Herrnstein Smith, 'In paratactic structure . . . thematic units can be omitted, added, or exchanged without destroying the coherence or effect of a poem's thematic structure.'[13]

In musical terms, paratactic structure allows the kinds of changes associated with *ars combinatoria*—exchanging or reordering units—as well as omitting or adding passages, without destroying the effect or coherence of the music. But it is important to bear in mind that Handel's music is paratactic only to a degree—certainly more so than Bach's music, whose constantly regenerating motifs and continuous surface is profoundly hypotactic. But we should not exaggerate: Handel's music is never truly 'choppy'—what is perhaps most striking, given the paratactic nature of his compositional method, is the apparent

[11] Sisman, *Haydn and the Classical Variation*, ch. 2.

[12] See Sisman, *Haydn and the Classical Variation*, 8. Originally quoted in Hugh Blair, *Lectures on Rhetoric and Belles Lettres* (repr. New York, 1826), 118.

[13] Barbara Herrnstein Smith, *Poetic Closure: A Study of how Poems End* (Chicago: University of Chicago Press, 1968), 98.

seamlessness of the surface of his music. It stands to reason, therefore, that an important category among his revisions would have to do with 'hiding the seams', or rendering a paratactic surface more hypotactic. This is a particularly interesting type of revision, for a continuous surface could be achieved in a number of different ways and for various reasons. The revisions examined here can be classified into three basic types: first, those in which parataxis is reduced for purely musical reasons, often achieved simply by eliminating cadences; secondly, those in which elimination of cadences is achieved through *ars combinatoria* techniques; and finally cases in which affective portrayal of the text provides the main reason that greater seamlessness is required.

Continuity and Cadential Elimination

Handel's revision of 'Your harps and cymbals sound' brilliantly illustrates the composer's routine concern with knitting together disparate elements in such a way that seams are hidden. As we saw, Handel first combines an independent a cappella vocal opening with a borrowed ritornello, then rewrites the end of the vocal opening in such a way that it is elided with the beginning of the ritornello. After revision, the vocal cadence serves as a link rather than as a point of articulation. Because cadences constitute a particularly tangible means of articulating musical surfaces, an obvious way to achieve greater continuity is to create elisions of the sort found in the revision of 'Your harps and cymbals sound', or to eliminate certain strong cadences altogether. This latter type of revision not only increases seamlessness, but also often embraces issues of harmonic structure and tonal balance.

   Corrections that postpone tonic arrival by eliminating cadences are particularly well represented in the oratorios. To choose just one example, in Dejanira's through-composed aria 'There in myrtle shades reclin'd' from *Hercules* a long passage that originally occurred in the autograph at bar 21 has simply been crossed out (see Ex. 7.8).[14] This passage consisted primarily of tonic and dominant chords, with a relatively strong cadence to the tonic in its bars 26 to 27. The cadence was strong enough, in fact, that the listener would expect another tonic cadence in the bars that follow; in the first version Handel instead made several deceptive moves at this point (in Ex. 7.8, bb. 27–8, and *HG*, bb. 22–4 = *HG* 4: 26, 2/2–4), which necessitated another return to the tonic later, in bb. 25–6. This original version is not harmonically

---

[14]   In the autograph this aria appears in E major (RM 20.e.8, fo. 14ʳ), but it was evidently transposed to G major before the first performance for the convenience of Miss Robinson. (See Dean, *Handel's Dramatic Oratorios*, 433.) In Ex. 7.8, I have transposed the excerpt to G for the sake of easy comparison with *HG*.

Ex. 7.8. Deleted passage from 'There in myrtle shades' in *Hercules*, BL RM 20.e.8, fo. 14^r

convincing: in the rejected passage the approach to the tonic is too strong to make the move to the subdominant persuasive. As a result the end of the piece (*HG*, bb. 21–6), which has the tonic as a goal, seems redundant, like a one-way rail journey to the same destination made, quite inexplicably, twice in succession. By cutting the passage, Handel mitigated the premature emphasis on the home key, resulting in an aria that is not only more continuous but more directed harmonically. Now nothing seems extraneous, which prevents any sense of *déjà entendu* on the part of the listener. Moreover, the final version is tonally balanced, consisting of eight bars that move to the dominant, seven bars that prolong the dominant (9–15), eleven bars moving back to the tonic (16–26), and a final ritornello that sustains the tonic key (26–8)—or in other words two tonal halves of fifteen and thirteen bars each.

Continuity and *Ars combinatoria*

In the A section of 'Daughter of gods', where Handel's 'block-like manipulation of materials' is apparent on a grand scale, rearrangement can be specifically linked to cadential elimination. This example embraces harmonic considerations while at the same time achieving greater seamlessness. His revisions concentrate on A2, or the second half of the A section of this da capo aria, bars 61–110 (*HG* 4: 68, 3/5 to 70, 4/1). The first autograph version of this section of the aria is transcribed as Ex. 7.9. In the original version the order of musical events differs considerably from the final published version, as Table 7.1 illustrates. Between the first and last versions of this section of the aria there existed at least one other. The first revision of the original was apparently to connect bar 70 to bar 95 (of the draft) in two steps, first by cancelling the original bar 71 and providing a new connecting bar. We can tell that this was Handel's first revision because he used the common mark 'NB'. It is reasonable to suppose that he later used the less common ⊘ because 'NB' was already in service. Second, he replaced bars 103–9 of the draft (shown at the end of Ex. 7.9) with bars 72–80 (draft), making adjustments to the original bar 102. (This revision was communicated by means of the sign ⊘). For reasons that will become clear below, Handel thus: (1) moved the original melisma on 'crowd' (draft, bb. 72–80) to a later point in the aria; (2) omitted the new 'bright liberty' motif that occurs over harmonies that emphasize and prolong the tonic, B flat (draft, bb. 82–5); and (3) omitted the long melisma on 'reign' (draft, bb. 87–94).

At some point, though it is impossible to say exactly when, Handel decided to restore the melisma (bb. 87–94 of the first version), for the original 'NB' at bar 95 has been crossed out and moved back eight bars to bar 87, which is marked 'NB' and 'stat' (presumably meaning 'stet' or 'restore'). This resulted in the final version of the aria, as published by Chrysander in *HG*, in which the original order of appearance of the two melismas has been reversed.[15]

---

[15] Theoretically other versions may have existed. One can imagine a version without melismas, for instance, if the original NB was being observed and the ⊘ signs had not yet been written. This is entirely speculative, however. We can only be certain of the versions above. In fact, I suspect that the time elapsed between the first and last versions was short.

EX. 7.9. Original version of A section of 'Daughter of gods' in *Hercules*, BL RM 20.e.8, fos. 34ᵛ–35ᵛ

Ex. 7.9. (*cont.*)

Ex. 7.9. (*cont.*)

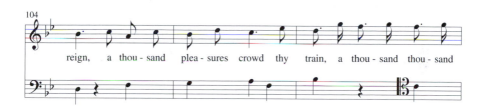

In all the revised versions, then, Handel chose to move the first melisma (b. 72 ff.) to a later point in the A section, and to eliminate the 'bright liberty' motif with its strong tonic emphasis (b. 82 ff.). Our attention should therefore focus on these items and their position in the aria.

The first melisma concludes with a great deal of emphasis on the dominant—with a dominant pedal, in fact. In the first version the F in the bass line was an octave higher and only sounded on the first beat, but it was a pedal nonetheless, resolving to an area that prolonged the tonic. This creates something of a crisis, because it is too early in the piece for such a strong emphasis on the home key.[16]

[16] It is true that Handel sometimes returns to the tonic at the start of A2, but not with so much emphasis.

TABLE 7.1. *Revision of 'Daughter of gods' A2 section*

Original:	HG 61–70 [Ex. 7.13]:	71–82 crowd −V ped.	82–86 Bright Liberty I	87–94 reign	95–102	103–9]	HG 99–10
Intermediate:	HG 61–71 [Ex. 7.13]:		95–102	95–102	72–82 crowd −V		HG 99–109
Final:	HG 61–71 [Ex. 7.13]:	87–94 reign		72–82] crowd −V ped.	HG 99–109 vocal cadence + Rit. 3 I		
HG		72–9	80–7	88–98			

The imperfections of this original version apparently led Handel to decide that his first melisma should be transplanted and bars 81–6 eliminated. In both the penultimate and the final versions, the dominant pedal thus occurs near the end of the piece. When it was moved, he lowered the F, which is now emphasized by reiteration on each beat. This is followed by a secondary dominant to V at the adagio (V^6_5/V–V in 97–8), and the resolution to the tonic at the end of the A section is strong indeed.

On a smaller scale, a correction probably motivated by similar concerns can be found in *Solomon*. 'Thrice bless'd that wise, discerning king' is a modified or half da capo aria with a modulatory first section (A), moving from i to III (bb. 1–44), a B section that reworks material from the A section and ends in v (bb. 44–61), and a final section (A') that repeats the text of the first section and returns to the tonic (bb. 61–84). Handel's revision occurs in the final section (Ex. 7.10).

In Handel's first version, the order of musical events suggests that the setting of the second line of text within the return of section A was initially a varied statement of the corresponding passage in the first section: but this was revised immediately; the fact that the final bar is incomplete indicates that he crossed out these bars before proceeding in the score. (This correction is not a cancellation, since, as we shall see, he ultimately restored these bars in a new order.) This setting of 'and mounts with virtue's eagle wing' contained essentially the same music as its appearance in the A section, bar 19 ff., that is, disjunct eighth notes in the voice against a violin passage combining motifs from bars 4 (the first three beats) and 6 (its middle two beats) of the ritornello. Beginning in the third bar of Ex. 7.10, 'fame' was set to a melisma first sung on 'adorn' in the B section, bars 54–7. The music for this melisma is first heard in the opening ritornello, bars 6–8.

In basic terms, Handel's revision once again simply changed the order of events. First he added a setting of 'and mount', etc. (bb. 66–7), clearly based on bars 25–6. Then he reversed the order of appearance of his original A' material. That is, the next event is the setting of 'fame' from the old version, i.e. bars 3–6 from the original passage (marked 'y' in Ex. 7.10), with minor changes and with the melisma now set to 'everlasting'. This is followed by the first two bars of the original (marked 'x' in Ex. 7.10).

One can easily see why the original passage required alteration. Its first two bars effected a cadence to A major (though the music did not pause here). By transplanting these bars, Handel delayed the tonic cadence until the end of the vocal part. He further enhanced the effect of this revision by altering the end of the passage to a striking deceptive cadence—striking because there is now almost continuous eighth-note motion in the bass before this cadence. The vi chord comprises a half note, which completely

EX. 7.10. 'Thrice bless'd that wise, discerning king' in *Solomon*, BL RM 20.h.4, fo. 56ᵛ

arrests the momentum of the piece, and this is followed by an authentic V–I cadence. By postponing the point of articulation from his first version, he created a more continuous harmonic movement, and he thereby ultimately strengthened the tonic resolution at the end of the piece.

In spite of his utilization of reordering on a large scale, Handel's compositional concerns manifested in the A section of 'Daughter of gods' and 'Thrice bless'd that wise, discerning king' are the same as those illustrated by 'There in myrtle shades': tonal balance and enhanced hypotaxis.

Continuity as Special Effect

Although creating a seamless surface was a routine concern of composers engaged in the conventional boundaries of musical discourse, such as within the independent sections of arias and choruses, the techniques of eliminating cadences and creating cadential elisions sometimes serve to produce connections between formal sections that are commonly distinct from each other. In this light the B section of 'Daughter of gods' from *Hercules* should be re-examined (see above, Ex. 5.3). I have suggested that Handel's new version of that aria is marked by greater continuity; it also reveals a transformation of discursive tonal planning into a more functional arrangement of keys. By ending in the minor mediant (D minor), the original, discursive version of the B section precluded a functional relationship between it and the A section, which is in B flat. Rather, as is typical of Handel's da capo arias, a tonal hiatus obtained. In the final version, he eliminated D minor and ended the B section in the subdominant: E flat. Although, as was pointed out earlier, E flat functions as a secondary dominant to A flat major (A flat is briefly tonicized on the last and first beats of bars 127–8, 128–9), this function is weak; a pedal on the pitch E flat is sounded throughout these measures. Furthermore, in bar 129, the E flat chord on the second beat moves directly to a dominant seventh of B flat in bar 130, which in turn resolves to the tonic—thereby achieving greater continuity than the first version.

This example demonstrates that the simple progression from tonic to dominant and back is a means through which greater continuity could be achieved. Functional tonality provides a way of sealing the gap between self-contained musical sections.

Handel's revisions in the original autograph version of 'Thou, God most high', a written-out da capo aria in *Belshazzar*, involve a number of compositional issues. Though the revisions engage a number of purely musical matters, such as thematic distribution, certain aspects of the revisions might in part have been influenced by concerns of text depiction.

The form of the aria is: A section (bb. 1–47), B section (bb. 47–62), and varied return of A (bb. 62–98). There are five major cuts in the autograph, all apparently made before the aria was fully orchestrated:

1. Beginning at the middle of the fourth bar of the original, Handel excised the last sixteen bars of the orchestral introduction, which included a weak cadence to the dominant and ended with an authentic cadence to the tonic (Ex. 7.11(*a*)), leaving only the head-motif to serve as the opening ritornello.

2. At bar 13 (of *HG*) he removed a passage that constituted a somewhat reharmonized repetition of the opening vocal statement, bars 4–12.

3. Two bars later, at bar 15 (of *HG*), two bars related to 14–15 were removed. This formed a more complete statement of the musical idea that accompanies 'through boundless space extends thy throne'.

Ex. 7.11. Deletions in 'Thou, God most high' in *Belshazzar*, RM 20.d.10: (*a*) fo. 6ᵛ; (*b*) fos. 7ᵛ–8ʳ

4. Starting at bar 28 (in *HG*) Handel truncated the original by twenty-two bars. These began with a continuation of the material for 'through boundless space', proceeded with recurrences at various pitch levels of the head-motif from the ritornello, and concluded finally with a statement of the second line of text (Ex. 7.11(*b*))

5. Five bars that refer to the music for 'through boundless space' were taken out of the concluding ritornello of the first A section.

Except for the revision of the opening ritornello, all the corrections bring about an omission or truncation of one of two thematic ideas, either the

EX. 7.11. (*cont.*)

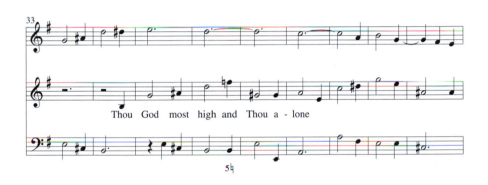

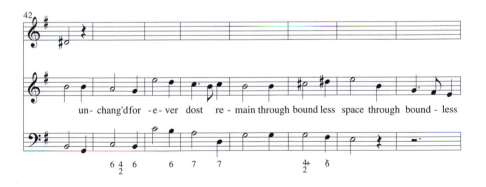

head-motif (listed as revision no. 2), or the motif associated with 'through boundless space' (nos. 3 and 5), or both (no. 4). Indeed, in the first version, the head-motif occurred perhaps too often. Similarly, the musical portrayal of 'boundless space' is perhaps more effective when it does not recur as frequently and at such lengths as in the original. Such thematic concerns may have been, if not the most significant, at least an important catalyst for Handel's corrections.

In some cases, however, thematic recall may not have been his main concern. And even where theme was almost certainly the most important factor, the tonal repercussions of the cuts are significant enough to warrant attention. After all, the importance of a revision in one musical parameter does not preclude the correction's importance in other domains. For instance, correction no. 2 was surely a way of extracting needless repetition; the original repeats the previous phrase and, even though the piece has just got underway, states the head-motif yet a third time. Surely the redundancy of the passage led Handel to amend his score. It is equally true, nonetheless, that the original passage does nothing to further the piece harmonically. Likewise, correction no. 3, which shortens the material for 'through boundless space', mitigates the emphasis on the dominant, B major. The original contained two cadences to B major, while the final version has merely a B chord: B has been reduced from a key to a chord. From a tonal standpoint, the first and fourth corrections above are by far the most interesting, however, and I shall begin with the first.

In its original form, the opening ritornello could be divided into two unequal halves. It began with an 'antecedent' phrase of four bars that ended in the mediant (G major), and concluded with a sixteen-bar 'consequent' phrase, culminating, as most of Handel's opening ritornellos do, in an authentic cadence to the tonic (E minor). He later simply excised the entire consequent phrase. As a result the ritornello is no longer a tonally closed entity, but a sort of harmonically open-ended 'up-beat' to the aria proper, and the ritornello and vocal entrance are thus organically linked. Furthermore, there is no strong cadence to the tonic until the vocal cadence near the end of the aria's first section (bb. 38–9), but the identity of the home key is maintained, among other means, by the doubled half-cadence in bars 11–14.

Correction no. 4 also furthers the piece's harmonic seamlessness. In bars 4 and 5 of the omitted passage there was an authentic cadence to B minor, followed by a modulatory section that moved through A minor (10–11 of the excised passage), B major (14–15), and G major (18–19). Particularly important for harmonic continuity is the omission of the strong cadence to B minor—a removal of a very significant point of articulation that is even more interesting in the light of the fact that the second section of the aria cadences to B minor. Besides achieving a more continuous harmonic flow, perhaps he wished to avoid harmonic redundancy.

In this revision Handel moves from a discursive or solar harmonic structure in his first version to a more functional one upon revision, and again this transition is related to continuity. The tonal plan of the original A section was i–III–v–i. The minor dominant is not a functional key, lacking the leading note of the major dominant. Thus it is more often found as a significant tonal area in Baroque pieces with a discursive arrangement than in the Classical period. By removing this key area, the simpler plan of the final version establishes a polarity between the minor tonic and major mediant, a more forward-looking key relationship that not only exemplifies the most common harmonic plan of the A sections of da capo arias in minor keys but becomes intrinsic to the tonal plan of the expositions of minor-mode sonata forms later in the century.

It is well known that the portrayal of the text is a crucial feature of Handel's vocal music. The text often determines the character of a part of a movement, and, in some cases, the entire piece. Such concern for text depiction might have motivated some of the revisions in 'Thou, God most high'. A characteristic of the setting of 'through boundless space' is that the accompaniment moves to dominant-seventh chords that progress to unexpected, even shocking, pitches rather than resolving in a conventional manner to their respective tonics. That is, 'boundlessness' is portrayed by eschewing expected cadential resolutions. By eliminating cadences, save those of extreme structural importance, Handel raises his word-painting to a higher level, portraying 'boundlessness' not only locally, but in the harmonic structure of the entire A section.

The chorus 'Wanton god of am'rous fires' in *Hercules* also illustrates both musical and textual reasons for altering cadence placement. In a number of places in the autograph, Handel revised and sometimes rebarred the original, replacing down-beat cadences with cadences to beat 3. Example 7.12 provides a typical example of one such altered passage.[17] The pronounced demarcation provided by strong cadences in the original version is out of character with the text: surely 'Wanton god of am'rous fires / wishes, sighs, and soft desires / . . . / o'er liquid air . . . and swelling main / extends thy uncontrol'd and boundless reign' calls for a rather seamless setting. Handel's ultimate setting, its graceful delicacy enhanced by weak-beat cadences, brilliantly reflects the images conveyed by the text.

---

[17] One might at first suppose that he revised these bars to remove the descending leap of a diminished fifth, but there are similar passages with diminished fifths between the same pitches that were not revised in other places in this chorus. These bass progressions are perhaps related to the text 'uncontrol'd and boundless reign'.

Ex. 7.12. Original and revised version of 'Wanton god of am'rous fires', bb. 23 ff. in *Hercules*, BL RM 20.e.8, fo. 71^r

In at least one fascinating case the normal functional key arrangement of an A section is made to 'spill over', as it were, into an aria's B section. The autograph of *Jephtha* contains a draft for the work's most famous aria, 'Waft her, angels, through the skies'. The draft is incomplete, but before he abandoned it Handel had completed part of the varied return of the A section (see Ex. 7.13). The plan of the original is as follows (x = first 2 bars of ritornello; y = bars 3–4 of ritornello; z = conclusion of the opening ritornello (bb. 5–7)):

EX. 7.13. Original version of 'Waft her, angels' in *Jephtha*, BL RM 20.e.9, fos. 99^r–100^v

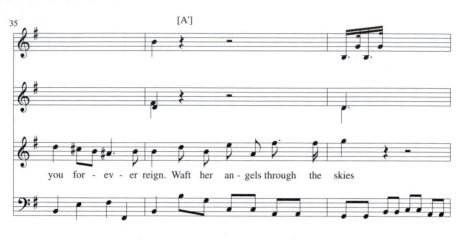

A section: A1					A2	
Rit. 1	[A Text	Rit. 2	A Text]	Rit. 3	[A Text]	Rit. 4
xyz		y		x		xy
I	I	I	I–V	V	–I	I

B section: –iii

A' section (incomplete):		A Text	Rit. 5	A Text
			y	
		I	I	I

Since a head-motif appears only at the beginning of the first and third statements of the text, we should think of this A section as being divided into two large sections, the second of which begins after the modulation to the dominant. Thus A1 includes two settings of the A text. This draft follows Handel's typical harmonic practice, with a modulation to the dominant and back in the A section and a modulation to the minor mediant at the end of the B section.

The final version of the aria is a da capo dal segno with an exact repeat of the A section (after the opening ritornello), but shorter than the first draft. Handel has eliminated the second half of the original A1 and recomposed the central ritornello and the B section, maintaining the music in essence but providing it with a new tonal orientation. A simple tonal plan results:

A section: Rit. 1	[A Text]	Rit. 2	[A Text]	Rit. 3
xyz		y		xz
I	–I	I	–I	I

B section: –V

A section (opening ritornello omitted)

In essence, he has eliminated the modulation to the mediant at the end of the B section and replaced it with the modulation to the dominant that originally occurred in the A section, which now does not modulate at all. Although the obvious goal of this extensive revision—practically a resetting of the text—was to shorten an aria that was becoming prolix, two details expose another aspect of the alteration. First (as in the first repeat of the A text in the first version) he omits the return of the head-motif at the beginning of A2, so that the distinction between A1 and A2 is blurred. Together with the lack of modulation and the fact that many cadences are elided, this makes for a more seamless A section. A similar concern for continuity may explain the B section revision. In the first draft Handel bypasses the opening ritornello in the return of the A section, moving directly from the B section statement to a vocal statement of the A section text. In the revised version this seamlessness is enhanced. By adding eighth notes in the bass at the end of the new B section, he effects a transition to the A section repeat, which begins directly with the voice rather than the ritornello. Since the lead-in includes a C♮ (the seventh above the dominant), it is impossible not to hear the dominant chord at the end of B resolve into the tonic at the vocal entrance. This effect could not be achieved with the mediant at the end of the B section.

The two versions of 'Waft her angels' show Handel moving from a solar tonal plan to a genuinely polar arrangement of keys in which the shift to new text is matched by a shift to the dominant. In the final version, the concept of a functional chord progression has been amplified to cover the important tonal areas of the aria, thereby achieving greater cohesion of structure; Handel has moved the modulation to V from the middle of the A section to the B section (which is in the dominant), thus making tonic/dominant opposition an important factor of the whole piece, which consequently possesses a less additive structure than the first version. The smooth surface of the final version better reflects the text's image of Iphis's flight to paradise ('Waft her, angels, through the skies', etc.).[18]

Handel's search for continuity represents the culmination of a number of compositional and stylistic issues raised in earlier chapters. First, his method of composition/revision involves a largely paratactic medium, for his process of borrowing, sketching, eliminating, sometimes adding, and often reordering materials typically involves manipulating short, discrete musical ideas. The fact that he based his compositions on brief, independent units links him to his younger contemporaries, who exploit similar materials, albeit in a musical style that is admittedly more short-breathed and, in terms of texture and harmony, more forward-looking than Handel's own musical language. His process of developing musical cells into complete musical compositions necessarily involved attempts to achieve continuity, weaving a number of diverse elements into a relatively homogeneous fabric. This need is perhaps especially important for a composer like Handel, who remained more devoted than his younger contemporaries to Baroque ideals of *Fortspinnung* and musical continuity, while still maintaining a somewhat more progressive style than his contemporary J. S. Bach.

---

[18]   Other facets of the revision also seem to result from a desire to depict the text more closely. The new B section includes a melisma on 'rise' not found in the first draft, which included only an upward leap on that word. More interestingly, the use of the dominant in the B section avoids modal contrast with the A section. Since the text of the B section describes Iphis after she arrives in heaven and thus heightens rather than contrasts with the A section text, it warrants neither a minor key nor contrast of mode. The use of the dominant for the B section—a move in the direction of more sharps—also characterizes much of the revised B section of 'Bless'd the day' (largely in E over a pedal until the cadence to C sharp minor), which also describes a state of increased bliss.

Striving for continuity, then, was one of Handel's daily concerns within the normal confines of musical composition. We thus find in his autographs ways of hiding the joints that become for him more or less standard: by cadential elimination, for example, sometimes also involving processes of reordering akin to *ars combinatoria* techniques, which typify his revisions as a whole. Yet we also find compositional changes that create overlaps between normative points of musical articulation, such as between the end of a ritornello and the opening vocal utterance, or between contiguous musical sections—thereby achieving an unusually high degree of hypotaxis. In many such cases heightened use of seamlessness was a response to the text, reflecting Handel's extreme concern with affective depiction of words and dramatic impact.

8

⌣⌢⌣⌢⌣

Texts, Musical Form, and Dramatic Impact

IN the course of composition, Handel frequently altered musical forms—a fact that distinguishes his compositional process from Bach's. According to Robert Marshall

corrections of 'form', in the most common meaning of that term, are practically nonexistent in the composing scores of [Bach's] vocal works. This is hardly surprising, since the form of the text and/or cantus firmus melody, i.e., the preexistent material, used in an aria or chorus essentially determined the basic musical form of the movement.[1]

It is certainly true that many of Handel's decisions concerning the basic formal structures of arias and choruses often must have occurred before he began actual composition, thus belonging to that vast realm called, ironically enough, 'precompositional activity'. However, pre-existent material—which in Handel's case amounts to two items: musical borrowings and the libretto—apparently had far less influence on him than on Bach in regard to the musical forms ultimately chosen. This is unquestionably the case with the borrowings. As we have seen from a number of previous examples, the musical model rarely seems to affect the form of the work based upon it; form represents one of the avenues through which Handel repays borrowings with interest. The role of the libretto in the generation of musical forms is, in Handel's case, a more complicated issue, however: to a degree the text helps define his musical forms, but he exercised some control over the text. In order to elucidate revisions of musical form, it is clear that something must be said about Handel's attitude towards and treatment of libretti.

Even when he chose old texts by authors no longer living (such as Congreve's *Semele*) Handel had a living adapter. Although Ruth Smith is undoubtedly correct that the artistic collaboration for Handelian oratorio was not of a Strauss–von Hoffmansthal intensity,[2] Handel nonetheless felt free to

---

[1] Marshall, *The Compositional Process of J. S. Bach*, 209.

[2] Smith, *Handel's Oratorios*, 3. Her excellent study includes a generally sensible discussion of Handel's collaboration with his librettists, but a fuller consideration of changes of text in Handel's autograph scores might have influenced certain of her conclusions.

eliminate lines of the libretto and to request changes from his librettists, a fact that apparently irritated Charles Jennens and, particularly, Thomas Morell.[3] In an undated letter Morell complains of 'what alterations [an Oratorio writer] must submit to, if the Composer be of an haughty disposition, and has but an imperfect acquaintance with the English language'.[4] He goes on to relate an amusing anecdote:

And as to the last Air ('Hail, wedded Love, mysterious Law' from *Alexander Balus*), I cannot help telling you, that, when Mr Handell first read it, he cried out 'D—n your Iambics'. 'Dont put yourself in a passion, they are easily trochees'. 'Trochees, what are Trochees?' 'Why, the very reverse of Iambics, by leaving out a syllable in every line, as instead of

> Convey me to some peaceful shore,
> Lead me to some peaceful shore'.

'That is what I want'. 'I will step into the parlour, and alter them immediately'.

Whether or not the details of this charming story are true is less important than what it tells us about the working relationship between Handel and the authors of his texts, which in this case seems to have been relatively intimate.[5]

Unfortunately, however, much of the creative discussion about texts must have occurred at a time prior to the beginning of the surviving written record of an oratorio's genesis.[6] We have access to two types of manuscripts that disclose certain aspects of this process: the manuscript librettos in the Larpent collection and the scores themselves, both autograph and manuscript.[7]

According to the Licensing Act of 1737, copies of plays and other entertainments to be performed on the British stage had to be submitted to the

---

[3] See Jennens's letter of 19 Sept. 1738 to Lord Guernsey in Deutsch, *Handel: A Documentary Biography*, 466. Jennens complains that Handel had rejected his original words for the end of *Saul* and replaced them with a 'Hallelujah'. As we have seen, Handel complained to Jennens about the length of *Belshazzar* and made specific suggestions about the end of that oratorio as well: 'The Anthems come in very properly, but would not the Words (tell it out among the Heathen that the Lord is King) Sufficient for one Chorus?'

[4] Deutsch, *Handel: A Documentary Biography*, 851. The letter is believed to date some years after Handel's death. Deutsch assigns it to *c*.1764.

[5] The interaction between Handel and his librettists has been detailed in recent studies. In addition to Smith, *Handel's Oratorios*, the most important of these include Anthony Hicks, 'Handel, Jennens and *Saul*: Aspects of a Collaboration', in Nigel Fortune (ed.), *Music and Theatre: Essays in Honour of Winton Dean* (Cambridge: Cambridge University Press, 1987), 203–27. It would seem from the existing evidence that Handel was more sympathetic to the opinions of Jennens than to those of Morell.

[6] It does not surprise me, therefore, that in his letters to Jennens concerning *Belshazzar* Handel is concerned with the practical matter of the text's extent rather than religious and political matters or the behaviour of the characters. (See Smith, *Handel's Oratorios*, 27.) If these matters were discussed (and one imagines that the behaviour of the characters, at least, might have been) it would have been more surprising if he had waited until after he set the first act to do so.

[7] See Dougald MacMillan, *Catalogue of the Larpent Plays in the Huntington Library* (San Marino: The Henry E. Huntington Library and Art Gallery: 1939), pp. v–xii, which underlies this summary.

Lord Chamberlain for licence two weeks before opening night. The first Examiner of Plays was William Chetwynd, who acted through deputies, first Thomas Odell (1738–49) and then Edward Capell (1749–81). On 20 November 1778 John Larpent was assigned the position, and he died in office on 18 January 1824. Official copies of all plays submitted for examination between 1737 and 1824 were in Larpent's possession at the time of his death, and were sold to John Payne Collier and Thomas Amyst. In 1854 it was announced that the Earl of Ellesmere had bought the collection, which thereafter resided in the Bridgewater House Library for sixty-three years, finally passing unheeded into the Huntington Library in 1917.

Among the wealth of plays in the Larpent collection are handwritten manuscript copies of fourteen of Handel's oratorio wordbooks (including librettos for all the oratorios covered in this study except _Hercules_) in the hands of four distinct copyists. These sources vary greatly in degree of interest. Many, perhaps all, came into contact with Handel, for he signed several dedications. At least one, _Alexander Balus_, seems to have been an early copy of the text that he may have used while composing the score.[8] This and a number of other manuscripts contain text changes in Handel's hand.

Among the works examined here, _Semele_ is perhaps the most interesting of these librettos. We can postulate a relative chronology for this libretto by comparing it with Handel's autograph score. It is apparently not the original text given to Handel to compose from, for a number of revisions in his autograph musical score had clearly occurred before this wordbook was made, there being no sign of these revisions in the wordbook. The most substantial example concerns the concluding chorus. In the autograph Handel had originally ended with a triple-time setting of Congreve's text 'Now mortals be merry and scorn the blind boy'. The manuscript wordbook contains only the new chorus, which underscores Winton Dean's observation that this revision of the score happened relatively early. But other autograph revisions were added to the libretto, and some changes in the autograph and conducting score apparently occurred after the wordbook had passed on to the Lord Chamberlain. For instance, the da capo is still present after 'Leave me, loathsome light', 'Behold in this mirrour' is still marked 'air', and the text 'I'll be pleas'd with no less / than my wish in Excess' did not settle down until after the conducting score was copied, possibly during rehearsal. This suggests that Handel had this libretto in hand for part of the composing process. In a sense, then, the _Semele_ libretto, too, was in part a 'working copy' during a part of

---

[8] Donald Burrows suggested this in 'Counting the Metre', read at a meeting of the American Handel Society at the University of Maryland in 1989.

the formative period before first performance. Thus the B section text of 'Come Zephyrs, come' (originally cavatina) is clearly a later addition to the wordbook, but the cancellation of the aria (which occurred before the first performance) is not indicated.[9]

If Handel did work from this text for a time, it might, of course, contain evidence of revisions found nowhere else. And so it does. For instance, apparently he considered adding recitative lines from Congreve, some of which were cued into the wordbook, only to be crossed out later. After the line 'She does her passion own' and just before 'You've undone me', for example, two lines from Congreve have been added:

> INO. What, had I not despair'd
> You never should have known.

Apparently Handel never set these lines.

Another set of omitted and changed lines may have to do with Handel's(?) fears about the text passing muster with the Inspector of stage plays. Winton Dean has remarked that the unorchestrated setting of 'Now mortals be merry' may have been rejected for its impropriety during Lent:

> Then Mortals be merry, and scorn the Blind Boy;
> Your hearts from His Arrows Strong Wine shall defend;
> Each Day and each Night you shall revel in Joy,
> For when Bacchus is born, Love's Reign's at an end.

This may have been a concern of Handel's for all of *Semele*, which is not only a mythological subject, unlike biblical oratorios of previous seasons, but a 'bauwdy opera', to quote Jennens.[10] Some of the changes may have been made to ameliorate the highly charged erotic content of the original. Thus Juno's instruction for coital union with Jove in his godlike form, which originally included the lines 'By this Conjunction / with entire Divinity / you shall partake of heav'nly Essence', was changed simply to 'you shall partake then of Immortality'. And 'destroy the curs'd Adulteress' becomes 'destroy the cursed Semele'. These revisions show something of the care with which Handel and/or the adapter of the libretto adjusted texts.

The three other extant wordbooks for the works surveyed in this study are less interesting for Handel's compositional process, and can be quickly summarized. Confirmation, if any were needed, that the 'Sinfony' in Act III of *Solomon* was added at a relatively late stage comes from the wordbook, where the word was clearly added later. Otherwise, the wordbook for *Solomon* seems

---

[9] This aria is discussed more fully in Ch. 9.
[10] See Dean, 'Charles Jennens's Marginalia', 162.

unfortunately to have been made at a late stage of the work's compositional history. There are virtually no changes in *Belshazzar* or *Susanna*.

The Composer and his Librettists

Handel's collaboration with librettists is also evidenced by the autographs themselves, where changes of text occur with some frequency. One of the most extensive of Handel's compositional revisions concerning an entire scene—the entertainment for the Queen of Sheba in *Solomon*—offers evidence concerning the creation of the libretto for this oratorio. As Dean first noted, Handel's pagination of the first act of *Solomon* discloses that the entertainment for the Queen of Sheba in Act III—the material beginning with the recitative preceding 'Music spread thy voice around' and ending with 'Thus rolling surges rise'—originally appeared in Act I. As he remarks, 'the masque was therefore not conceived as an entertainment for the Queen of Sheba but for Solomon's own queen'.[11] This is substantiated not only by Handel's pagination, but also by the text of Solomon's recitative at the start of the entertainment:

> Well my fair Queen, in converse sweet,
> We'll spend the time in soft retreat;
> Sweep, sweep the string to sooth my blooming fair
> and rouse each passion with th'alternate air.

After transplanting the entertainment to Act III, Handel cancelled the first two lines of recitative and changed 'my blooming fair' in the third line to 'the Royal fair' to refer to the Queen of Sheba.

This musical transfer, an instance of Handel's 'cut and paste' method on the largest conceivable scale, has significant ramifications for the genesis of the entire oratorio. Dean notes that a plausible reason for the change was to reduce the great length of Act I, and suggests that the change 'must have happened before the composition of Acts II and III'.[12] It is quite possible, in fact, that the change occurred before Handel had received the text for at least the third act, if not both Acts II and III. Having rejected the entertainment scene from Act I, he may have requested of his unknown librettist a third act that would allow him to use the music for the entertainment; or the librettist may have suggested such a change if Handel complained of the first act's length, as he did in the case of *Belshazzar*. We know, in fact, that Handel

---

[11]   Dean, *Handel's Dramatic Oratorios*, 530.   [12]   Ibid.

began composition of *Belshazzar* before receiving its third act text, there is no reason that the case could not be the same for *Solomon*. If so, *Solomon* illustrates the extent of Handel's collaboration with a librettist during the creation of the libretto.

If Handel enjoyed influence on the wordbook, it is clear why it is problematic to speak of the text as the primary determinant of form. He could (and did) request changes from the librettist when he deemed it necessary. The strongest evidence for this aspect of the composer/librettist collaboration comes from correspondence of James Harris, which has only recently come to light. After he had seen a draft of the libretto that Harris and Jennens had based upon Milton's poems *L'Allegro* and *Il Penseroso*, Handel proposed reworking the poems. Jennens wrote to Harris:

He seem'd not perfectly satisfy'd with your division, as having too much of the Penseroso together, which would consequently occasion too much grave musick without intermission, & would tire the audience. He said he had already resolv'd upon a more minute division, which therefore I left him to make with the assistance of your plan; & this morning he brought me the first part so divided, in which I made some corrections, chiefly of Smith's blunders in writing; & he took it back with great satisfaction, & I dare say sat down to compose as ever he came home.[13]

There can be no doubt, then, that Handel exerted control over his texts. Moreover, while it is undeniable that the structure of the text determines to some extent the form of an aria and the degree to which the form might be changed, it does so only to a limited extent.[14] Although in some cases it would be impossible for a da capo aria to become a strophic aria without a change of text, for example, many texts could serve a da capo aria or, if the repeat of text is ignored, a two-part through-composed aria equally well. The following examples, in which Handel altered musical form in a fundamental way without changing the text, illustrate the degree to which his librettos offered formal flexibility.

Formal Freedom

Belshazzar contains two fascinating instances in which Handel abandoned his original da capo format for less common forms. Both these revisions, which

---

[13] See Rosemary Dunhill, *Handel and the Harris Circle* (Hampshire: Hampshire County Council and the Author, 1995), 7–8, which underlies this discussion.

[14] It might seem at first that a more detailed study of Handel's texts alone could take us close to his precompositional considerations. However, none of the extant manuscript wordbooks precisely preserves the texts with which Handel was faced when he first began work, and we cannot reconstruct details of those original texts.

are undoubtedly related to one another, were made at a relatively late stage of the oratorio's genesis, after the conducting score had been copied. The first of these, Daniel's 'Lament not thus', began life as a full da capo aria, the first section of which comprises three statements of the text, the first modulating to the dominant, the second returning to the tonic, and the last maintaining the tonic key. The B section cadences in the minor mediant, and in Handel's original conception this was followed by a full da capo repeat. Later he curtailed the length of the aria by inserting the B section between the second and third textual statements in the first section:

A1   A2   A3 | B section | da ❌apo
I–V   –I   –I | –iii |

This revision is characteristically economical, requiring precious little rewriting. Handel added only four bars, 24–7, which confirm the tonic arrival with another vocal cadence and a brief ritornello in the new key, on the bottom system of the folio.[15]

The resulting form, which covers the same amount of text as a full da capo in less time, probably belongs among a number of revisions designed to accommodate the ungainly length of Jennens's wordbook for *Belshazzar*. Handel's often-quoted letter of 2 October 1744 to his librettist Charles Jennens addresses this matter:

I receiv'd the 3rd Act, with a great deal of pleasure, as you can imagine, and you may believe that I find it a very fine and sublime Oratorio, only it is realy too long, if I should extend the Musick, it would last 4 Hours and more. I retrench'd already a great deal of the Musick, that I might preserve the Poetry as much as I could.[16]

In fact, Handel's musical solutions for the problem of the oratorio's length might explain why there are an unusually large number of such forms in *Belshazzar*. While there are only five da capo arias—somewhat surprising in the light of the fact that the preceding three oratorios, *Semele*, *Joseph*, and *Hercules* contain fourteen, nine, and thirteen da capos respectively—there are two other written-out da capos in addition to 'Lament not thus'—'Thou, God most high' and 'Can the black Aethiop change his skin'—as well as two modified da capos with modulatory first sections. All these structures represent an abbreviated replacement for da capo forms.

Eric Weimer has pointed to three structural modifications of da capo aria form, which had grown to enormous length, in operas composed between 1720 and 1780:

It is scarcely an oversimplification to explain the history of large-scale aria forms in mid-eighteenth-century opera seria in terms of an ongoing attempt to prune dead wood from an inexorably expanding organism: first by repeating only half of the A section (the 'half da capo' aria), then by inserting the B section in the middle of the A section (the 'modified da capo' aria), and finally by dispensing with a repeated A section altogether (the 'two tempo' aria).[17]

Although Handel seems to have had no aesthetic difficulties with the musical viability of da capo arias, it is striking that all the aria forms that Weimer describes abound in Handel's oratorios. And in the case of *Belshazzar*, at least, it is clear that Handel used some of these forms precisely because of that 'inexorably expanding organism', da capo form. Although his use of multiple aria forms in the oratorios is often viewed as a factor that sets them apart from his operas, it would seem that his oratorios in fact reflect certain developments in eighteenth-century opera more clearly than his own operas do.

Daniel's second aria, 'O Sacred Oracles', underwent a transformation that occurred in precisely the manner that Weimer describes. Its first section (or A section) was originally a standard two-part structure, with the first statement of text accompanied by a modulation to the dominant and the second statement of text returning to the tonic. Again, Handel cancelled the return of the A section and moved the B section into the middle of the A section, this time after the dominant has been established by voice and continuo and then reinforced by the internal ritornello:

A1   ↓   A2   B section

I–V   –I   –iii

The resulting form, a 'modified da capo', can be understood in two distinct ways. As a ternary form, it is sometimes regarded merely as a 'variation' of the full da capo aria form—which is borne out by Handel's use of these forms to replace full da capos in *Belshazzar*.[18] In this sense the modified da capo is essentially like the written-out da capo—simply a substitute for full da capo arias. Moreover, even modified da capo arias with modulatory first sections do not always rely on tonic–dominant polarity. For instance, 'Alternate hopes and fears' in *Belshazzar* modulates to the minor dominant at the end of the A section, which reflects a Baroque conception of harmony.

[17] Eric Weimer, *Opera Seria and the Evolution of Classical Style 1755–1772* (Ann Arbor: UMI Research Press, 1984), 27–8.

[18] Marshall regards modified da capo forms simply as one type of da capo aria, because the structure of the text is ternary (*The Compositional Process of J. S. Bach*, 210–11). Bach composed modified da capo forms more commonly than Handel (see Marian Whapples, 'Bach, Handel and the Recapitulation Aria', *Journal of Musicology*, 14 (Fall 1996), 475–513).

On the other hand, 'O Sacred Oracles' offers a different view of these forms, which in particular cases should be regarded as expanded two-part or binary forms. The 'modified da capo' with an A section that modulates to the dominant (or, in minor keys, to the relative major) is more forward-looking than a written-out da capo such as 'Lament not thus'.[19] In fact, this aria form—perhaps a relative of sonata form—became common in operas written in the second half of the century.[20]

Handel's revisions of form in these *Belshazzar* arias might be explained in terms of Heinrich Christoph Koch's *Versuch einer Anleitung zur Composition*.[21] Elaine Sisman offers a tri-partite description of Koch's compositional method:

He begins with the phrase (Absatz or Satz), outlining its possible constructions. Two or more phrases combine to form a period (Periode), the intermediate level. And combining this period with other periods creates the third level, which is a type of form. For example, if the period is combined with one or two other periods, and the whole arranged into two repeated sections, a dance form results. If the period or group of periods . . . is successively repeated with elaborations in which one may discern the original melody (Hauptmelodie), variation form results. If the period is regularly alternated with contrasting periods, rondo form results. And if the periods are expanded into principal periods (Hauptperioden), sonata form results.[22]

The principle underlying Koch's description—the essential relatedness of all musical forms—clearly applies to Handel's creation and alteration of forms in the oratorios, although the forms themselves changed over the course of the century. Handel's method of composition is clearly 'additive', and his process of revision, which frequently involves expanding, deleting, or rearranging material, is clearly based on a method of construction identical with that described by Koch.

Changes of Text and Musical Form

The preceding discussion discloses that even when he made no traceable changes of the original text, Handel enjoyed freedom of formal choice, often

---

[19] Handel altered 'Rejoice greatly' in *Messiah* from a full da capo to a modified da capo aria in precisely the same manner. See Larsen, *Handel's Messiah*, 220.

[20] Charles Rosen has warned against viewing this structure as a sort of sonata form, primarily because 'the B section . . . may be distinguished from a development section in various ways: by its being in a different tempo from A1 and A2 (generally slower) and with a different time signature, by its harmonic character and its presentation of new material . . .'. See Rosen, *Sonata Forms* (New York: W. W. Norton & Co., 1988), 57–8. In 'O Sacred Oracles', however, and in Handel's arias generally, the B section is often not in a different tempo or metre from the A section, and it frequently restates or 'develops' A material in contrasting keys. In some senses Handel might be closer to the Classical period than the mid-century composers Rosen has in mind.

[21] See Koch, *Introductory Essay on Composition: The Mechanical Rules of Melody, Sections 3 and 4*, trans. Nancy Kovaleff Baker (New Haven and London: Yale University Press, 1989).

[22] Sisman, 'Small and Expanded Forms', 447–8.

not choosing the form most obviously dictated by the structure of the text. There are cases in which changes in the text appear together with formal structure of the music. If the text proved too restrictive in limiting formal choices, Handel—or, submitting to the composer's instruction, the librettist—altered it. However, it is rare that lines are actually changed for the sake of musical form; generally either the repeats of lines suggested by the text are manipulated, or lines were deleted or restored. Many revisions that involve changes of text still show the process of sectional manipulation akin to that Koch described.

The ease with which Handel could, by simply omitting or restoring lines, alter the libretto as well as the musical form is clear from the history of the rejected aria 'Come Zephyrs, come' in *Semele*. Congreve's text for Act II, scene 2 of *Semele* begins with the following text for Cupid:

1 See, after the Toils of an amorous Fight,
2 Where weary and pleas'd, Still panting she lies;
3 While yet in her Mind She repeats the Delight,
4 How Sweet is the Slumber that Steals on her Eyes!
5   Come Zephyrs, come, while Cupid Sings,
6   Fan her with your Silky Wings;
7   New Desire
8   I'll inspire,
9   And revive the dying Flames;
10   Dance around her
11   While I wound her,
12   And with Pleasure fill her Dreams.
    [A Dance of Zephyrs, after which Semele awakes and rises.]

Handel first set only lines 5 to 9 of this text. The omission of the first four lines probably reflects a conscious attempt to reduce the amount of simple recitative, to which English audiences objected. The oratorios in general have as little recitative as possible, and lines of recitative written in but never set are frequently encountered in the autographs. More significantly, perhaps, he omitted the most explicitly sexual lines, possibly in an attempt to make the text acceptable to the Inspector of stage plays as well as his audiences.

Lines 5 to 9 were originally set as a cavatina. At some later point he restored the last three lines of Congreve in an inserted B section, which was then followed by a dal segno repeat of the first part.[23] One of the most

---

[23] This is apparent both from the autograph score, where fo. 55, on which the middle section appears, is clearly an insertion, attached to fo. 56 with red sealing wax, as well as from the manuscript wordbook, in which the B section text has been squeezed in.

sublimely beautiful compositions to flow from Handel's pen, this one aria for Cupid in all of *Semele* was cancelled before the first performance. Its music resurfaced the next year in *Hercules*, and its transformation for that work will be discussed in the following chapter.

Choruses allowed Handel even more formal freedom than arias. He and his librettists generally reserve da capo forms for arias, and choral texts commonly prescribed no particular musical form. In *Solomon* a transformation of two levels can be seen: Handel changed both the form of 'Swell the full chorus' at the end of Act II and his original plan to effect a larger ABA form by having statements of the chorus surround the aria 'Beneath the vine'.[24]

'Swell the full chorus' has a very complicated history; the end of Act II of *Solomon*, where the chorus occurs, poses knotty editorial problems that have not been sufficiently realized, much less resolved. Unfortunately, we cannot simply compare Handel's sketch with Chrysander's edition of the chorus (*HG* 26: 200–6), for Chrysander's *Gesamtausgabe* might not represent a version of the chorus that Handel knew. In order to grasp his revision of the piece we must first address these editorial issues.

In the autograph, 'Swell the full chorus' occurs twice, directly following Zadok's aria 'See the tall palm' and recurring at the end of the act after the aria 'Beneath the vine'.[25] In his edition Chrysander eliminated the entire first statement of the chorus, so that 'Swell the full chorus' occurs only at the end of the act.[26] Even within this single chorus, however, differences between the autograph and Chrysander are numerous. In the autograph the chorus begins with an orchestral ritornello of four bars (if ritornello is not too grand a term for this brief opening), whereas Chrysander, following the conducting score, eliminates the orchestral opening and begins directly with the first vocal utterance. Thereafter the two versions correspond until bar 30 of the autograph and bar 26 of Chrysander. At this point in the autograph (fo. 81ᵛ), Handel originally brought back the ritornello, but he later cancelled these bars (Ex. 3.8). This completes the chorus's A section.

Originally the A section led to a B section (*HG* 26: 204–6). Chrysander concludes the chorus with a literal 'dal segno' return of the A section (the dal segno omits the first two bars from Chrysander's A section) following the B section. But the autograph continues with an abbreviated return of the A

---

[24]   In Ch. 3 I demonstrated how Handel expanded a short sketch to create 'Swell the full chorus'. Here I wish to show how he altered the form of his first version.

[25]   See RM 20.h.4, fos. 79ᵛ–86ᵛ.

[26]   Here Chrysander's edition follows the conducting score and the printed libretto rather than the autograph.

EX. 8.1. 'Swell the full chorus' in *Solomon*, BL RM 20.h.4, fos. 83ʳ–84ʳ

Ex. 8.1. (*cont.*)

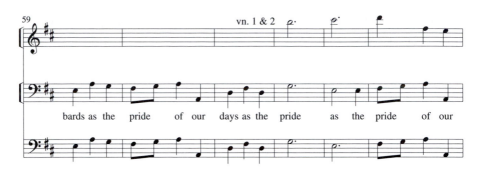

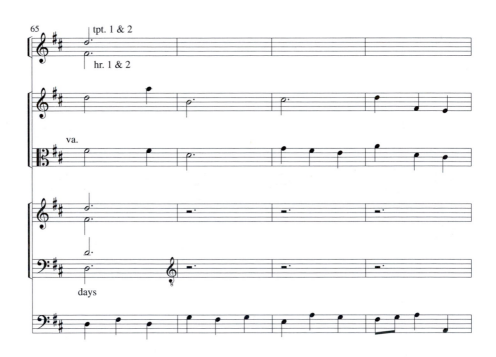

EX. 8.1. (*cont.*)

Ex. 8.1. (*cont.*)

section, followed by a varied statement of the B section, largely in B minor but concluding in F sharp minor (see Ex. 8.1). Finally, the autograph version concludes with a repeat of the A section, omitting its first twelve bars. As Dean points out, the original version of the chorus is in a sort of rondo form.[27]

In the autograph, this first statement of the chorus is followed by a recitative, 'The shepherd shall hail him' (*HG* preface), which in turn precedes the aria 'Beneath the vine'. After the aria, Handel wrote down the opening vocal exclamation of 'Swell the full chorus' with an instruction to repeat the chorus beginning with the dal segno mark.[28] As stated above, Chrysander eliminates the first statement of the chorus. A different recitative, 'No more shall armed bands', following 'See the tall palm', introduces 'Beneath the vine'. Only then do we get 'Swell the full chorus' without the opening ritornello. In short, the first version consisted of several large musical sections, and Handel apparently produced the final version by eliminating some of them. However, all the primary sources disagree about what Handel's ultimate version was.

In the autograph it is clear enough what the cuts are: Handel took out the B′ section and the abbreviated return of the A section that preceded it, and moved the dal segno return to the end of the first B section, restoring to it several bars that were cut from the final A section return in the longer version. The rondo has become an ABA form by subtracting blocks. All these cuts in the autograph were made in the chorus that stands before the aria, and this first appearance of the chorus was not cancelled in that score.

The conducting score suggests a further sequence of revisions. Though nothing in the autograph indicates it, in the conducting score the first appearance of the chorus has been cancelled. Furthermore, when it appears after the aria, the chorus encompasses only the A section. Apparently Handel communicated verbally with his copyists about these changes.

The librettos are different again. The printed libretto contains the text for the entire chorus, including the B section—but since this text served the B′ section as well, it is impossible to tell whether this version is the rondo or the ABA—after (and only after) the aria. In the manuscript libretto, however, the text appears both before and after the aria.

The ultimate authority should be the conducting score, which was presumably used as the source for parts. Chrysander follows this score in positioning

---

[27] Dean, *Handel's Dramatic Oratorios and Masques*, 530.

[28] Even this raises a problem. There are two dal segno marks in the A section of the first statement of the chorus, one of which was cancelled. For now, I wish to lay aside the question of which sign Handel's later instruction refers to.

the chorus only after the aria, but he follows the autograph in regard to the chorus's form. His reasons for using the ABA version are admittedly aesthetically viable, if not historically certain. But Handel apparently reduced his rondo first to an ABA form and then to an A section.

The foregoing discussion of revisions underscores an important aspect of Handel's compositional process. On the level of form Handel's music is 'additive', composed by joining together discrete sections, just as Koch described later in the century. We have seen several examples of changes of form involving the manipulation of large sections: among others, the addition of a B section to a cavatina to create a full da capo aria, the transformation of da capo arias into half and modified da capo arias, the cancellation of rondo sections to create a tri-partite (ABA) structure, and the further cancellation of the B section and A section repeat to create a simpler form. Handel's autographs display the multitude of possibilities offered by combination, subtraction, and addition of discrete musical sections.

Internal Changes

Other formal changes arise not out of manipulating whole sections, but out of internal revisions within sections. Through more involved means of recomposition the independent musical sections can undergo important changes in character that affect the identity of the outer form.

Handel expanded the chorus that opens Act II of *Solomon*, 'From the censor curling rise', in a manner that gives a different shape to the form.

> 1 From the censor curling rise
> 2 Grateful incense to the skies;
> 3 Heaven blesses David's throne,
> 4 Happy, happy Solomon!
> 5 Live, live for ever, pious David's son;
> 6 Live, live for ever, mighty Solomon.

Handel set this text in a through-composed double chorus. The first four lines are predominantly homophonic with antiphonal exchanges between the two choirs, modulating from tonic to dominant. The fifth line begins a new, fugal section, consisting of a fugato and its varied restatement, each time ending with a homophonic tag which brings back the fourth line of the text. The resulting form consists of five sections distinguished by texture: homophony (ll. 1–4)–fugue (l. 5)–homophony (l. 4)–fugue (l. 5)–homophony (l. 6). In Handel's original setting, the final section, a setting of the final line of text, freely recalls musical material from the first section in orchestral ritornelli while the chorus presents a new, elongated homophonic idea. He ultimately altered his original scheme by repeating the first vocal entrance at the beginning of this section. In the middle of the last bar of *HG* 26: 131, which was originally followed by the middle of the second bar of *HG* 26: 135, the composer inserted a page into the autograph that repeats twelve bars from the vocal entrance followed by two bars that provide a smooth transition to the material that follows.[29] As a result, the beginning of the section is clearly heard as a return, with a complete restatement of the text. The final section as a whole more strongly manifests the character of a musical restatement as well, albeit one that is worked out differently than the original appearance. This example reminds us, once again, that Handel sometimes created musical refrains and returns where none existed in the text—just as he could avoid suggested returns of text (i.e. da capos) if the need arose.

The chorus 'O Joacim' at the end of Act II of *Susanna* (*HG* 1: 145–52) was also expanded. Originally the piece consisted only of a homophonic common time introduction of twelve bars closing in B flat followed by a fugue in G minor (which was longer by two pages in the first draft—this version was cancelled very early on, before even the vocal parts were concluded), with an entirely different text (see Ex. 8.2):

> O piety, unfading light,
> Thou eldest born of Heav'n,
> To guide us thro' this gloom of night
> Thy friendly ray be giv'n.

As Dean has pointed out, the autograph reveals that Handel decided to change the text before recomposing the piece. Although the revisions of text and music therefore seem, to some extent, to be independent, the new text is identical in structure with the old, so that no musical changes are necessary to accommodate it:

> Oh Joacim, thy wedded truth
> Is warranted of heav'n:
> And to thy faith illustrious youth
> Shall due regard be giv'n.

This text directly follows Joacim's resolution to save Susanna; thus the new text refers more specifically to the drama on a human level. Handel reset the introductory part of the chorus, transforming it in fascinating ways.

First, he altered the metre from common time to 3/4. The new setting retains the melodic and harmonic structure of the original, at least for the first

---

[29] As mentioned in Ch. 2, Handel provided the bass line only for the repeated material, which he marked 'per tutto' to instruct the copyists to reproduce all the parts.

Ex. 8.2. Original opening of 'O piety' in *Susanna*, BL RM 20.f.8, fo. 84^r

Ex. 8.2. (*cont.*)

un - fad - ing   Light   thou   eld - est   born   of   Heav'n

several bars. This version obviously changes the way that the text is stressed, but it is not clear that the metrical change is simply a response to the new text; the change of metre might also relate to the particular manner in which Handel expanded the piece. In the new version, the homophonic introduction is interwoven with imitative passages derived from the opening movement of Suite V of Muffat's *Componimenti musicale*.[30] Handel retained the metre of Muffat's fugue, and possibly altered the metre of the introduction to match it.[31] The intertwining of the two pieces gives the opening greater scope and importance. Formerly a brief homophonic introduction prefacing a fugal movement that constitutes the chorus proper, the opening of the new version acquires the status of a complete section in itself. It is, in fact, longer than the fugal section that follows.[32]

[30] I am grateful to John Roberts for drawing my attention to this borrowing in a letter of 17 Jan. 1989.

[31] It is impossible to retrace the order of events. He might have decided to incorporate the Muffat either before or after the metrical change. The large amount of borrowed material makes it perfectly plausible that he might have altered the metre of his material to fit the music he wished to appropriate; this would probably have been easier than rewriting Muffat's fugue in common time.

[32] At a later stage, Handel altered two passages near the end of the introduction. These ended on D major, altering the harmonic relationship between the introduction and the section that follows it from the original version's B flat/g to D(V/g)/g. The second version of the introduction at first included a statement of the fugue subject in C minor, leading to an authentic cadence in that key. A tonicization of G

To summarize, Handel's revisions of musical form may be said to fall into two groups: first, those brought about through adding, deleting, or recombining sections—large-scale manifestations of the techniques related to *ars combinatoria* that were discussed in previous chapters; and second, those brought about by revisions within sections that are significant enough to change the movement's character in such a way as to influence our perception of the outer form. Ironically, the one complete change of text we have seen ('Oh Joacim') apparently has no bearing on the musical form, at least in terms of structure. It is through manipulation of text repeats and adding or deleting lines that Handel brings about changes in musical form.

To maintain, as I have here, that the text does not govern the musical form as strongly in Handel as in Bach is certainly not to deny that a profound relationship between text and music exists. However, thus far our discussion has explored the flexibility that lies within that relationship between music and text. We have focused predominantly on just one aspect of this relationship: the relation of musical form and the structure of the text. There are obviously many other aspects of the libretto that play a role in the music. In the remainder of this chapter I should like to turn to the libretto as harbinger of the drama and explore two other aspects of the text that have significant ramifications for musical form: the way in which a change in musical form might better suit larger dramatic issues, such as the structure or dramatic direction of a scene, and the ways in which changes in musical form can enhance musical characterization.

Scenic Structure and Dramatic Impact

As a dramatic entity, oratorio relies on the cumulative effect of scenes and numbers within scenes for its theatrical coherence. On the whole, critics have tended to deny that early eighteenth-century musical dramaturgy possesses either coherence or dramatic vitality. Handel's late oratorios have thus been criticized for their similarity to Italian opera seria,[33] which is traditionally viewed as merely an undramatic chain of da capo arias separated by recitative:

---

minor and material in G minor were necessary to make the half-cadence in that key convincing. In the final version this subdominant area is removed—Handel rewrote the two preceding bars (*HG* 1: 149, bb. 2–3) and provided three new bars (next three bars in *HG*)—perhaps because, coming at this point in the section, it weakened the tonic. Once this first passage was removed, he replaced the second passage with three bars that move more directly to the half-cadence. As a result the final version ends clearly in G minor—there is no question that D is heard as V of G minor at the end—and in less time than the original. The link to the fugal section that follows is thereby strengthened.

[33] Dean complains of the mechanical da capo arias and the regular structure of the first acts of *Jephtha* and *Theodora*. See Dean, *Handel's Dramatic Oratorios*, 597.

In *secco* recitative, each little scene presented at least one character with new information or a new situation; his emotional reaction to it occupied the aria to which the scene
built. Such scenes and such feelings were relentlessly multiplied and balanced . . . The
composers simply concentrated their attention on a series of 'aria situations'; they were
not concerned with the necessary intricacy of plot, for all the details were handled by
means of discussions, destined to be set in neutral, devitalized *secco* recitative.[34]

Handel's practice even in the most opera-like of his oratorios actually suggests
a far less myopic focus than this: his long-range musical view seems to have
encompassed entire scenes. Far from concentrating on arias alone and out of
context, certain of Handel's revisions seek to enhance the cohesiveness of
scenic structure, and to alter the dramatic direction. In this section I shall concentrate on changes of form that can best be understood in the light of other
revisions within the scene.

Susanna, *Act I, scene 1*

A complex series of extensive revisions occurred in Act I, scene 1 of *Susanna*.
Including the overture, all of the first four pieces were either radically
recomposed or replaced with new pieces, as were arias later in the scene. To
a large extent these aria substitutions and changes of form relate to dramatic
issues, and most involve interrelated changes of text that might have been
spearheaded by Handel.

After the overture, the oratorio begins with a choral lament over a chromatically descending tetrachord bass (*HG* 1: 8). In the original version Handel
set only the first two lines of text ('How long, oh Lord, shall Israel groan /
in slavery and pain?'), at least down to bar 63. At this point came a strong vocal
close, followed by an instrumental ritornello (Ex. 8.3). The musical form of
the first section of the chorus was A (1–29) B (29–47) A' (47–end). The B section is distinguished by the use of a new, ascending ground in C major, contrasting with the outer sections in A minor. While a ritornello at this point
would result in an ABA' form—certainly common in Handel's scores—it is
not likely that he intended to end the chorus with this ritornello and set the
two remaining lines in a new chorus; for this would mean that the text of the
opening chorus consisted of two unrhymed lines. It is more probable that he
planned to set the final two lines in a new, separate section—thus opening
this oratorio, like many others, with a choral block.

Like the textual changes in other parts of the scene, the last two lines

34 Joseph Kerman, *Opera as Drama* (new and rev. edn., Berkeley: University of California Press,
1988), 48.

Ex. 8.3. 'How long, oh Lord' in *Susanna*, BL RM 20.f.8, fo. 6ᵛ

metaphorically foreshadow dramatic events in the main action of the oratorio, by asking for deliverance from oppression:

> Jehovah! Hear thy people's moan
> and break th'oppressor's chain!

The new ending of the chorus accommodates this text and marks a dramatic musical change from what precedes it. Several factors contribute to
this surprising change so late in the piece: it abandons the ground, changes
mode (at first) from minor to major (A–D), utilizes the upper register in
the strings (which includes a strident unresolved leading note in bars 64–6),
employs block chords, and—with the cancellation of the original instrumental ritornello—all this occurs quite suddenly. Handel also decided to
use these two lines of text in the body of the chorus. He retexted the B
section, thus providing a correlation between musical and textual form in
the final version:

Original version		*Final version*			
Text:	1–2 (3–4?)	Text:	1–2 3–4	1–2	3–4
Music:	ABA′ ——	Music:	A B	A′	C

The revised ending of the chorus was added before the score was 'filled up'.
The extensive revisions of the next two pieces, an aria and a duet, however,
belong to a later stage, after orchestration. Both also involve changes of text,
and internal evidence suggests that the revisions relate to each other.

In the first version, the opening chorus was followed by the following lines
of recitative for Joacim:

> Our crimes repeated have provok'd his rage,
> and now he scourges a degen'rate age.

The recitative cadenced to B minor, followed by an expressive E minor largo
for Joacim:

> Heartfelt sorrow, constant woe
> from our streaming Eyes shall flow;
> till the Lord has heard our grief,
> till the Lord shall send relief.

This brief through-composed air gains much of its expressiveness through
Neapolitan harmonies and points of imitation. Its sentiment links Joacim with
the suffering Israelites; in fact, the text essentially restates that of the chorus.

Handel and, apparently, his librettist ultimately replaced this aria with an
entirely different piece, a da capo aria in E major (*HG* 1: 12–16). The musical change is profound, the dramatic change even more so. Now the chorus

is followed by the recitative text above, but rather than cadencing to B minor, it includes two further lines, closing in G sharp minor:

> My wife, my fair Susanna, come,
> and from my bosom chace this gloom.[35]

Joacim's new aria text bows to the on-going national oppression, but in the B section his sorrow gives way to wedded bliss:

> Clouds o'ertake the brightest day;
> beauteous faces, blooming graces
> soon submit and feel decay.
> But true faith and wedded love
> banish pain and joys improve.

The aria substitution quickens the pace of the drama. As a result of it, we move away from the issue of national mourning to the relationship of the two lovers more quickly than in the first draft. Moreover, the second version more clearly defines the character of Joacim, whose primary role throughout the drama is that of lover and helpmate to Susanna. It is vicariously through her, more than through the larger political situation, that Joacim will suffer. The revised version accurately delineates his role from the very beginning.[36]

This revision might qualify certain of Ruth Smith's conclusions about Handel's interaction with librettists. On the basis of the information given to us by letters of Handel and anecdotes by Jennens and Morell (admittedly scant), Smith notes that Handel seems concerned primarily with the extent of texts, not dramatis personae, religious or political issues, nor narrative content and verbal detail.[37] It is unlikely that Handel made the changes we have just seen in *Susanna* in blind complaisance to the issues those revisions seem to address, or at least affect. It seems more likely that the changes required collaborative efforts on the parts of both composer and librettist.

A profound change of musical form occurred in the duet that follows,

---

[35]   Originally the recitative text continued, but of the following lines the first two were never set; the last four lines (for Susanna) were for the time being also cancelled, but later Handel set them after the aria, to introduce the duet:

> tho' wrung with the Oppressor's chain,
> when near my fair, my Heart forgets its pain.
> SUSANNA. Oh Joacim! when thou art by,
> my soul dilates with new-born joy;
> Down my pale cheeks the tears no longer run,
> but fly like dew before the morning sun.

[36]   We cannot be precisely sure of the respective roles of composer and librettist here. One imagines that Handel spearheaded the revisions and involved his librettist in the process.

[37]   See Smith, *Handel's Oratorios*, 27–8.

'When thou art nigh' (*HG* 1: 17–23), where a form related to the written-out da capo underwent substantial reworking. Both music and text were revised—apparently at the same time—but the change of text seems to have little bearing on the outer form. The eighth of the duet's ten lines originally read: 'Nor behold through the land one so happy as I', which Handel changed to 'And chace every cloud that would darken the sky'. The sentiment is similar but the new line directly alludes to the first line of the previous aria ('Clouds o'ertake the brightest day'). In fact, the duet simply serves dramatically as a demonstration of the relationship described in the aria.

The change of text required a minimal amount of rewriting, though Handel took advantage of the opportunity, for instance, of providing 'chace ev'ry cloud' with an expressive melisma. Nonetheless, his formal transformation of the duet goes far beyond what the new line of text required. The original bifolio that stood between folios 11 and 14 survives in FM MUS MS 259, and this contains the interior of the duet's first draft (Ex. 8.4). We are thus able to reconstruct the first version of the duet.

The first two-thirds of the duet in its original form might comprise a typical (though vast) da capo form. The A section modulates to V and returns to the tonic, and there is a fermata over the final note of the ritornello. The B section ends in the minor mediant, exemplifying Handel's most common harmonic practice.[38] If he originally intended to compose a full da capo or a dal segno structure, however—which is possible but not demonstrable—the plan was abandoned by the end of the B section. Here we get a return of the opening text with an extensively recomposed musical 'return'; although the musical material is familiar from the A section, it is significantly abbreviated and begins in the dominant rather than the tonic, which is reserved until later.

Perhaps Handel felt that the structure of this duet was unbalanced. He almost certainly found it too long, for the second version is much shorter—and thus the revision might relate to the duet's dramatic function. The material of the two versions is similar enough to allow us to see that certain passages have been excised. For instance it is clear in the British Library autograph that when he went back to rewrite the duet he eliminated seventeen bars beginning at bar 34 (transcribed in Ex. 8.5), a passage in E (V) that overlapped the first lines of text for each character. In the new version this is replaced by four bars in V based on the second important melodic idea from the ritornello (though the direction of the sequence is reversed); the V area is greatly reduced. This represents the most significant change in the first section. Near its end the vocal cadence material is rewritten.

---

[38]   See Harris, 'Harmonic Patterns in Handel's Operas'.

EX. 8.4. First draft of 'When thou art nigh' in *Susanna*, FM MUS MS 259, pp. 77–8, BL RM 20.f.8, fo. 14ʳ

Ex. 8.4. (*cont.*)

Ex. 8.4. (*cont.*)

RM 20.f.8, fo. 14r

so hap-py as I, with joy on their wings the young mo-ments shall

with

fly–

forte

nor be - hold through the land one

Ex. 8.4. (*cont.*)

The B sections of the two versions of the duet are identical for the first twenty-six bars (*HG*, bb. 111–36), until the cadence to B minor (ii), after which the two versions substantially diverge. The B section of the original includes another thirty-one bars, which ultimately cadence in C sharp minor (iii), followed by a return of the A text, as noted above. In the second version the entire C sharp minor area has been removed—a type of revision familiar from the previous chapter. Although music from the A section returns, it is quite different from the original return, and the A text never comes back. The forms of the pieces are outlined in Table 8.1. Handel's revision has involved

Ex. 8.5. 'When thou art nigh' in *Susanna*, BL RM 20.f.8, fo. 11ʳ⁻ᵛ

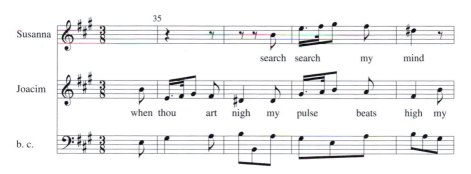

a change of form. The original might be described as a somewhat unusual written-out da capo aria, whereas the revised version is a two-part form that is rounded by a musical return at its end. In terms of proportions the two sections are more nearly equal than were the three in the original. Handel has produced a more well-balanced piece. Moreover, the course of this revision

TABLE 8.1. *Revision of 'When thou art nigh'*

First version			
Text:	A	B	A
Music:	a	b	a′
	I	vi ii iii	V I
Final version			
Text:	A	B	
Music:	a	b	new a′
	I	vi ii	V I

reflects a common practice in the oratorios: the cavatina (AA′) or two-part musical form with textual form AB, rather than da capo form, constitutes the backbone of certain oratorios (such as *Saul*). In many cases either form can serve the same text.

Moreover, this revision of form makes sense in the light of the preceding aria substitution. As pointed out above, the duet exemplifies the relationship described in Joacim's new aria. While Handel wished to illustrate this relationship at length in the first version of the scene, when the duet introduced the issue of the love between Joacim and Susanna, such a long duet was not necessary with Joacim's new aria in place. Taken together, these revisions thus show a concern for dramatic as well as musical proportions.

One other aria substitution in this scene is significant for drama. There are two versions of Susanna's 'Would custom bid' in the autograph score, but originally there was none; apparently even the first version was inserted into the score. In the first draft Chelsias's 'Peace crown'd with roses' was set as an air, which was later omitted, and the aria text appeared as recitative. Perhaps the suppression of Chelsias's aria and the insertion of 'Would custom bid' are related changes.

The inserted aria gives Susanna the chance to reflect on her first impressions of Joacim. The first setting of the inserted text was an expressive siciliano in B major. Dean reasonably suggests that this version may have been suppressed in order to avoid two consecutive sicilianos.[39] Of more significance to the drama, it is striking how the final version, a hymn-like triple-metre piece, reflects the chaste and pure love expressed by the text. This aria is similar to 'With thee th'unshelter'd moor', a cavatina in *Solomon*, both aesthetically and dramatically. The earlier version of 'Would custom bid' may express the pain of passionate love—but the time for suffering has not yet descended upon Susanna,

---

[39]   Dean, *Handel's Dramatic Oratorios*, 551. He provides an excerpt from the original version.

and in the revised version we are instead given a glimpse of the innocence of her love. This change, too, results in a greater focus on the relationship of the two lovers.

In sum, the extensive revisions of this scene seem to have a threefold goal: to foreshadow the events of the drama, to accentuate the nature of the relationship between Susanna and Joacim, and to underscore Susanna's purity. The compositional process here demonstrates that Handel was concerned to find the right match among drama, text, and musical form and expression.

As a composer of extended vocal works, then, Handel's musical concerns were obviously not limited merely to individual pieces. To achieve musical and dramatic cohesion throughout an oratorio, it was necessary for him, like all dramatic composers, to consider the cumulative effect of his music over a large span of time such as a scene or even an entire act. Handel at times reworked entire scenes by altering musical forms or formal elements; in conjunction with aria substitutions, these changes transform the drama. Although the revisions alter each of the set-pieces in fascinating ways, their cumulative effect on the entire scene is perhaps the most important result. We shall not understand such revisions if we insist that Handel concentrated only upon 'aria situations'.

Semele, *Act III, scene 1*

One aspect of the relationship between libretto and musical form that arose in the preceding discussion of *Susanna* demands further attention: the issue of dramatic characterization. Manipulating musical convention to reflect more effectively the dramatic events is a well-known *morceau favori* of Handel's. Revisions of musical form that toy with our expectations can sometimes alter or enhance our perception of a dramatic event or character.

Changes of musical form altering the dramatic pace of a scene as well as dramatic characterization occur in Act III of *Semele*, in the arioso 'Somnus awake' and the aria 'Leave me, loathsome light'.[40] Handel created the symphony and recitative at the beginning of the act out of a process of successive transformation.

John Roberts has pointed out that the symphony (HG 7: 153) is based on the aria 'Sonno placido nume' from Alessandro Scarlatti's *Il Pompeo* (Ex. 8.6).[41] One of the reasons Handel chose this particular aria as a source may be, as Roberts remarks, that the Scarlatti aria is about sleep, and the *Semele* scene occurs in the cave of the god of sleep, Somnus.

---

[40] Dean, *Handel's Dramatic Oratorios*, 385–6.   [41] Roberts, *Handel Sources*, vi, p. x.

Ex. 8.6. Alessandro Scarlatti, 'Sono placido nume' from *Il Pompeo*

Handel's symphony begins with a close parody of Scarlatti, with altered orchestration. Scarlatti began with a typical arrangement of melody in violins with accompaniment in violas and basses. Handel instead gives the melody to cellos and basses. He also extends Scarlatti's opening bars, coming to a caesura in bar 4, whereas Scarlatti elided the beginning of the piece (1–4) with the next section—the point when the melody is given to the bass with accompaniment in upper strings, a dispensation that Handel follows.

In Handel's original draft of this piece (whose inner leaves survive in the

Fitzwilliam), the voices enter during the symphony, thus constituting an arioso (Ex. 8.7). This first version takes much of its material throughout from Scarlatti. The rising chromatic lines of the first version, for example (b. 17), are also in Scarlatti (fo. 77^r), and both pieces end in D major.

EX. 8.7. Original version of 'Somnus awake' in *Semele*, FM MUS MS 259, pp. 35–6, BL RM 20.f.7, fo. 80^r

Ex. 8.7. (*cont.*)

Handel's revision of the piece is altogether remarkable. He wrote a new ending for the symphony, comprising three bars after bar 15 that move, surprisingly, to G minor. Roberts has suggested that this ending may have been prompted by Scarlatti's ending, where the D cadence sounds like a dominant cadence in G minor.[42] The 'allegro e forte' section, where the voices enter, seems at first glance an entirely different movement, both from the symphony and from the first version. The tempo and dynamic marking 'allegro e forte' obviously contrast with the 'larghetto e piano per tutto', and the orchestra plays predominantly diatonic, triadic sixteenth notes rather than drowsy eighth notes and chromaticism as in the first setting. Dean astutely suggests that Handel originally failed to heed Congreve's original stage directions: 'A Soft Symphony . . . Then the Musick changes to a different Movement.'[43]

[42] Roberts, *Handel Sources*, vi, p. x.   [43] See Dean, *Handel's Dramatic Oratorios*, 386.

Ex. 8.7. (*cont.*)

and lift up thy heavy lids of lead.

Raise thy reclining head.

In spite of these dramatic surface changes, however, the new version is clearly based on the earlier one. In fact, the essential melodic/harmonic framework of the original is maintained, as Ex. 8.8 shows; the voice parts and harmonic progression (D–G–E^6–A) in the two versions are largely the same until the end, where the earlier version cadences in D and the later in A. This fascinating case brings to mind Steven LaRue's discussion of metrical changes, where despite extensive rhythmic and metrical alterations Handel generally retains the melodic structure.[44] In this case, however, neither the metre nor the melody has changed, yet the differences between the two versions lend the new piece an entirely different character. In terms of drama the second version is more convincing. Beautiful as the original was, one could not seriously hope to rouse the sleeping Somnus with it.

The aria of Somnus, 'Leave me, loathsome light', might also have been

---

[44]   See LaRue, 'Metrical Reorganization' 477–90.

Ex. 8.8. Comparison of original and revised versions of 'Somnus awake' in *Semele*, FM MUS MS 259, pp. 35–6, BL RM 20.f.7, fo. 79ʳ

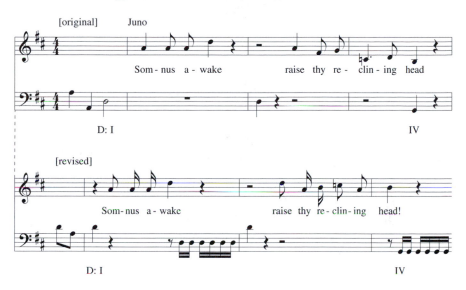

Ex. 8.8. (*cont.*)

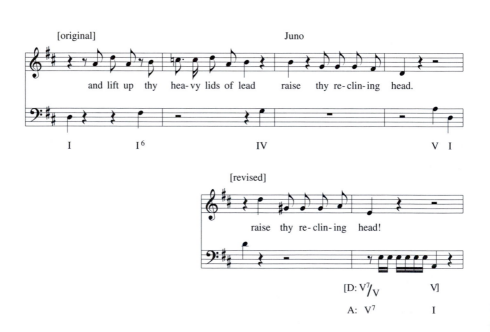

influenced by the Scarlatti original in some general ways. It, too, is in D major, and it begins, like the Scarlatti, with a long D in the voice. Moreover, both pieces are characterized by conjunct accompaniment. But these shared characteristics may have much to do with the shared *Affekt*—the portrayal of sleep—the commonality between the two, then, being more or less coincidental. In any event, the similarities between the opening symphony and Somnus's aria create a need for dramatic contrast in the intervening recitative, which the new version provides.

Handel also revised the formal structure of Somnus's 'Leave me, loathsome light'. Initially the score was marked 'da capo dal segno' after the second section, with a new ritornello for the repeat. The lethargy of Somnus is reflected in the music by the fact that neither the A section nor the B section effects a true modulation. The second version enhances this musical portrayal of Somnus's character: Handel cancelled the dal segno mark and the new ritornello, and wrote 'sleeps again'.[45] In the revised version the god of sleep returns to his slumber prematurely, before repeating the first half of the aria— a device sometimes found in Handel's operas.[46] As a result the aria is tonally open-ended, moving from D major for the A section to F sharp major at the aria's end.

Taken together, these revisions quicken the pace of the drama, rendering it more convincing and gripping. The attempt to rouse Somnus is accomplished with a flourish in the second version, a flourish that contrasts with the timelessness of the music for the slumber-ridden god, whose drowsiness takes precedence over 'proper' musical structure—a dramatic ploy of the highest order. Handel's revisions of this scene illustrate his concern for dramatic integrity.

Hercules, *Act III, scene 3*

If we find an enhancement of dramatic characterization of Somnus in *Semele*, in *Hercules* we find a psychological progression, the climax of which is achieved by Handel's revision of the mad scene. Without question a dramatically compelling scena—and one of the most unusual formal structures in Handel's oratorios—is the famous mad scene for Dejanira in Act III, scene 3 of *Hercules*. Having learnt that she has unwittingly brought her husband Hercules to his death, Dejanira goes mad, displaying her virtuoso vocal technique in an electrifying scene.

---

[45]   Dean, *Handel's Dramatic Oratorios*, 385.

[46]   Examples of sleep scenes that employ similar musico-dramatic devices can be found in *Orlando*, *Arianna*, and *Giustino*, but only Somnus's aria does not end in the tonic.

Because madness asserts its presence by undermining normal procedures, scholars typically define mad scenes by contrasting them with what they are not. Ellen Rosand, for instance, rightly describes the mad scene from Act II, scene 7 of *Orlando*, where Orlando goes mad because of his love for Angelica, by contrasting it with the most conventional form of opera seria, the da capo aria.[47] Whereas most of Handel's arias are marked by unity of *Affekt* (to use a now unpopular term), with the only shift of emotion coming, if at all, with the B section, mad scenes are characterized by shifting affections—a musical depiction of unstable minds. This is as true for Dejanira's mad scene as for Orlando's.

The mad scene in *Hercules* shares a number of other features with its famous predecessor in *Orlando*. Both begin with an accompanied recitative suitable to the heightened emotional tension of the scene, followed by a set-piece. Both the accompagnata and the set-piece are characterized by abrupt and unexpected shifts of mood and music, including changes of metre, tempo, and key. In both scenes Handel's setting intensifies the emotional discontinuity of the scene by imposing a number of local musical contrasts.

In addition to their avoidance of typical da capo form, there are a number of specific formal similarities between the set-pieces in *Orlando* and *Hercules* that allow us to begin to speak of the 'form of madness' in Handel. Dejanira's 'See the dreadful sisters rise', like Orlando's 'Vaghe pupille', adopts rondo form, but its structure is more complex than the simple rondo (ABACA + ritornello) found in *Orlando*. Again there is a recurring musical refrain, linked to Handel's decision to restate lines ('See the dreadful sister's rise', etc.), though this is not a refrain in the original text. This forms a rough formal outline more complex than that of 'Vaghe pupille' (see Table 8.2). Moreover, as in *Orlando*, the first episode (B—'Hide me from their hated sight / Friendly shades of blackest night!') comprises a triple-time lament over a descending tetrachord ground, but with a diatonic rather than a chromatic bass.

In *Hercules*, however, Handel is apparently concerned with obscuring formal clarity—of both text and music—to a greater degree than in 'Vaghe pupille'. He repeats lines of the text freely, making Dejanira's guilty vision of the furies obsessive, and her state of mind even more unpredictable than Orlando's. Many of the sections of the piece are tonally open, and the refrain, extended differently each time it occurs, appears in different keys. (See Table 8.2.) Section A (Concitato) modulates from E minor towards G

---

[47] The mad scene in *Orlando* has been discussed against the backdrop of opera seria conventions in Ellen Rosand, 'Operatic Madness: A Challenge to Convention', in Steven Paul Scher (ed.), *Music and Text: Critical Inquiries* (Cambridge: Cambridge University Press, 1992), 241–87.

TABLE 8.2. *Musical structure of 'See the dreadful sisters rise'*

Bar (HG)	Section	Lines of text	Tempo	Metre	Keys
30–44	A	1–4	Concitato	4/4	E minor to A minor to V/vi in D major
45–60	B	5–6	Lento e piano	3/4	B minor
60–87	⎡A′	1–4	Concitato	4/4	G major
	⎣B′	5–6	Lento	3/4	V pedal in G major
88–105	C	7–8	Concitato	Alla breve	G minor to B minor (becomes V of E minor)
106–37	⎡A″	1–2	Tempo I	same	E minor
	⎣C′	7–8	same	same	same
137–43	Ritornello		same	same	same

major, as we would expect, but it is not achieved—instead V of D major resolves deceptively to an F sharp major chord. At this point section A stops abruptly and section B appears in B minor, with changes in metre, tempo (Lento e piano), and dynamic level as well. Section A′ (Concitato) appears suddenly in G major (*HG* 4: 225, last system) and is rounded off by an abbreviated return of B section material (Lento) without the ground and over a G pedal. Section C (Concitato—*HG* 4: 227), a setting of the last two lines of the text ('No rest the guilty find from the pursuing furies of the mind'), is particularly far-reaching in its modulation: the furies pursue Dejanira from the flat side (G minor) to the sharp side (B minor); the final chord is altered to B major to prepare the immediate appearance of the concluding section in E minor, which begins with A″ in E minor and leads with no significant break to a recurrence of the text and musical material from section C in the tonic key.

The fact that the contrasting sections share material also contributes to the formal irregularity of this scene. Section A′ ends with material related to section B; the material of section C (such as the falling sixteenth notes in the strings) is similar to the A sections, and text and material from the C section recurs in the final appearance of A′. Handel thus obfuscates divisions between the primary sections of the aria. The resulting structural ambivalence relates to his most significant revision of the piece.

The ambiguity about where the 'aria' begins demonstrates the degree to which Handel succeeds in blurring the distinction between recitative and aria. This is less true of the first version (Ex. 8.9). He originally composed a clear cadence at the recitative text (after 'black Tisiphone'), so that there was little

EX. 8.9. Dejanira's mad scene in *Hercules*, BL RM 20.e.8, fos. 113ᵛ–114ʳ

Ex. 8.9. (*cont.*)

question as to where the accompagnata ended. Moreover, the aria began with a ritornello that presented the main theme of the A section. Later he revised the piece by simply removing the recitative cadence and the aria ritornello.

The success with which Handel's revision obscures the expected distinction between recitative and aria can be gauged by Chrysander's edition of *Hercules*. In that edition the aria proper might seem to begin with the 'concitato' section at the end of page 222 of *HG* 4, but this interpretation is open to question.[48] I shall present an alternative view here—though the interesting point is not which reading is correct, but the fact that there can be any disagreement at all on a point that is usually undebatable. The double bar at the end of page 222 of *HG* 4 is Chrysander's rather than Handel's, and even though we hear a preview of material that occurs later in the set-piece (*HG* 4: 229, bb. 3–4), the first 'concitato' quickly moves from aria to recitative style.[49] The set-piece, it seems to me, begins on the bottom system of page 223 ('See the dreadful sisters rise', etc.). This view is supported by the text, for only at 'See the dreadful sisters rise' is there a change from decasyllabic blank verse to pairs of rhyming lines of irregular lengths:

> Where shall I fly! where hide this guilty head!
> Oh fatal error of misguided love!
> Oh cruel Nessus, how art thou reveng'd!
> Wretched I am! by me Alcides dies!

---

[48] Apparently Winton Dean considers this Concitato the beginning of the 'aria' in its final version. See Dean, *Handel's Dramatic Oratorios*, 427–8. My thoughts about the beginning of the aria are in accordance with Walther Siegmund-Schulze, 'Die Dejanira-Szene im Oratorium Hercules', in his *Georg Friedrich Händel: Thema mit 20 Variationen* (Halle (Saale), 1965), 105–8.

[49] Admittedly there is evidence to support Chrysander's reading: the bar of rest preceding this point in the score and the new clefs and key signature.

These impious hands have sent my injur'd lord
Untimely to the shades! let me be mad!
Chain me, ye furies, to your iron beds,
And lash my guilty ghost with whips of scorpion!
See! see! they come! Alecto with her snakes!
Megaera fell, and black Tisiphone!

See the dreadful sisters rise!
Their baneful presence taints the skies!
See the snaky whips they bear!
What yellings rend my tortur'd ear!
  Hide me from their hated sight,
    Friendly shades of blackest night!
Alas! no rest the guilty find
From the pursuing furies of the mind!

Which of these interpretations is preferable, however, is perhaps less interesting than the remarkable fact that there could be ambiguity about so basic a matter.

In Dejanira's mad scene Handel thus undermines one of the most salient and pervasive conventions of early eighteenth-century musical dramaturgy. By eliding two separate pieces and thereby obscuring the distinction between recitative and aria, he creates a continuous dramatic 'scena' that furthers Dejanira's mental decline. Just as the insane Dejanira's vision of the furies departs from reality, her aria obfuscates formal clarity, and her scene as a whole actually avoids the 'normal' procedure of moving from recitative to aria. The traditional boundaries of musical discourse cannot contain Dejanira's dementia. By subverting the norms of musical structure madness asserts its presence, and that it does so by subverting the norms of musical structure is only what we expect: in all periods 'operatic' madness represents what might be called a convention of unconvention. But Handel's choice of musical form—and his elimination of the boundary between aria and recitative, even allowing material to be shared between the two—is unique in his works, and perhaps in the whole history of musical madness.

Handel's revisions of form in his oratorios, then, cannot be understood as a purely musical phenomenon; we must analyse musical changes in relation to the libretto—its structure, the drama it conveys, and the characters it presents. Oratorio (or opera) engages multiple modes of discourse, which may either cohere or disagree, but the interrelationships among them cannot be ignored. Simply put, Handel did not allow one layer of discourse to lord it over the other. His revisions of musical form seem to have occurred for a number of different reasons, including proportion, balance, plot, and individual characterizations; but Handel was never a powerless composer forced to follow the artificial restraints of a libretto that 'imposed' certain musical structures (or specific revisions of those structures). Instead, the flexibility of his use of musical forms—forms crafted with an eye towards their interactions with other dimensions of oratorio—represents a significant component of his capacity to create viable musical drama.

9

Musical Imagery as Drama

PREVIOUS chapters have suggested that a complete understanding of Handel's compositional process must allow for paradoxes. Certain issues require us to take this observation a step further: the generalizations that we draw about Handel's compositional process, extracted from individual cases, at times may assume a dialectical shape; for normative processes that appear to be contradictory or opposed actually disclose a similarity in compositional approach.

Such is the case with text-setting. Handel's musical art seems often to have been inspired by images in the text, images that he takes pain to portray in his music, often adjusting or changing such effects during the process of creation (as the first part of this chapter reveals). On the other hand, he sometimes transfers an entire musical setting from one text to an entirely different text (the subject of this chapter's second part)—on the surface a process that should presumably be anathema to a composer who attempts to create a kind of musical discourse that resonates with textual images.[1] However, Handel generally transforms the music to suit its new text and dramatic situation. In his case, then, both these processes reveal a single compositional concern with creating a cogent symbiosis between text and music.

Musical Imagery

Handel's musical autographs suggest that the process of visualizing stage action inspired the composer's creative muse.[2] Although the oratorios were

---

[1] A similar manner of formulating the issue is already present in a discussion of how the poet should adapt suitcase arias to new texts in Pier Jacopo Martello's *Dialogo sopra la tragedia antica e moderna* of 1715: 'But tell me this: what will you do if in lieu of an aria of indignation, which is what you had there before, there is now to be inserted an aria that expresses love? Will you set indifferent words to it? But if the composer was not a blockhead, he will have written music suitable to the original expression, quite unadaptable to the other.' See Piero Weiss, 'Pier Jacopo Martello on Opera (1715): An Annotated Translation', *Musical Quarterly*, 66 (1980), 378–403 at 398.

[2] This point was first suggested by Winton Dean. See *Handel's Dramatic Oratorios*, 36.

not intended to be staged, he regularly included elaborate stage directions in his composing scores. As Dean puts it, 'the evidence strongly suggests that in the heat of creation Handel saw Saul, Hercules, Belshazzar, and the rest striding the boards, and that such a vision controlled the form and gestures of the music itself'.[3] In other words, the imaginative impulse fired by scenic descriptions may in part account for the sensational pictorial imagery in Handel's dramatic music.

Since the act of composition for Handel must often have begun with contemplation of the text, the creation of particular musical images to suit it in many instances belongs to the early stages of the creative process. This must have been the case, for instance, in the aria 'With fond desiring' from *Semele*, where Semele's vocal line, unsupported by basso continuo except at the major cadences, is doubled by violin. The use of this monophonic texture aptly reflects the text 'Love and I are one'. Similarly, a famous example of word-painting in *Joshua* goes back as far as the written record will take us. An early draft of 'O thou bright orb', left incomplete, already contains the sustained pitch A that depicts the stationary sun—an effect Handel preserved in the final setting.[4]

Of course, it is easier for us to examine those instances in which pictorial imagery was created during a later compositional stage. Handel adds word-painting or increases the effect of a particular image in his music with some frequency. To choose a simple example, near the end of the chorus 'Righteous Heav'n beholds their guile' at the close of Act I of *Susanna*, Handel originally composed a typical supporting bass (see Ex. 9.1). Early on (probably before writing the upper parts), however, he decided that the bass line should take part with the upper strings in a flurry of sixteenth notes resonating with the fury of the text 'wrath divine outstrips the wind'. Accordingly, he changed the bass line to sixteenth notes, thus rendering mimetic the entire fabric of the orchestral postlude to the chorus.[5]

In other cases Handel completely alters the manner in which he depicts text, choosing a new means of portraying it, as we can see from an aria in *Hercules*. Iole's 'My father, ah!' comprises a two-part aria, the first part of

---

[3] See *Handel's Dramatic Oratorios*, 36.

[4] See FM MUS MS 259, pp. 65–6. This version is notated in longer rhythmic values than the final version, but is otherwise quite similar. Since the final setting is marked 'allegro', the change in notation might indicate an increase of tempo—no doubt welcomed by the trumpet soloist who sustains the A!

[5] In this case he takes the word-painting a step further. In Winton Dean's view, 'perhaps Handel reached the practicable limits when he set the words "Tremble, guilt, for thou shalt find Wrath divine outstrips the wind" in *Susanna* to a double fugue, with one subject to each line of the poem, in such a way that the second, in notes of half the length, repeatedly "outstrips" the first' (*Handel's Dramatic Oratorios*, 63).

Ex. 9.1. 'Tremble guilt' in *Susanna*, BL RM 20.f.8, fo. 48ᵛ

which is a tragic, recitative-like setting of Iole's memory of her father's death, a common-time larghetto in C minor (*HG* 4: 75–7, first system). Iole's blessing of her father, 'Peaceful rest', which forms the aria's second part, is contrastingly in triple metre and the key of the relative major (E flat) (*HG* 4: 77, 2/1 to p. 79).

The autograph contains a revision near the beginning of the second part, 'Peaceful rest' (bb. 7–17 of this section). Handel evidently rewrote this passage before continuing to compose the score, because the passage ends with an incomplete bar, even in voice and continuo (Ex. 9.2). This original version of the vocal entrance is static both in melody and bass. Note particularly in this passage of nine bars the four statements of the cadential formula (7–8, 9–10, 12–13, 14–15; the third statement is slightly varied), which preclude any sense of forward momentum. It might be that this lack of forward movement was meant to portray the text 'peaceful rest'.[6]

Handel rejected this version in favour of different musical imagery. He eliminated one of the cadences in bars 7–10 of the draft, after which the vocal line appears in conjunction with a restatement of bars 1–8, so that no cadence

---

[6] If such is the case, then this example resembles 'Cease ruler of the day' (discussed below). There, too, in an attempt to portray text in music Handel essentially brought the piece to a halt before it began— a technique he sometimes employs to good effect. For example, in the duet 'Caro/Bella! piu amabile beltà' near the end of the third act of *Giulio Cesare* the vocal entrance, in common time rather than the predominant 12/8, allows for a static moment of timelessness as the lovers address each other before they begin the duet proper.

EX. 9.2. 'Peaceful rest' in *Hercules*, BL RM 20.e.8, fo. 39ʳ

occurs again until the end of the phrase (*HG* 4: 77–8, bb. 16–17). The voice starts with repeated pitches (G and A♭) to depict 'peaceful rest' and thereafter ascends to a high point in bar 16, providing a sense of climax and (in bb. 16–17) return. This revised version not only achieves greater continuity in both its melody and harmony, but also a sense of forward drive that was missing in the first version.

It is clear from these examples that Handel carefully weighed the measure of his imagery, a process that could extend through several phases of the genesis of a work. And if musical imagery sometimes plays a traceable role in his compositional process, this merely underscores the large role that word–painting has in Handel's dramatic music, even when its genesis cannot be reconstructed.

Both the frequency and the manner in which Handel employs musical imagery has not always won him admirers. In *An Essay on Musical Expression* of 1752, Charles Avison distinguishes two basic ways in which music can reflect text. The first he calls 'Imitation', the depiction of movement (ascent, descent, flying, etc.) or non-musical sounds (laughter, etc.), whose purpose, he pejoratively remarks, is to fix 'the Hearer's Attention on the Similitude between Sounds and the Things which they describe, and thereby to excite a reflex Act of Understanding [rather] than to affect the Heart and raise the Passions of the Soul'.[7] The second kind of text depiction is 'Expression', which is a broader and, for Avison, a far nobler thing: 'such a Concurrence of Air and Harmony, as affects us most strongly with the Passions or Affections which the Poet intends to raise . . . the Composer is not principally to dwell on particular Words in the Way of Imitation, but to comprehend the Poet's general Drift or Intention, and on this to form his Air and Harmony'.[8]

In 1753, the year after Avison's essay first appeared, William Hayes, Heather Professor of Music at Oxford University, anonymously published his *Remarks on Mr. Avison's Essay*, in which he argued that, contrary to Avison's claim, Imitation and Expression are by no means contradictory, as certain works by Handel (notably *L'Allegro, il Penseroso ed il Moderato*) demonstrate. Apparently in response to Hayes the second edition of Avison's *Essay* (1753) makes explicit complaints against Handel.[9] In a famous passage, Avison criticizes Handel, among other things, for 'condescending to amuse the vulgar Part of his Audience by letting them hear the sun stand still' in *Joshua* and for his portrayal of the stalking of a giant in *Acis and Galatea*.[10]

---

[7] Charles Avison, *An Essay on Musical Expression* (London: C. Davis, 1752), 57. Imitation of nature became a popular topic among 18th-c. writers on music, including James Harris, 'A Discourse on Music, Painting, and Poetry' in *Three Treatises Concerning Art* (1744), and such writings increased during the second half of the century.   [8] Ibid. 61.

[9] These were to be echoed in other 18th-c. publications. According to Oliver Goldsmith in 1760, Handel 'has been obliged, in order to express passion, to imitate words by sounds, which tho' it gives the pleasure which imitation always produces, yet it fails of exciting those lasting affections, which it is in the power of sounds to produce'. See Oliver Goldsmith, 'On the Different Schools of Music', *British Magazine* (Feb. 1760); available in *Collected Works of Oliver Goldsmith*, ed. Arthur Friedman, iii (Oxford University Press, 1966), 93. Avison's points (without his specific references to Handel) are summarized in Edward Lippman, *A History of Western Musical Aesthetics* (Lincoln and London: University of Nebraska Press, 1992), 101–3. There is some confusion there, however. Although Lippman cites only the 1752 edition of the *Essay*, he discusses material (including the five observations) that first appeared in the second edition of 1753, some of which I take to be Avison's reaction to Hayes's attack.

[10] Avison, *An Essay on Musical Expression*, 2nd edn. (London: C. Davis, 1753), 63, 65–7. This passage is reprinted in Enrico Fubini, *Music and Culture in Eighteenth-Century Europe*, trans. Wolfgang Freis, Lisa Gasbarrone, and Michael Louis Leone, trans. ed. Bonnie J. Blackburn (Chicago and London: University of Chicago Press, 1994), 310–19.

A particularly apt vehicle for demonstrating the usefulness of Avison's observations—and for vitiating certain of his criticisms on their own terms—is 'Cease ruler of the day to rise' from *Hercules*. Earlier in the drama the hero Hercules swore that the sun would cease to dawn, the moon 'be blott'd from her orb ere he prove'd false' to his wife Dejanira. The neurotic Dejanira, however, believes that the captive Iole rather than she herself is the object of her husband's affections. In 'Cease ruler of the day' Dejanira gives vent to her feelings over Hercules' supposed infidelity. Although Handel chooses to depict the passion of melancholy in this expressive aria, the text might as easily have invited a rage aria from the composer:

> Cease, ruler of the day to rise,
> nor, Cynthia, gild the ev'ning skies,
> to your bright beams he made appeal,
> with endless night his falsehood seal.

As we saw in the previous chapter, however, Handel is careful to depict Dejanira's vacillating emotional states in Act II of *Hercules*—from jealousy to angry ridicule, from melancholy to joy. With characteristic dramatic insight he responds not merely to the surface meaning of the aria text as a whole, but to the emotional state of the character singing at a particular point in the story: he reads between the lines. One might argue that this exemplifies Avison's Expression taken to another level—one that recognizes the importance of musical drama, which plays no role in Avison's discussion.

In its present form there is some word-painting in the aria, such as the melodic ascent to the word 'rise', depicting the movement of the sun, and the melismas on and repetition of 'endless night', but the original version contained much more 'Imitation'. As Ex. 9.3 shows, the first word of the aria, 'cease', was followed by a rest in all parts, and there were far longer melismas on 'endless'. At a late stage, after the conducting score had been copied, Handel decided to eliminate these instances of word-painting from the aria each time they occurred (see *HG* 4: 169–71). Perhaps the composer felt that the blatant depiction of these specific words detracted from the considerable expressive power of the aria, in essence that Imitation detracted from Expression.

'Cease ruler of the day' shows that the basic concepts of Avison's *Essay* would not have been lost on Handel, but, contrary to Avison's claims, Handel did exercise discernment over when Imitation was not appropriate. Indeed, the *raison d'être* of the revisions of this aria could be explained with Avison's own words: 'the musical Composer, who catches at every particular Epithet or Metaphor that the Poet affords him, to shew his imitative Power, will

Ex. 9.3. 'Cease, ruler of the day to rise' in *Hercules*, BL RM 20.e.8, fo. 80ʳ

never fail to hurt the true Aim of his Composition, and will always prove the more difficent in Proportion as his Author is more pathetic or sublime' (68–9).

It is perhaps not enough that Handel's musical revisions seem to defeat Avison's criticism on its own turf. There still remains the more important question of whether we should confine our investigation of word-painting to the criteria Avison suggested. In fact, he raised several specific points about word-painting. First, 'when *Sounds* only are the Objects of Imitation' the mimetic part should occur only in the accompanying instruments, because 'it is probable, that the Imitation will be too powerful in the *Voice* which ought to be engaged in *Expression* alone'.[11] Second, when music imitates motion both the vocal and instrumental parts should coincide in their imitation. Avison considered the portrayal of motion to be a dangerous undertaking, for 'the Intervals in Music are not so strictly similar to animate or inanimate Motions, as its Tones are to animate or inanimate Sounds' (63). Thus certain manifestations of this kind of imitation will be more successful than others: 'little jiggish Slurs are less like the Nod of Alexander, than Shakes and Trills are to the Voice of the Nightingale' (65–6). Third, imitation should not be employed to represent objects 'of which Motion or Sound are not the principal Constituents' (66). His final points embrace larger aesthetic issues: that music should never imitate disagreeable sounds, and that the composer should be careful in judging when imitation was appropriate to a given setting.

Handel, of course, left behind no specific writings about imitation, though one remark of the composer concerning word-painting has recently come to light. Katherine Knatchbull claimed that Handel himself communicated to her before the first performance of *Israel in Egypt* that 'the storm of thunder is to be bold and fine, & the thick, silent darkness is to be express'd in a very particular piece of musick'.[12] Moreover, Handel's stance on the relationship of words and music was expressed most cogently in his music. It is clear from virtually every page of his dramatic vocal music that his judgement of the appropriateness of word-painting not only disagreed with Avison's, but was governed by very different concerns.

Avison's disapproval of much of Handel's word-painting may result from overlooking the importance of dramatic musical gestures for musical theatre. His discussion, though it succeeds in identifying the portrayal of textual images as a particularly salient component of Handel's music, never mentions drama, and his inability to grasp the relation of imitation—actually far too

---

[11] Avison (1753), 61.   [12] Dunhill, *Handel and the Harris Circle*, 6.

limited a term for Handel's musical imagery, which transcends mere word-painting—to drama is his central failure as a critic of Handel.

This important role that musical imagery plays in the dramatic component of Handel's vocal works is readily evident in his scores. Perhaps more than any other composer, Handel possessed a keen ability to portray movement in music, and the dramatic vitality of the result far outstrips Avison's disapproval of this sort of word-painting. Indeed, most of us are less offended than Avison by the sun standing still in *Joshua*, and more attuned to its dramatic impact.

To paraphrase Dean, Handel not only 'visualized Saul, Hercules, Belshazzar, and the rest striding the boards', he transferred this vision into the very 'form and gesture of the music itself'. This quality of his music is reflected in the critical language employed to describe it, from 1752, when Avison first noted the importance of imitation in Handel, to the present. The following excerpt concerns an aria in which a multiplicity of images combine in dramatic discourse (*HG* 4: 27–32):

In 'Where congeal'd the northern streams' Handel combines two ideas, the frozen landscape and the resolution of Hyllus' search, in a remarkable mood-painting. The rigid quaver movement (*Andante larghetto e staccato*) in the bass, the cold E natural in the first bar of the G minor theme, the accented crotchets for 'With adventurous steps I'll tread', and the *staccato* repeated semiquavers for 'bound in icy fetters' each make their contribution; the climax comes when the voice for four bars is frozen to the note G, joined by the upper strings in unison, while the bass heaves like the ocean beneath the polar ice and momentarily breaks surface with a clashing A flat.[13]

Granted, pictorial interpretations can be grafted onto, if not made to fit, almost any passage of music. The interpretation quoted above, however, is likely to be meaningful to a broad compass of listeners, for the language reflects the tacit dramatic vitality of Handel's oratorios, which results in part from the dramatic role played by his musical imagery. It is, in fact, the dramatic qualities in the music itself that defines unstaged oratorio as a dramatic genre. The 'drama *in* music' of the oratorios and the care with which Handel achieved it constitute one of the sources of their musical and dramatic success. In the case of 'Where congeal'd the Northern Streams' we are led to experience Hyllus' search for his father in foreign climes—in fact we are led into the mind of the character:

> Where congeal'd the Northern Streams,
> Bound in icy Fetters, Stand;
> Where the Sun's intenser Beams
> Search the burning Libyan Sand;

[13]   Dean, *Handel's Dramatic Oratorios*, 421.

> By Honour, Love, and Duty led,
> With advent'rous Steps I'll tread.

It is beyond the scope of this chapter to examine Handel's word-painting in its totality. But to limit ourselves to the vantage point of his compositional revisions, it is possible to examine an important way in which word-painting plays a dramatic role: by portraying unstaged and unstageable presences. 'Where congeal'd' has already provided one example: the music paints the future landscape as Hyllus imagines it and his actions therein—in short an unstageable scene. We shall examine two other kinds of presences that Handel is able to represent musically: the presence of fate and the presence of supernatural phenomena. In both cases these imaginative constructions appear as almost animate beings—as 'characters', if you will—within the musical discourse.

In depicting fate the musical imagery, in Edward Cone's terms, serves as the conveyer of 'the composer's voice'. There are cases when the orchestra's musical imagery may convey something to the audience of which the living characters on stage are oblivious. The aria 'Virtue my soul shall still embrace' near the beginning of *Jephtha* (*HG* 44: 27–31), for instance, contains such a moment of musical irony, or what Carolyn Abbate (though admittedly addressing a profoundly different repertoire) calls musical narrative, 'a unique moment of performing narration within a surrounding music'.[14] Jephtha has agreed to fight to free his countrymen from the Ammonites, who have held them captive for eighteen years. His first aria expresses the good result he naively expects to result from his virtue:

> Virtue my soul shall still embrace,
> Goodness shall make me great.
> Who builds upon this steady base,
> Dreads no event of fate.

At this dramatic moment Jephtha is happily unaware of how much he has to fear from fate: that ultimately, as a result of a foolish vow, he will trap himself into the obligation of offering his own daughter as a sacrifice. That God should expect him to carry out this vow becomes a central crisis of the story ('How dark, oh Lord, are thy decrees' but 'whatever is, is right'). In its happy-go-lucky manner, the A section of 'Virtue my soul' reflects Jephtha's ignorant but blissful state of mind at the beginning of the drama. In the B section, however, Handel creates a disjunction between the text and the music's

---

[14] Carolyn Abbate, *Unsung Voices: Opera and Musical Narrative in the Nineteenth Century* (Princeton: Princeton University Press, 1991), 19.

voice. 'Who builds upon this steady base, / Dreads no event of fate' evokes a sustained pedal first on B, then on E. Handel surely intended the pun between 'base' and 'bass'.

In Baroque music pedal-points are often associated with stasis, firm grounding, or timelessness. The pedal is, for example, typically a feature of pastoral settings because in its lack of motion it suggests repose, the peacefulness of the Arcadian existence. Pedal-points are accordingly quite prominent among the pastoral elements that express 'the sweets of life, unwounded by its cares' in Joseph's Act II aria 'The peasant tastes the sweets of life' from *Joseph and his Brethren*. In 'Virtue my soul' the pedal seems at first similarly wedded to Jephtha's unworried, peaceful state of mind—a result of the 'steady base' (bass) upon which he is grounded.

Handel soon reverses all associations of steadfastness the pedal might evoke, however, revealing that the text and the musical word-painting are both false. Above the pedal a motif appears in the violins that is clearly based on an accompanimental idea in the A section, but in its new appearance it is extremely disjunct, with jagged leaps and many dissonant pitches. This material seems actually to force the pedal up a half-step to E#, ironically, at a moment when Jephtha refers to the 'steady base'. The sense of foreboding created by this music surely reflects the future dire events of fate that will lead to a crisis. One might say that the passage functions as a proleptic narrator, foretelling future events of which Jephtha has as yet no clue. The passage contrasts with the surrounding music in a manner that Abbate considers typical of narrative moments:

[These moments] can be identified by their bizarre and disruptive effect. They seem like voices from elsewhere, speaking (singing) in a fashion we recognize precisely because it is idiosyncratic . . . A musical voice sounds unlike the music that constitutes its encircling milieu.[15]

In the original version Handel allowed this 'fate motif' to pull the music far afield tonally, to F sharp minor—a striking departure from the A section's G major tonic (Ex. 9.4).[16] There is such a thing as too bold a gesture, however. Handel rejected this unusual harmonic relationship, apparently, before finishing the first draft, replacing it with a more typical B section ending in

---

[15]　Ibid. 29.

[16]　If he originally intended for this F sharp minor cadence to serve as the end of the B section, it would have created a very rare harmonic relationship with the A section. In her analysis of the relationships of the concluding cadences of A sections and B sections in 711 arias from twenty-eight of Handel's operas, Ellen Harris did not find a single instance of I/vii. (See Harris, 'Harmonic Patterns in Handel's Operas', 89.)

EX. 9.4. 'Virtue my soul' in *Jephtha*, BL RM 20.e.9, fo. 16ʳ

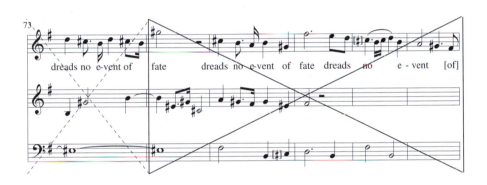

the mediant (B minor).[17] His omission of the seven-bar passage affecting the move to F sharp minor by no means obliterates the presence of the prophet-ic musical voice; it is merely an instance of fine tuning. The musical depic-tion of fate was obviously part of Handel's intention from the beginning; the issue disclosed by the revision concerns the degree to which this musical depiction should influence the tonal direction of the aria.

At this moment in *Jephtha* it is as though an 'other' voice has entered the music, circumventing the effect of the pedal as a naive word-painting device and suggesting that Jephtha's sense of security is ill-founded. Handel's use of musical imagery thus transcends what Avison meant by Imitation of nature as well as the more modern term 'word-painting'. If it is not Imitation, how-ever, it nonetheless illustrates another way in which Handel's musical imagery can assume a dramatic role.

Handel's capacity to suggest the appearance of a supernatural phenomenon within the musical discourse is gloriously displayed in the famous handwrit-ing scene in *Belshazzar*. In Act II, scene 2 the inebriated Belshazzar challenges the God of Judah to vindicate his injured honour. In a striking early use of instrumental recitative, a hand appears and writes on the wall (adagio e stac-cato, ma piano), leaving behind it 'types unknown'. Belshazzar and the chorus of Persians see the hand and respond to it in a scene remarkable for its structural fluidity and dramatic flow (*HG* 19: 156–9). Although there is no stage action, there is no question about the dramatic vitality of the music.

In fact, the actual appearance of the hand is so convincing in its first occur-rence that Handel was forced to revise a later number within this scene, when Daniel emerges to interpret the handwriting (Ex. 9.5). In the original setting of the interpretation—of which much music and text were cut—Handel attempted to evoke the memory of the hand by recalling the instrumental recitative when Daniel says 'From Him the hand was sent'. Yet the portray-al of the hand as an actual presence was so strong that Handel apparently could not evoke its mere memory without suggesting that it has appeared again. More than likely the composer abandoned the attempt to evoke the memory of the hand and removed the instrumental recitative in this scene because of the difficulty of distinguishing between presence and remem-brance in musical terms.

One of the functions of Handel's imitation, then, is to personify abstract 'characters', non-human and otherwise unstageable presences—a function of

---

[17] The example actually contains three distinct versions. Handel first composed eleven bars that would have cadenced to F sharp minor (bb. 68–78 in Ex. 9.4). He then cancelled the last five of these bars (74–8) and intended to follow bar 73 with bar 79. He then eliminated bars 73 and 79, and changed the bass line of bar 80 to follow bar 72.

EX. 9.5. First setting of Daniel's interpretation in *Belshazzar*, BL RM 20.d.10, fo. 115ᵛ

utmost importance in a dramatic medium such as oratorio. In *Jephtha* Handel
took pains to tailor that image to a particular moment in the drama; in Act II,
scene 2 in *Belshazzar* he created a musical image that he could not transfer
to a new context. Such instances possess ramifications for other aspects of
Handel's compositional process. For the picture of Handel's music that
emerges from these examples—a picture that suggests the dramatic centrality
and seeming immutability of musical imagery—seems at first to be negated by
the existence of retexted arias. Part of the reason for the ensuing discussion,
however, is to problematize this simplified manner of formulating the issue.

Musical Adaptions to New Texts

In the light of our discussion heretofore, it might come as a surprise that the
autographs of Handel's oratorios abound not merely in rejected drafts that

were ultimately replaced by new settings of the same text, but also transfers of music, originally intended for one text, to an entirely new text.[18] The process of revising and reusing old music seems to raise a fundamental compositional problem: if, as the preceding examples illustrate, Handel's musical ideas are to be associated with concrete textual ideas, then how can the same music serve different texts? Similarly, if musical imagery is wedded to drama, how can it be transferred to a new plot? The answers to these questions will vary depending upon the case at hand. There are times when musical images are so strongly associated with specific textual images that they cannot be used in other contexts, such as the appearance of the hand in *Belshazzar*.

In other cases the music is largely non-pictorial, and a transfer can easily be made to a text with a similar layout. Such was the case when Handel simply reused the fugue that originally ended Act II of *Semele* as 'Zaphnath Egypt's fate foresaw' in *Joseph and his Brethren*. As I have argued elsewhere, the music was probably almost precisely the same in both settings.[19] Neither text offers much in the way of word-painting.

In still other cases, however, the word-painting is significant enough to emerge as a concern but, for at least two reasons, not an insurmountable obstacle when Handel recomposed and rearranged old music to suit a new text. First, musical images are not entirely piece-specific; because of the abstract nature of musical discourse, the same image is sometimes suitable for various contexts. Secondly, Handel's transfers often involve a large amount of rewriting, so that new images can be accommodated. We can explore the procedures that emerge during such undertakings in three resettings that involve transplanting music from one text to another (see Table 9.1).

The composition of the aria 'How bless'd the maid' from *Hercules* can be traced through its use of material from the rejected aria 'Come Zephyrs come', originally intended for *Semele*.[20] There are several significant alterations of the original aria, many of which relate in part to the use of different texts. To cite the most prominent instance, in 'Come Zephyrs come' the

---

[18] It will not surprise anyone familiar with the literature on parody in Bach and Handel, which began in the 1920s. To cite only a few major writings on this topic, see Arnold Schering, 'Über Bach's Parodieverfahren', *Bach-Jahrbuch* (1922), 49–95; Ludwig Finscher, 'Zum Parodieproblem bei Bach', in Martin Geck (ed.), *Bach-Interpretationen* (Göttingen: Vanderhoeck und Ruprecht, 1969), 94–105; and Hans-Joachim Schulze, 'The Parody Process in Bach's Music: An Old Problem Reconsidered', *Bach*, 20 (1989), 7–21. A few works on Handel's parody procedures (excluding the voluminous literature on borrowing—see Ch. 3) include Bernt Baselt, 'Zum Parodieverfahren in Händels frühen Opern', *Händel-Jahrbuch* (1975), 19; Hill, 'Handel's Retexting', 284–9; Ellen Harris, 'Integrity and Improvisation in the Music of Handel', *Journal of Musicology*, 7 (1989), 301–15; and LaRue, *Handel and his Singers*, 177–81.

[19] See Hurley, 'The Summer of 1743'.

[20] This aria is published only in the piano-vocal score, ed. Anthony Lewis and Charles Mackerras (Oxford: Oxford University Press, 1972).

TABLE 9.1. *Musical transfers*

Semele (1743) 'Come, Zephyrs, come'	→	*Hercules* (1744) 'How bless'd the maid'
Solomon (1748) 'Golden Columns', 1st setting'	→	*Solomon* (1748) 'Will the sun', 2nd setting
Susanna (1748) ''Tis not age's sullen face', 1st setting	→	*Susanna* (1748) 'Chastity, thou cherub'

triple-time B section, wondrously imitative of dance, admirably suits the words:

> Dance around her
> While I wound her,
> And with pleasure fill her Dreams.

The B section of 'How bless'd the maid', however, differs in poetic imagery and therefore required new music:

> Though low, yet happy in that low estate,
> And safe from ills, which on a princess wait.

Handel composed an entirely new B section which, except for its key, bears no resemblance to its forebear (*HG* 4: 108–9). His employment of word-painting in the new B section, the text of which has little potential for musical imagery, is more localized and less interesting than in the earlier aria; 'low' and 'happy' are contrasted, but otherwise the music is non-descriptive. This move towards less word-painting typifies the resetting of this aria.

The first sections (or A sections) of the two compositions are in large part very nearly identical. In fact, Handel may have begun by copying directly the first page (or first thirty bars) of 'Come, Zephyrs, come', making only minuscule alterations.[21] More significant changes begin in bar 31, where Handel replaces his original passage of eight bars with nine new bars, again most likely a result of the intimate mimetic relationship of music to text in *Semele*, where 'fan her with your silky wings' evokes undulating sixteenth notes in the voice and violins (bb. 31–9). (See Ex. 9.6.) This particular musical image

---

[21] The second beat of the vocal entrance in 'How bless'd the maid' originally carried a dotted sixteenth note followed by a thirty-second note, like 'Come, Zephyrs, come', but Handel changed this to a single eighth note. This may support the argument that he began by copying. Otherwise there is just one alteration: in bar 9 of 'How bless'd' the first violin begins with G, making a linear connection to the A of bar 7, rather than with a C, as in 'Come, Zephyrs, come'.

Ex. 9.6. 'Come, Cupids, come' in *Semele*, BL RM 20.f.7, fo. 54ᵛ

ill serves the *Hercules* text—'with sweet content in humble cell, from cities far removed'—which inspired no word-painting. Typically, the new passage has the same harmonic goal as the music it replaces, so that substitution does not harmonically affect the remainder of the aria.

Too exquisite to discard from the body of the aria, the 'silky wings' material is reserved for an appropriate place in 'How bless'd the maid', at the start of the second half of the A section, where it graphically depicts 'murmuring rills' (bb. 56–61 = *HG* 4: 106, bb. 2–8). The appearance of this material at the beginning of A2 parallels musically the original aria, with one divergence. In *Semele* this third statement of the passage flirts with the minor mode by lowering the third of the chords in bars 60 and 61—a highly satisfying, if subtle, harmonic variation that is missed in the *Hercules* aria.

Besides 'internal substitutions', or replacing old passages and musical sections with new ones, the transformation of 'Come, Zephyrs, come' into 'How bless'd the maid' also involved musical 'insertions'. These, too, relate to the new text for the A section of 'How bless'd the maid', which consists of six lines divided into two stanzas, each consisting of two eight-syllable lines and one six-syllable line in the pattern 886 886 (aabccb). The first section of 'Come, Zephyrs, come' consists of one line of eight syllables, and two lines each of seven and three syllables, in the pattern 87337 (aabbc). With such different poetic structures, it is no wonder that the two settings differ. The new text for the second aria may have prompted the insertion of three bars not in the original at bar 64 (*HG* 4: 106, 2/3). This brief passage allows the last line of text to be heard in its entirety before it undergoes internal repetitions.

A more significant insertion, certainly the most important structural change in the A section, is the expansion that takes place near the end of the aria. At bar 80 Handel repeats the second half of the A section text once again, recalling material from the start of A2 (56–62) and then concluding with the vocal cadence derived from *Semele* (compare bb. 79–82 of *Semele* with *Hercules*, bb. 91–4). This expansion helps preserve textual coherence. In the original *Semele* aria Handel had repeated the A section text in the second half of the aria's A section, as was the normal practice, but in *Hercules*, owing in part to the longer text, the text has been stated in its entirety only once by the end of A2. In the expansion Handel brings back the first line, and then repeats some of the A2 text, so that the meaning of the text is not lost.

This expansion sets off a chain reaction—yet another substitution. The closing ritornello in *Semele* recalls the 'silky wings' passage again, but in *Hercules* this same passage ('murmuring rills') had just been stated. Consequently Handel uses a different concluding ritornello, clearly to avoid stating this already familiar passage too frequently—a recurring type of revision often found at the ends of A sections, as we have seen.[22]

The resulting aria shows no sign of the rewriting it has undergone. (It must be confessed that certain features of the original—the incredible B section and the subtle modal shifts the third time the 'silky wings' material appears—are great losses.) The primary aesthetic difference between the two arias, however, lies in the profound change in the relationship between words and music, which, in regard to word-painting at least, is more intimate in 'Come, Zephyrs, come'.

Handel's recasting of music from 'Come, Zephyrs, come' for 'How bless'd the maid' reveals two processes that typify his musical substitutions. First, musical images that originally served to reflect a specific word or image are sometimes capable of reflecting other textual images equally well. In such cases Handel 'reassigns' the old musical image to new text. The reinterpretation of the 'silky wings' image as 'murmuring rills' illustrates how brilliantly this process can sometimes succeed. Second, and on the other hand, all texts do not provide the same opportunities for word-painting, and a new text obviously might alter the mimetic power of the music. While both 'Come, Zephyrs, come' and 'How bless'd the maid' contain 'imitation' in Avison's sense, the 'silky wings'/'murmuring rills' passage being a prominent example, the *Semele* aria is by far the more 'imitative' of the two. In particular, the rhythmic figure played by the violins in the first two bars as well as the ethereal figure in the bass, bars 2–3, depict the movement of the zephyrs. Handel used a similar musical 'topos' (to apply Heinichen's terminology)[23] in the aria 'Aure deh per pietà' from *Giulio Cesare* (1724).[24] (See *HG* 68: 104 ff.) The textual similarities between this and 'Come, Zephyrs, come' are striking:

---

[22] See Ch. 4.

[23] Johann David Heinichen, *Der General-Bass in der Composition* (Dresden, 1728), 24–94. Relevant passages are discussed in George Buelow, 'The Loci Topici and Affect in Late Baroque Music: Heinichen's Practical Demonstration', *Music Review* 27 (1966), 161–76. See also Ratner, *Classic Music*, 9–30.

[24] The passages are not similar enough to be designated as a borrowing, however. A study of Handelian topoi has never been undertaken, but it might prove a useful way of understanding his music.

Aure deh per pietà
Spirate al petto mio
Per dar conforto oh Dio
Al mio dolor.

Sweet Breezes with your gentle Gales,
In Pity cool my troubled Breast.[25]

In 'How bless'd the maid', the musical material from *Semele* no longer depicts breezes.[26] Instead, the delicate orchestration must be taken as expressive of the utopian existence of the humble maid—or, on another level, of Iole's delicacy and innocence. In Avison's terms, we have moved from 'Imitation' in *Semele* to 'Expression' in *Hercules*; while it might be argued that in an abstract sense (and in terms of the efficacy of much of its musical imagery), 'Come, Zephyrs, come' is superior to the aria derived from it, 'How bless'd the maid' is perhaps the more 'expressive' aria. Both dramatically and musically, Iole's aria is more personal and intimate, Cupid's more decorative and external. Perhaps the most striking impression of all is the integrity of each aria despite much common ground; Handel carefully crafts and recasts his music to fit each dramatic context.

Many of these same issues arise from investigation of a musical substitution in *Solomon* that provides us with the rare opportunity of tracing a melisma from its birth to the decline of its mimetic significance. As noted above, Handel transferred the music from the first setting of the priest Zadok's aria 'Golden Columns' to the final setting of the Queen of Sheba's 'Will the sun forget to streak' (*HG* 26: 298–303). In Chapter 10 I shall explore some of the reasons why this complex instance of resettings and substitution came about. For the moment it will suffice to examine the process of transferring music to a new text, the story of which begins with the first version of 'Golden Columns'.

Unfortunately, the first setting of 'Golden Columns' does not survive in its entirety. Folio 117 of the *Solomon* autograph in the British Library contains on both its sides most of the introductory ritornello (Ex. 9.7(*a*)), and the aria's concluding ritornello survives on fo. 126ʳ (Ex. 9.7(*c*)). Since fo. 117 is the end of a gathering while fo. 126 is the beginning of one, the central part of the first setting of 'Golden Columns' must have been contained on a separate, intervening gathering. Among the Handelian materials at the Fitzwilliam is a bifolio containing the 'middle' of the aria (Ex. 9.7(*b*)), and

[25] Harris, *The Librettos of Handel's Operas*, iv. 68–9.
[26] Another previous example of this topic is Seleuce's 'Dite, che fa, dov'è l'idolo mio' in *Tolomeo*, Act II, scene 6. This music is a recognizable forerunner (again not a borrowing) of 'Come, Zephyrs, come'. The English translation in the original libretto refers to zephyrs in an amorous context. See Harris, *The Librettos of Handel's Operas*, v. 40–1.

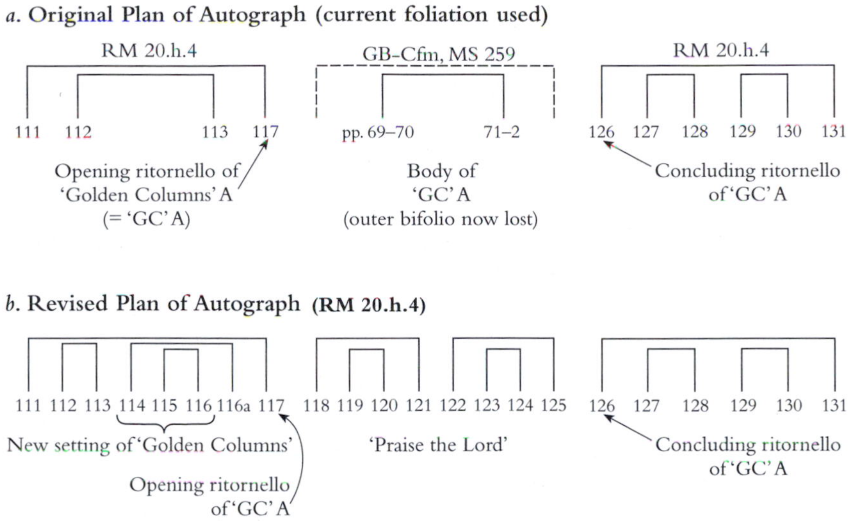

a. **Original Plan of Autograph (current foliation used)**

b. **Revised Plan of Autograph (RM 20.h.4)**

FIG. 9.1. Folio gatherings in Act III of *Solomon*

the physical characteristics of the paper suggest that this bifolio once formed part of the autograph.[27] The Fitzwilliam bifolio once formed the inner leaves of a gathering of four folios positioned between folios now numbered 117 and 126, and the outer bifolio of this gathering is now missing (see Fig. 9.1).[28] Even with this material, then, the original aria is not complete. If we divide the aria into five parts (physically rather than musically), its second and fourth parts are missing. Nonetheless, the surviving material is substantial enough to allow us to explore Handel's compositional revisions. The composer's most substantial alteration of the first setting of 'Golden Columns' is the addition of the ascending melisma that depicts 'swells'. The aria originally did not take advantage of this opportunity for imitation (see Ex. 9.8). Perhaps at the same time, Handel made a related change in the medial and concluding ritornellos (see Ex. 9.9). In addition to rebarring the passage, which need not concern us, he introduced in the third version of the medial ritornello a theme identified by John Roberts as a borrowing from a Telemann aria, 'Unbegreiflich ist dein Wesen' (see Ex. 9.10).[29] Although the

[27] For specific paper information see Burrows and Ronish, *Catalogue*, 210, 238.

[28] When Handel revised 'Golden Columns' he removed the entire gathering, replacing it physically (as opposed to musically) with fos. 118–25, containing the chorus 'Praise the Lord'. The new setting of 'Golden Columns', the musical replacement of the original aria, was inserted before fo. 117 (fos. 114–16).

[29] John Roberts, 'Handel's Borrowings from Telemann', 170. Ellwood Derr has discussed the relationships between the second setting of 'Will the sun' and its Telemann source (see 'Handel's Procedures', 116). The aria can be found in Telemann, *Musikalische Werke*, iv, ed. Fock, 289–91.

EX. 9.7. First version of 'Golden Columns' in *Solomon*: (*a*) RM 20.h.4, fo. 117ʳ

Ex. 9.7. (*cont.*)

missing leaves prevent us from knowing with certainty, it seems likely that the revised medial ritornello introduces this material for the first time in the aria.

Handel revised the concluding ritornello in a similar manner (Ex. 9.7(*c*)). After the head–motif, the original version continued with a statement of the

Ex. 9.7. (*cont.*)

passage associated with 'swells' discussed above; thus the concluding ritornello would have reflected the revised beginning of A2. In the new version,
Handel substitutes for the 'melisma' a restatement of the Telemann material,
this time developed somewhat. By limiting this Telemann material to the
orchestra, the revised ritornellos bring about a clearer distinction between the
vocal sections (as far as can be seen) and the purely orchestral sections of the
aria, and the melisma thus never loses its imitative status, remaining closely
aligned with the text 'swells with state'.

Ultimately Handel decided to scrap this setting of 'Golden Columns' altogether, resetting the text to entirely new music, and salvaging the discarded
music for a new version of 'Will the sun forget to streak'. Adapting Zadok's

EX. 9.7. First version of 'Golden Columns' in *Solomon*: (*c*) BL RM 20.h.4, fo. 126ʳ

Ex. 9.7. (*cont.*)

music for Sheba's queen involved a transposition from G minor to E minor, as well as a number of notational changes. 'Golden Columns' was originally marked larghetto, but Handel changed this to 'Andante'. In keeping with this revision, 'Will the sun' B, again marked Larghetto, is notated differently, its rhythmic values half that of 'Golden Columns' A; but the relative tempo

Ex. 9.8. First setting of 'Golden Columns' in *Solomon*: addition of melisma

markings andante and larghetto would indicate that the two arias proceed at the same pace.

In addition, the orchestration of 'Golden Columns' A, with its divided viola parts, was somewhat more elaborate than 'Will the sun' B. The second violins originally played sixteenth notes against the eighth notes in the violas. In the new aria, Handel simplifies the role of the accompanying parts, opting for steady sixteenth notes that mitigate the accompanimental bustle of the original.

EX. 9.10. Comparison of (*a*) Telemann, 'Unbegreiflich ist dein Wesen', and (*b*)
Handel, 'Golden Columns' A

(*a*)

(*b*)

As far as we can tell from the surviving leaves of 'Golden Columns' A, the
two pieces closely correspond in musical content and form—a fact that
reflects the physical characteristics of the two aria texts; a direct musical substitution could easily be brought about because both consist of eight seven-
syllable lines (see texts below). Moreover, the Queen of Sheba's aria is fairly
bland in regard to *Affekt* or expressiveness, and could accommodate a wide
variety of settings, if the opportunities for word-painting are overlooked.

> Golden Columns, fair and bright,
> Catch the mortals ravish'd sight;
> Round their sides ambitious twine
> Tendrils of the clasping vine:
> Cherubims stand here display'd,
> O'er the ark their wings are laid:
> Ev'ry object swells with state,
> All is pious, all is great.
>
> Will the sun forget to streak
> Eastern skies with amber ray,
> When the dusky shades to break
> He unbars the gates of day?
> Then demand if Sheba's queen
> E'er can banish from her thought
> All the splendor she has seen,
> All the knowledge thou hast wrought.

Certain revisions made in the process of accommodating the new text
deserve our attention, however. Bars 25–8 of 'Will the sun' B comprise
three inserted bars not included in 'Golden Columns' A (b. 29). This

change illustrates Handel's concern for an effective setting of the new text. Whereas the second part (beginning after the internal ritornello) of 'Golden Columns' began with the seventh line of text, the second part of 'Will the sun' begins with a repeat of the first line of text. In 'Golden Columns' the seventh and eighth lines are independent and extractable ('Ev'ry object swells with state / All is pious, all is great'), but Handel could not have begun a new section of 'Will the sun' with its seventh line—the middle of a sentence—without making nonsense of the text.

The entire text is not repeated in the second half of 'Will the sun'; the first two lines are presented, but lines 3 and 4, which simply modify the complete thought of lines 1 and 2, are omitted here. The inserted bars are settings of lines 5 and 6, which begin the consequence ('Then demand if Sheba's queen', etc.). In short, Handel telescopes the text without sacrificing coherence.

Besides the issue of text distribution, the musical insertion improves the text-setting in one other important way. If we compare the first halves of the arias once again, it is striking that the melisma is somewhat more convincing in the first version, where its rising sixteenth notes on 'swells' well depict 'Ev'ry object swells with state', than in the final setting, where the melisma happens to fall on 'taught'. The melisma has not quite become a mere decorative ornament rather than a specific mimetic device, for it still presumably expresses the abundance of knowledge that Solomon has taught.[30] But it is less convincing than before. Handel's retexting of the second half of the aria, however, allows the melisma to regain some of its original descriptive power at least once: as a result of the added bars, the melisma falls on the word 'splendor' (though its next occurrence is again with 'taught').

One of the reasons that the melismas do not seem out of place in the new setting is that they are arguably not intended to be primarily descriptive, or at least that they need not be heard merely as such. On a dramatic plane the melismas may be experienced as a communication of the Queen of Sheba's effusive, even sensuous, gratitude—a reading that is in keeping with the expressive qualities of the aria on the whole—rather than as attempts to highlight specific words. Again Handel has transfered music from a primarily descriptive and decorous text ('Golden Columns') to a more heart-felt and personal expression (in 'Will the sun'). The result is justly one of the most celebrated of his arias.

If both of these examples show a quantitative decline in the use of musical

---

[30] This sort of displacement of a descriptive melisma is sometimes found in music of English composers. Ellen T. Harris has pointed out that elaborate embellishment of wholly unimportant words is a regular stylistic feature of Matthew Locke's music. She interprets this feature as a means of avoiding obstruction of communication of the text—'a bow to declamation'. See Ellen T. Harris, *Henry Purcell's Dido and Aeneas* (Oxford: Clarendon Press, 1987), 90.

EX. 9.11. First setting of ''Tis not age's sullen face' in *Susanna*, BL RM 20.f.8, fo. 22^r

imagery, there are also cases in which the new text rather than the original offers greater opportunities for word–painting, opportunities that Handel pursues. In other words, he does not always move away from imitation towards expression, but is quite capable of taking the opposite route. Such an example can be found in *Susanna*. The end of the original setting of '''Tis not age's sullen face' is found on fo. 22ʳ of *Susanna* (Ex. 9.11); the preceding portion of the aria was apparently written on pages that have not survived. The recitative text beginning 'Oh wondrous judge', also on fo. 22, was not set to music. The presence of the recitative text on fo. 22ʳ indicates that the aria fragment was not merely a precompositional draft, but was actually intended for the autograph score. The fact that the remainder of the bifolio (fos. 22ᵛ–23ᵛ) was blank when Handel decided to use it in the first act indicates that he must have rejected this draft early on, before preceding to the piece that follows it in Act III.³¹ (It is also clear, in any case, that he must have rejected this draft before writing Daniel's next aria, 'Chastity, thou cherub' (*HG* 1: 184–7), for it uses material from the original.)

It was Winton Dean who, with some surprise, first noted the relation of 'Chastity, thou cherub' to the rejected draft of Daniel's earlier air, '''Tis not age's sullen face':

Incredible as it may seem, the last eleven bars of the first draft of ['Chastity, thou cherub'], so happily wedded to the words 'Gentle as the dawn of light, Soft as music's dying strain', were in fact composed to the second and third lines of [''Tis not age's sullen face'], 'Wrinkled front and solemn pace, That the truly wise declares'. The music may have been suggested by Daniel, but it had no connection with chastity.³²

Although the original setting 'had no connection with chastity', it is not inappropriate to the text. And, typically, Handel alters the score to depict the new text more affectively. These points emerge when the differences between the settings are considered.

The musical form of the original apparently differs from the later settings. Both the second setting of '''Tis not age's sullen face' and 'Chastity, thou

---

³¹ Eventually he composed a new setting of 'Would custom bid' on the blank sides following the rejected draft. He inserted this new aria into Act I between fos. 21 and 24, which contained the old, unorchestrated version of 'Would custom bid', ultimately attaching fo. 22ʳ to fo. 21ᵛ with red sealing wax. These facts are significant for understanding the genesis of *Susanna*. Apparently, the new setting of 'Would custom bid' was a relatively late addition, certainly after he had begun Act III, even though the first setting was not orchestrated. Of course, even the first setting of 'Would custom bid' was an insertion, forming no part of the original score. More than likely the substitution of the second setting in Act I occurred during the 'filling up' period, after the entire skeleton draft had been prepared.

³² Dean, *Handel's Dramatic Oratorios*, 554. In my reading only eight bars (not eleven) are shared between the two pieces: the sixth to thirteenth bar of the original (see Ex. 9.11) are almost precisely the same in the two versions. The preceding bars do not occur in 'Chastity, thou cherub', and the concluding ritornellos differ.

cherub' are da capo arias, but the rejected draft was not. Clearly the text that would eventually comprise the B section in the new aria was already written, for part of it occurs at the beginning of the draft ('oft she flies from silver hairs'). Its setting is fairly modulatory, tonicizing G minor and F major, foreshadowing its ultimate setting as a B section.

There also seems to have been a significant change in orchestration. It is possible, in fact, that the original was a continuo aria, and that Handel might have intended for strings to play the closing ritornello. Even the final setting of this text is lightly accompanied, and features only voice and continuo for long stretches; perhaps the sparse accompaniment, often linked in the aria to a 'walking bass', was related to the idea of old age.

At any rate, the string accompaniment is an important addition to the eight-bar passage in 'Chastity, thou cherub'—quite apart from such musical additions as the lovely suspensions, the very existence of accompaniment is employed mimetically. When 'music's dying strain' is mentioned in this passage, for instance, the strings drop out, and at one point the continuo drops out, though it did not when the music was set to a different text. These changes surely constitute part of the reason that the second setting seems 'so happily wedded to the words'. Of course the music is by no means out of character in its first use, where age's 'solemn pace' is represented by the repeated eighth notes and stepwise motion in the melody. When this text was reset, the stepwise motion was retained, but age's pace was slowed to quarter notes (see *HG* 1: 168–9).

In short, Handel fashions the music in an appropriate way for each setting, and the comparison pinpoints another recurring text-setting device. The repeated eighth notes and stepwise motion were used to depict pacing in the rejected draft, and this passage is ultimately associated with dawn in 'Chastity, thou cherub'. In *Theodora* a text which combines these images, pacing and dawn, is set to repeated eighth notes, often marked by stepwise motion: Irene's 'As with rosy steps the morn advancing drives the shades of night' (*HG* 8: 66 ff.) Perhaps we have uncovered another Handelian topos.[33]

The question posed at the outset—how music replete with text-specific imagery can be transferred to entirely different texts—rests on an assumption that has turned out to be ill-founded in its implication that transplanting music from one text to another is as simple a process as, say, moving from verse to verse in a strophic song. For a composer less concerned with onomatopoeia

---

[33] While musical features may become text-specific, they need not be exclusively so. The characteristics described here are obviously not associated with pacing and dawn in all their occurrences throughout Handel's career.

and other mimetic devices the process might have been almost as mechanical as that. And admittedly, even Handel's transfers are occaionally quite straight-forward; but more often his interest in imbuing his music, whether a new set-ting or old, with musical imagery led to more involved processes. As we have seen, these processes can have various results, depending on the case in ques-tion. Sometimes his attempt to reassign musical images to new texts was at least as successful as in 'newly composed' works (never an entirely safe term with a composer with such predilection for borrowing as Handel); in other cases the original work might constitute a *paradis perdu* of imagery that will never be regained; at still other times a new text invites new word-painting, and the final setting is richer in effective imitation than the original. Given the extent to which Handel alters his music during such transferrals, then, there is no rea-son to assume that the success of the operation depends upon position (first vs. last) in the process. We should thus be wary of attempts to define what Handel's substitutions and self-borrowings 'mean' before the actual process of rewriting has been explored—a warning that applies as well to his practice of borrowing from other composers. Only one thing is clear: given the effort expended in transferring music, it is unlikely that it represented an 'easy way out' for the composer.

Finally, Avison's dichotomy between imitation and expression is mislead-ing. As Avison's first critic Hayes also pointed out, musical imagery is not opposed to expression. Furthermore, the measure of a work's expressiveness in opera and oratorio depends largely upon its dramatic function, which Avison failed to explore. Yet the dramatic context of a piece was of primary importance to Handel, who balanced imagery and expression (insofar as they can be separated) to suit it. It is above all the integrity of each piece—whether old or new, descriptive or emotive—and its effectiveness within its own con-text that demanded his greatest attention and that has won him a place among the most celebrated musical dramatists.

IO

Singers and the Creative Process

IN his important book on *Messiah*, the late Jens Peter Larsen argued that unlike the opera, in which the drama was forced to yield to brilliant solo singing, the dramatic integrity of oratorio required the submission of the solo singers. Indeed, he attributes much of the dramatic success of oratorio to its freedom from the vanity of prima donnas:

English singers and those acclimatized by a long stay in England were not stars like the Italian opera soloists, and they could not make the unyielding demands of such stars. Opera was, and continued to be, a musical star performance. It was the brilliant singing, not the dramatic entity, which supported it. Oratorio had another aim. Sustained by an all-embracing idea, it had the right to demand that the soloists and the choir subordinated themselves to this idea. It was impossible to demand this sub-ordination of the Italian opera stars; they were accustomed to prominence, not to submission. To continue to use them in oratorio would have placed considerable obstacles in the way of fulfilling this demand.[1]

Quite aside from its ill-concealed bias against opera seria, Larsen's notion that aesthetic differences between oratorio and opera result largely from the degree to which Handel responded to his singers' demands is misleading.[2]

It is true that Handel did not always compose his oratorios for particular soloists, whereas he had often been in a position to choose opera librettos with a specific cast in mind.[3] In the case of the 1741 works, *Samson* and *Messiah*, for instance, Handel composed 'generic' solo parts (for soprano, alto, tenor, and bass) without any particular individuals in mind because he did not yet know who would comprise his Dublin (or London) cast.[4] This was not

[1] See Larsen, *Handel's Messiah*, 35.
[2] Larsen's low opinion of the dramatic integrity of Handel's operas appears most blatantly in his 1988 lecture to the American Handel Society, now published as 'The Turning Point in Handel's Career', *American Choral Review*, 26 (1989), 55–62.
[3] C. Steven LaRue in *Handel and his Singers* suggests that during the Royal Academy period Handel typically decided upon his cast before choosing his opera librettos.
[4] It is not entirely clear whether Handel knew about his Dublin trip when *Samson* was drafted. He did not perform *Samson* in Dublin, and left the score in draft stage when he turned to *Messiah*, adding the

necessarily his normative or preferred procedure during the entire oratorio period, however; in fact, Handel's letters to Jennens indicate that the composer had a particular cast in mind as he wrote the music for *Belshazzar*.[5] Therefore we must admit the existence of at least two practices during the 1740s. During those periods when Handel maintained largely the same cast of soloists for several seasons, it seems reasonable to suppose that his compositional aims included striving to match his music to the individual abilities of his singers. In any case, their individual vocal qualities ultimately affected Handel's music, regardless of exactly when he first knew who his soloists would be; for once he became certain of his cast he commonly revised his scores to suit the vocal capacities of individual soloists.

It is not necessary to explore the revisions Handel made for all his oratorio singers in order to illustrate this thesis. The following discussion will undertake a more feasible task, exploring compositional changes made for three singers: Giulia Frasi, Thomas Lowe, and Sibilla. The first part will focus mainly on Frasi, Handel's leading soprano from the 1749 season until his death, and his use of her as an exponent of the 'pathetic style' as defined by Charles Burney; after a brief summary of the careers of Frasi and Thomas Lowe, this first section will turn to certain interrelated resettings that involve transferring music from Lowe to Frasi—a procedure that can be understood in the light of Frasi's 'mournful muse'. Finally, in its second part I shall evaluate some revisions made for a singer with entirely different capabilities than Frasi, Sibilla. In addition to revealing how Handel could respond appropriately to such different singers, with stark contrasts in his process of revision and musical style, the examples cited expose the false dichotomy in Larsen's approach: the needs of the singers do not always clash with the 'higher aim' of oratorio; very often revisions made to suit a soloist also enhance both drama and music.

Giulia Frasi

Larsen evaluates Giulia Frasi's importance to Handel as follows:

A few years later [in 1748] Frasi and Galli became Handel's permanent women-stars and for a time the alto-castrato Guadagni was also singing in his oratorios. This might

other solo parts after his return from Ireland. Donald Burrows has recently argued that Handel might have composed solo parts for soprano, alto, tenor, and bass because he did not yet know who the cast would be for the next *London* season. See Burrows, *Handel: Messiah* (Cambridge: Cambridge University Press, 1991), 12–15.

   [5] See the letters of 9 June and 2 Oct. 1744 in Deutsch, *Handel: A Documentary Biography*, 591, 596. The alterations required by an unexpected change of cast are discussed in Dean, *Handel's Dramatic Oratorios*, 454–5. The Novello edition of *Belshazzar* by Donald Burrows restores Handel's intended pre-performance version.

seem to mean that the Italian element—and thus the Italian opera style—had once again become dominant as it had been in the oratorios of the early 1730's. But these three singers had grown accustomed to English traditions and to Handel's special style, in quite a different fashion from their Italian predecessors. Frasi and Galli were not—like Cuzzoni and Faustina—international stars. They could not demand that the composer and the style of performance should be at their whims; they were singers of a different class, who had to learn to accept the tasks assigned to them.[6]

Larsen's viewpoint, which has never been directly refuted, is correct in part but overlooks certain important facts. On the one hand, it is true that Frasi had grown accustomed to English traditions. Indeed, Charles Burney's article devoted to Frasi in Rees's *Cyclopedia* suggests that many of her gifts were ideal for English oratorio:

Having come to this country at an early period of her life, she pronounced our language in singing in a more articulate and intelligible manner than the natives; and her style being plain and simple, with a well-toned voice, a good shake, and perfect intonation, without great taste and refinement, she delighted the ignorant, and never displeased the learned.[7]

In *A General History of Music* Burney documents Frasi's popularity as a singer of English works in her later years:

I can recollect no English operas in which the dialogue was carried on in recitative, that were crowned with full success, except the Fairies, set by Mr. Smith in 1755, and Artaxerxes, by Dr. Arne in 1763 [2nd February 1762]; but the success of both was temporary, and depended so much on the success of singers, Guadagni and Frasi in the one, and Teducci, Miss Brent, and Peretti in the other, that they never could be called stock pieces, or, indeed, performed again, with any success, by inferior singers.[8]

If Frasi was not an international star, then, she was nonetheless celebrated in England. In 1764 J. C. Smith wrote of her, 'For if She [Miss Fromantel] was to sing, you must take away the part from Mrs. Frasi, who is a much more Capital Singer than the other'.[9]

However, Larsen fails to take into account the extensive involvement of Frasi, Galli, and Guadagni in Italian opera. Frasi was an Italian immigrant who had studied with the composer G. F. Brivio in Milan. She joined the opera company at the King's Theatre in the Haymarket in 1742, where she sang

[6] Larsen, *Handel's Messiah*, 38.

[7] See 'Frasi, Giulia' in Abraham Rees, *The Cyclopaedia; or, Universal Dictionary of Arts, Sciences, and Literature*, xv (41 vols., Philadelphia: Samuel F. Bradford and Murray, Fairman, & Co., c.1820).

[8] Charles Burney, *A General History of Music*, ed. Mercer. ii. 681.

[9] Quoted by Larsen, *Handel's Messiah*, 193.

Italian operas in Italian.[10] Even though Frasi had lived in England for some years before she first sang for Handel in 1748 and her pronunciation of English was allegedly better than that of native speakers, her accomplishments as an Italian singer were nonetheless noteworthy. Burney remarks of Frasi's participation in a 1745 performance of the pasticcio *L'Incostanza Delusa* that Count St Germain's 'Per pietà bell'idol mio' was sung by 'Frasi, first woman, and encored every night'.[11] Although she did not achieve international renown, Frasi's continuing involvement in Italian opera during her years in England was known to Handel.[12]

In fact, *pace* Larsen, at least one feature of the Italian opera style that becomes predominant in the late oratorios, the use of the da capo aria form, might well relate to the participation of immigrant Italian singers like Frasi who remained active in Italian opera. For one thing, singers experienced in the Italian opera would have been acquainted with the sort of ornamentation the da capo required. As Larsen himself first noted, Handel's use of the da capo form in oratorio, though never as pervasive as in opera, varied from time to time. It is striking that the smallest number of da capo arias occurs in an

[10] These included Galuppi's *Enrico* (Costanza), a role not listed in Sartori's catalogue of librettos (see below); Porpora's *Temistocle* (Roxana); Galuppi's *Sirbace* (Nerena); and two pasticcios, *Gianguir* (Mahobeth) and *Mandane* (Emira) in 1742–3; Lampugnani's *Alfonso* (Garzia); Handel's and Lampugnani's *Rossana* (Tassile); Veracini's *Rosalinda* (Ernesto); Lampugnani's *Alceste* (Olinto); and *Aristodemo* (Timotele) by Pescetti and others in 1743–4; Gluck's *La Caduta de' Giganti* (Brireo); Galuppi's *Il Trionfo della continenza* (Quinto Flaminio); and the pasticcio partly by Brivio and St Germain, *L'Incostanza Delusa* (Corina— not listed by Sartori) in 1745; *Alessandro nell'Indie* (Timagene); the pasticcio *Annibale in Capua* (Bomilcare) and Terradellas's *Mitridate* (Arbate) in 1746; Paradies's *Fetonte* (Teone); Terradellas's *Bellerofonte* (Assiane— a role also overlooked by Sartori), *Lucio Vero* (Lucilla), and *Rossane* (Cleone) in 1747; Hasse's *Didone* (Selene) and *La Semiramide riconosciuta* (Tamiri) in 1748, to stop with the year Handel began to use her regularly. See *The London Stage 1660–1800*, 11 vols. Part 3 (1729–47), ed. Arthur H. Scouten, Part 4 (1747–76) ed. George W. Stone, Jr. (Carbondale: Southern Illinois University Press, 1965–8), v. 398–9; C. Taylor, 'Handel's Disengagement', 176–7; and Claudio Sartori, *I libretti italiani a stampa dalle origini al 1800*, 6 vols. (Cueno: Bertola & Locatelli, 1993), ii. Frasi sang many male roles in 1744–6, which misled Sartori into identifying a 'Signor Frasi' in London during those years. The libretti often identify the singer as 'La sig. Frasi'. Interestingly, Frasi seems not to have sung male roles when paired with Galli, who often sang them.

[11] Burney, *A General History of Music*, ii. 844. See also Deutsch, *Handel: A Documentary Biography*, 607.

[12] Another of Burney's assertions is fraught with problems. He claims that Frasi's *Cheval de bataille* was the aria 'Tremende occuri attroci [*sic*]' in Pergolesi's *Olimpiade*, which was still enthusiastically received ten years after the opera's run ended (Rees, *Cyclopedia*, s.v. 'Frasi, Giulia'). The *General History of Music* makes it clear that this London performance of *Olimpiade* was in fact a pasticcio called *Meraspe, o l'Olimpiade*, and that Frasi sang the aria originally performed by Monticelli (*General History of Music*, iv. 555). 'Tremende oscuri atroci', found in Act II, scene 6 of *Meraspe*, represents a retexting of Pergolesi's 'Torbido in volto e nero' from his *Olimpiade*. Burney owned a copy of the aria with the original text in manuscript, but he did not know what it was (ibid.). It is impossible that Frasi sang this aria in the forms that have survived in Walsh's edition of *Meraspe* or in Pergolesi's score—presumably the versions Burney knew; in both its versions the aria's range extends to high C, well above Frasi's limit of high A, and this cannot be fixed by simple transposition. If she sang the aria at all, it was in a revised form no longer in existence.

oratorio with the largest English cast, *Saul*. In the last oratorios, from *Alexander Balus* to *Jephtha* (excluding *Solomon*) Handel's use of da capo arias increases dramatically from earlier years; the da capo plays a small role in the preceding period (in *Belshazzar* to *Joshua*). Although many issues may have influenced Handel's aims in utilizing the da capo, singers were surely among these influences.

Frasi first sang for Handel in a revival of *Judas Maccabeus* in 1748, and it was first in *Solomon* and *Susanna* that he composed new music for her.[13] In *Solomon* she sang the parts of both queens and first harlot (who is faced with the prospect of her child's death). Thereafter Handel casted her consistently as an innocent heroine who is faced with the threat of her own demise: she sang the title-role in *Susanna*, who after resisting an attempted seduction is accused of fornication and condemned to death; the title-role also in *Theodora*, a Christian martyr who refuses to worship Roman gods and chooses death rather than becoming a temple prostitute; and she was the first Iphis in *Jephtha*, who is doomed to become a human sacrifice as a result of her father's foolish vow to God. Although Frasi was apparently a versatile singer, she excelled in expressive music, judging from the high number of slow, declamatory arias of lamentation that Handel gave to her—including 'Can I see my infant gor'd' in *Solomon*; 'Bending to the throne of glory' and 'If guiltless blood' in *Susanna*; 'Fond flattering world, adieu', 'With darkness deep', 'When sunk in anguish', and 'To thee, thou glorious son', in *Theodora*; and in *Jephtha*, 'Happy they' and 'Farewell ye limpid springs'. All these pieces exemplify what Charles Burney called the pathetic style in music.

Although Burney considered the pathetic style to be so familiar as hardly to need explanation, he defined it as a kind of theatrical music that tends to 'move the great passions, particularly those of grief and sorrow'.[14] In *Dr. Burney as Critic and Historian of Music* Kerry Grant cites Burney's song 'Constancy' (1753) as an example of the pathetic, listing several specific features of that style. Among these are: (1) a text that evokes pity, with reference to death, grief, sorrow, tears, etc.; (2) minor mode; (3) slow tempo; (4) melodic dissonance such as tritones (especially on expressive words such as 'sigh') and leaps of a minor seventh; (5) the underlying harmony, rich in seventh chords of various sorts, often in their most dissonant inversions, and the Neapolitan sixth chord; and finally (6) appoggiaturas.

---

[13] She had sung in *Rossane* in 1743, had performed Handel arias in concert in 1746, in the Handel pasticcio *Lucio Vero* in Nov. 1747, *Judas Maccabeus* in Feb. 1748. *Solomon* was composed 5 May–13 June 1748 (perf. 17 Mar. 1749); *Susanna* was composed 11 July–24 Aug. (perf. 10 Feb. 1749).

[14] Grant, *Dr. Burney as Critic and Historian of Music*, 32–4. The song 'Constancy' is reproduced on p. 33.

While the pathetic style encompassed a great deal of variety, and should not be limited to those traits found in 'Constancy', Handel's essays in the pathetic do exhibit many similar features.[15] To choose one example from arias composed for Frasi, 'With darkness deep' from the prison scene in *Theodora* (*HG* 8: 109–11) is a setting of a text that is profoundly pathetic, with references to darkness, woe, night, death, and the grave. In F sharp minor and marked 'largo e staccato', its harmony is rich, with numerous seventh chords (bb. 1 and 3—circle of fifths with seventh on each down-beat). Note also the minor-seventh leap in the melody in bars 10–11 (*HG* 4: 110, 1/2–3). An additional expressive feature is the low tessitura in the violins at the beginning, no doubt associated with death and the grave. What constitutes the pathetic varies by composer and piece: as a rule, Handel rarely employs appoggiaturas as Burney did, but he frequently uses sigh motifs of seconds (as in the symphony at the beginning of the prison scene, or in 'Fond, flattering world, adieu').

Thomas Lowe, who typically assumed Handel's tenor roles of secondary importance, was a singer of quite a different sort than Frasi. Trained by Arne, Lowe specialized in English productions. He had been in Handel's company in 1743 for *Samson* (Israelite and Philistine man and Israelite Officer), before departing for Ireland.[16] Upon his return to England, Lowe acted and sang at Drury Lane until 1748, when he joined Handel's company again. He was the first Jonathan in *Alexander Balus* and the first Septimius in *Theodora*. The music Handel conceived for him is typically dance-like and melodious, with florid moments occasionally arising; even his sporadic minor-key arias are never profoundly tragic. Burney wrote that Lowe 'had the finest tenor voice I ever heard in my life, for want of diligence and cultivation, he never could be safely trusted with anything better than a ballad, which he constantly learned by his ear'.

The qualities and capabilities of these two singers help to explain certain of Handel's revisions in *Solomon* and *Susanna* made before their first performances. In two cases he took music from tenor Thomas Lowe and after recomposing it for new texts gave it to soprano Giulia Frasi (see Table 10.1).

The final act of *Solomon* houses a complex exchange involving four different

---

[15] Burney describes many of Handel's opera arias as pathetic in his *General History of Music*. An examination of those arias reveals the same traits.

[16] For information on Lowe, see Dean, *Handel's Dramatic Oratorios*, 657; Philip Highfill *et al.* (eds.), *A Biographical Dictionary of Actors, Actresses, Musicians, Dancers, Managers and Other Stage Personnel in London, 1660–1800* (Carbondale, Ill.: Southern Illinois Press, 1978), s.v. 'Lowe, Thomas'; and Rees, *The Cyclopedia*, s.v. 'Lowe, Thomas' by Charles Burney; and Judith Milhous and Robert Hume, 'Librettist versus Composer: The Property Rights to Arne's *Henry and Emma* and *Don Saverio*', *Journal of the Royal Music Association*, 122 (1997), 52–67.

TABLE 10.1. *Musical transfers involving Frasi and Lowe*

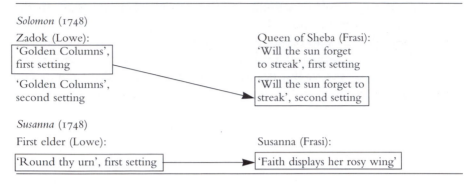

Solomon (1748)

Zadok (Lowe):   Queen of Sheba (Frasi):
'Golden Columns',   'Will the sun forget
first setting   to streak', first setting

'Golden Columns',   'Will the sun forget to
second setting   streak', second setting

Susanna (1748)

First elder (Lowe):   Susanna (Frasi):

'Round thy urn', first setting   'Faith displays her rosy wing'

settings. Rejecting his first settings of 'Golden Columns' and 'Will the sun forget to streak' and replacing them with new settings, Handel reused the music from the first setting of 'Golden Columns' (Ex. 9.7) for the second setting of 'Will the sun'. Aspects of this musical transfer were examined in the last chapter, but the question why this particular aria substitution came about remains to be answered. Indeed, the revision produces many effects, all of which might have played a role in Handel's decision to make this change. First, the text of 'Golden Columns', though primarily descriptive, seems better suited to the fast, 'fair and bright' D major aria (*HG* 26: 262) than to its minor-mode, slow-moving first setting. (The texts of these two arias are given in Ch. 9.) Because the Queen of Sheba's aria, on the other hand, is fairly bland in regard to *Affekt* or expressiveness, it could accommodate a wide variety of musical settings. Furthermore, the substitution of the new setting of 'Golden Columns' may have resulted from a desire to create more musical contrast between the arias of Zadok and the Queen of Sheba. Moreover, with the aria 'Pious king and virtuous queen', three of the last four successive arias of the oratorio were minor-mode compositions marked 'larghetto'. Resetting 'Golden Columns' and inserting 'Praise the Lord' (if, as Dean suggested, this chorus formed no part of the original conception) also help to establish a more festive mood for the final part of *Solomon*.

These observations may help to explain why Handel chose to reset 'Golden Columns', but why the music of the rejected aria was reused in 'Will the sun' is a different matter. While the first setting of 'Golden Columns' differs in *Affekt* from the new setting and from the inserted chorus ('Praise the Lord'), it is not so far in terms of expressiveness from the original setting of 'Will the sun forget to streak' (Ex. 10.1). While one is in common time, the other in triple metre, one ornate, the other simple, the minor key, slow

EX. 10.1. First setting of 'Will the sun forget to streak' in *Solomon*, BL RM 20.f.8, fos. 128ᵛ and 131ʳ

Ex. 10.1. (*cont.*)

tempo, and the compositional technique of setting each line of text to one musical phrase ending in some sort of cadence (including half-cadences and Phrygian cadences) establish commonality of *Affekt* between the two works. The music of 'Golden Columns' won out because it is the more impressive of the two arias. In neither case does the text prescribe the 'aria patetica', but the passionate music of 'Golden Columns' 1 and 'Will the sun' 2 encompasses many features of the pathetic (see Ex. 9.7 and *HG* 26: 298–303). In addition to the solemn tempo and minor mode, note the rich harmony, with seventh chords in third inversion (bb. 2–3 in *HG*; b. 3 in Ex. 9.7), as well as melodic dissonances such as the tritone ascent from b to f♯ over a diminished seventh chord in bar 5 of *HG* (Ex. 9.7(*a*), b. 10).

Perhaps the most compelling reason for this substitution is that Handel seized the opportunity to give Frasi the sort of slow, solemn air at which she excelled. The second setting of 'Will the sun' perfectly reflects her capabilities, judging from her Handelian repertoire on the whole, but seems somewhat ill suited to Lowe's typically less serious style. More *comme il faut* for Lowe is the new setting of 'Golden Columns', which features a relatively unadorned vocal line, a more sprightly tempo, and major mode, all reflecting the style of his first aria in *Solomon*, 'Sacred Raptures cheer my Breast'.

A similar case occurs in *Susanna*. Act III contains the concluding bars of an early setting of 'Round thy urn' for the first elder (Ex. 10.2). The manuscript evidence is confusing and requires explanation, for fo. 95^r, on which the conclusion of the draft is found, is the third side of a bifolio. Presumably the rest of the aria proceeded the end, but the present condition of the folio suggests that fo. 94 was blank after the first version of 'Round thy urn' was completed. The mystery is easily accounted for: originally the folio must have been folded the other way round, so that fo. 95^r was the first page, followed by fo. 94 (see Fig. 10.1). Most of the aria was written on preceding pages, which were discarded, but the bifolio with three and a half blank sides (bifolio 95/94) was saved for future use. Handel must have reached for the surviving bifolio while composing the new version of 'Round thy urn', refolding it so the blank folio was first and, when he reached the F minor fragment, simply composing the new setting of the aria around it.

The second setting of 'Round thy urn', while in many ways different from the original, retains certain of its features: duple metre and a minor key. Moreover, the first time it occurs in the air, the text 'never ceasing, still increasing, with the length of time shall grow' is set to a passage resembling the original, with the rhythmic pattern of two shorts and two longs in the melody accompanied by a chromatically ascending bass (Ex. 10.3). But in the new setting, the word 'grow' is given a melisma in its later occurrences, thereby enhancing the relationship of words to music in the final version.

The music of this rejected air was ultimately used in Susanna's 'Faith displays her rosy wing', or so the surviving fragment would suggest (cf. Ex. 10.2 with *HG* 1: 161, 2/1–3/5).[17] The only significant difference between the two is a sort of embellishment of the cadential bars, to match the different text. Interestingly, 'Faith displays' immediately precedes 'Round thy urn' in Act III, and the former shows no sign of revision.

With its minor mode, its melody permeated by leaps of minor sevenths and 'sigh motifs' of seconds, and its wide-ranging harmonic setting with diminished chords and Neapolitan sixths, 'Faith displays her rosy wing' exemplifies the pathetic style. Moreover, it possesses a feature characteristic of Handel's most serious works: obfuscating the structural juncture between the opening ritornello and vocal entrance so dramatically that one wonders if the opening

---

[17] Since the beginning of the draft has not survived, we cannot state with certainty what differences there might have been between the two versions. The music that survives is almost identical with the new aria, and this suggests to me that the two arias were probably much the same.

EX. 10.2. First setting of 'Round thy urn' in *Susanna*, BL RM 20.f.8, fo. 95^r

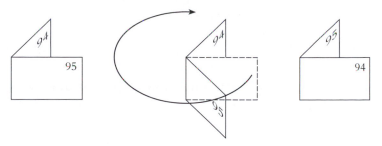

FIG. 10.1. Refolding of original b:folio 95/94

EX. 10.3. Second setting of 'Round thy urn' in *Susanna*, BL RM 20.f.8, fo. 94^r

of thy woe, ne- ver ceas- ing still in -creas-ing, with the length of time shall grow

should be perceived as a ritornello at all.[18] It may come as a surprise that this music was first given to the first elder, an altogether unsympathetic, hypocritical character. But it is not as odd as it at first seems. The first elder assumes a false stance in 'Round thy urn', feigning lamentation for the ensuing death of Susanna. As she points out in the recitative after his aria: ''Tis thus the crocodile his grief displays, sheds the false dew, and while he weeps betrays.' The transfer of this material to Susanna, who sings a different text, alters the dramatic context of the music significantly. In recitative she welcomes death, and her aria text celebrates and embraces it:

> Faith displays her rosy wing,
> Cherubs songs of gladness sing,
> virtue clad in bright array,
> streaming with eternal day,

[18] This musical phenomenon takes on a programmatic function in the *Theodora* chorus 'He saw the lovely youth / Death's early prey / Alas! too early snatch'd away'. The 'interrupted' opening ritornello might also depict the vicissitudes of fate in 'How dark, oh Lord, are thy decrees' in *Jephtha*. Interestingly, both these examples resonate with 'Faith displays', where Susanna has just learnt that, owing to the vicissitudes of fate, she is to be death's early prey. At the very least the 'interrupted' opening ritornello is clearly associated with tragedy in each case.

whispers in my ravish'd ear:
innocence shall never fear,
welcome to this bright abode,
seat of angels, seat of God.

As we have seen, however, the music tells a different story; a lament, it embodies Susanna's sadness at having to die. While in the first setting of 'Round thy urn' the music was true to the text but not the character's actual feelings, now music is true to the character's feelings rather than the text, rendering the drama more convincing. This dramatic situation—a heroine claiming joy in death in words while the music contrastingly portrays her troubled inner state—occurs several times in Handel's late oratorios: for instance, in Theodora's 'Fond, flattering world, adieu' (where earthly values rather than life are rejected) and Iphis's 'Happy they' in *Jephtha*, both of which roles as well as the role of Susanna were sung by Giulia Frasi. This disjunction between text and music becomes interesting in the light of Burney's puzzling assessment of Frasi, written some forty years after he had taught her: that when she first came to England, 'she was young and interesting in her person, had a clear and sweet voice, free from defects, and a smooth and chaste style of singing; which, though cold and unimpassioned, pleased natural ears, and escaped the censure of critics'.[19]

Burney's description of Frasi as 'cold and unimpassioned' seems surprising in the light of the sort of music Handel wrote for her. Admittedly he refers to the period before Frasi sang for Handel, whose training might have developed her abilities as a tragic heroine; or perhaps Burney is simply inaccurate (which is sometimes true of his descriptions of singers). It is perhaps not impossible, however, that the dichotomy between text and music found in many of Frasi's arias might account for the apparent discrepancy. Perhaps there was an element of restraint when Frasi sang emotionally charged arias that Handel wished to exploit; detachment in the face of death was a heroic quality celebrated in plays of the period.

According to Ian Donaldson's analysis, 'the cult of Sensibility' in eighteenth-century drama was stimulated by a feeling of hostility towards a contemporary revival of interest in the teachings of the Stoics. Donaldson maintains that the situation in which a person becomes 'aware of the imminence of his or her own death laid a strong hold on both philosophical and imaginative minds of the age . . . All writers on the passions in this period readily conceded [unremarkably] that this was among the situations that provided the

---

[19] Burney, *A General History of Music*, iii. 841. This statement is repeated in Abraham Rees, *The Cyclopedia*, xv.

supreme test of self-control.'[20] He cites as an example of simultaneously indulging and restraining passion Nicholas Rowe's pathetic tragedy *Lady Jane Grey* of 1715. On the eve of her execution Lady Jane reads 'Plato's *Phaedon*, / Where Dying Socrates takes leave of Life, / With such an easy, careless, calm Indifference, / As if the Trifle were of No Account'. As the play goes on, however, it becomes apparent that Lady Jane's own indifference is unlike that of Socrates. Her restraint is maintained only with difficulty, and is continually threatened by the force of her passion.

This literary convention of 'heroic restraint' is of relevance for *Susanna*. Having learnt that she has been sentenced to death from the crowd chorus that begins Act III ('The cause is decided the sentence decreed / Susanna is guilty Susanna must bleed'), Susanna becomes the quintessential sentimental heroine. No better illustration of the paradox of both indulging and restraining emotion could be found than 'Faith displays'. The added expressive dimension made possible by musical theatre permits the representation of several passions simultaneously; while the music makes it clear that Susanna is suffering from emotional turmoil, the text shows self-control in spite of her emotions. If Frasi's singing was unimpassioned in such situations, it must have enhanced the audience's perception of her restraint. In spite of the attempt to restrain emotion, the aesthetic remains that of the pathetic, for the heroine's effort in the face of overpowering feelings heightens the pathos of the moment.[21] Thus a web of discourses marked by disjunctions—that between music and text balanced by that between inner turmoil and outer restraint—parallels the seeming paradox of an exponent of the pathetic style whose singing was 'cold and unimpassioned' to one listener. But by the principle of Occam's razor, it is perhaps more likely that Burney was simply wrong—or that Frasi's expressive abilities increased after her very first years in England.

In any case, Burney's memoirs shed light on an aspect of Handel's biography that relates to the genesis of the oratorios. It is thought that during his operatic career Handel may have entertained the opinions of his singers, who might have seen their music in some form before the opera's completion, before settling on their arias. Certain anecdotes from Burney's memoirs relating to the days when he was Frasi's teacher suggest the existence during the oratorio period of a similarly intimate professional relationship between

---

[20] Donaldson, 'Cato in Tears: Stoical Guises of the Man of Feeling', in R. F. Brissenden (ed.), *Studies in the Eighteenth Century* (Toronto: University of Toronto Press, 1973), 378.

[21] Iphis's 'Happy they' is also an excellent illustration of this emotional paradox. Though Iphis sings 'with content I will resign', the beginning of her aria is fragmented and the metre is aurally uncertain until several bars into the piece. Handel's setting suggests that this 'contentment' is a sentiment maintained only with difficulty.

Handel and his singers. Although these episodes are related in a way that casts Burney himself in a more positive light than Frasi or Handel, they offer a fascinating glimpse into Handel's activities during the oratorio period:

> Handel himself . . . used to bring an Air, or Duet, in his pocket, as soon as composed, hot from the brain, in order to give me the time & style, that I might communicate them to my scholar (Frasi) by repetition; for her knowledge of musical characters was very slight . . .[22]

Another anecdote gives an account of Handel demonstrating a piece to Frasi (not a freshly composed one, but one she was to sing in a revival).

> At Frasi's, I remember, in the year 1748, he brought, in his pocket, the duet of *Judas Maccabeus*, 'From these dread scenes', in which she had not sung when that Oratorio was first performed, in 1746 (*sic*). At the time he sat down to the harpsichord, to give her and me the time of it, while he sung her part, I hummed, at sight, the second, over his shoulder . . .[23]

Although these anecdotes demonstrate above all the care with which Handel prepared his singers for performance, it seems reasonable to suppose that during these private rehearsals or lessons he would have taken note of any changes the singers needed or requested—particularly with pieces 'hot from his brain'. Since Handel typically composed his oratorios months before the first performance, there was time to alter the score if needed, that is, to make precisely the sort of revisions examined above.[24]

The musical revisions that Handel made for Frasi tempt us to speculate, in the absence of hard evidence, about her impact on the direction of Handel's artistic output. In his last three oratorios Handel pursued a profoundly different path than he had in the 'military' oratorios composed after *Belshazzar*. In fact, *Susanna*, *Theodora*, and to some extent even *Jephtha* mark a substantial departure from the works of the 1740s on the whole (with the exception of *Semele* and *Hercules*), which focus on males.[25] Frasi's roles in *Susanna* and *Theodora* are

---

[22] *Memoirs of Dr. Charles Burney 1726–1729*, ed. Slava Klima, Garry Bowers, and Kerry S. Grant (Nebraska: University of Nebraska Press, 1988), 92.   [23] Ibid. 95.

[24] In spite of Burney's aspersions on Frasi, Handel's enthusiasm for her is borne out by the autograph of *Susanna*. Besides the aria substitution discussed in this section, he inserted two new arias for her into his original score: 'Would custom bid' and 'Guilt trembling'.

[25] Frasi was, in this sense, the new 'La Francesina'. Between 1744 and 1746 Elisabeth Duparc, called La Francesina, had sung the roles of victimized women such as Semele, Iole in *Hercules*, and Nitocris in *Belshazzar*. Both Frasi and Francesina had sung serious roles in Italian operas on the London stage.

One of Francesina's areas of vocal expertise was the birdsong aria, which may have influenced an aspect of Handel's oratorio production. In 1739 through 1741 she sang in *Acis and Galatea*, in which she would have sung 'As when the dove' and 'Hush, ye pretty warbling quire'. Thereafter she sang 'Sweet Bird' in *L'Allegro* and 'The morning lark' from *Semele*. 'The morning lark', taken from Congreve's elegy 'To Sleep' and refashioned into a da capo text, was inserted into Congreve's *Semele* libretto for Handel (Brian Trowell,

unique among the oratorios in featuring a heroine suffering because of her resistance to the threat of sexual assault.[26] Even in the absence of documentary evidence one begins to wonder if Frasi's expertise in the aesthetic of pity might have played some role in Handel's choice of subject for these works. The possibility seems all the more likely in the light of his operatic practice. C. Steven LaRue has recently suggested that the singers had an enormous impact on the creation of Handel's operas.[27] It is difficult to believe that his artistic values and practice changed so dramatically in his later years that he no longer took into account the qualities of his singers—even in the most operatic of his oratorios.

Sibilla

Another singer whose abilities influenced Handel's creative process—but in a manner profoundly different in nature than did Frasi's—is Sibilla (or Mrs Pinto), Handel's second soprano in 1748 and 1749. Sibilla made her debut in Arne's *Comus* in 1743, later performing in the same composer's *Rosamond*, *The Temple of Dullness*, and Lampe's *The Dragon of Wantley*. She joined the King's Theatre in 1747, appearing in Handel's pasticcio *Lucio Vero*, in Hasse's *Didone* and *Semiramide riconosciuta*, and in *La ingratitudine punita*.[28] She sang in *Alexander Balus*, *Susanna*, and *Solomon*.[29]

Handel's music for Sibilla seems to exploit her experience in ballad opera. Her experience and abilities may even have influenced his rewriting of 'Ask if yon damask rose'. There are altogether three versions of this aria, as Dean has pointed out.[30] The first version is certainly the longest (Ex. 10.4).[31] After

---

'Congreve and the 1744 *Semele* libretto', *Musical Times*, 111 (1970), 993–4). One wonders if this was done specifically for Francesina. This matches Burney: 'It was for the natural warble of this singer that Handel composed his English airs of execution, such as "Sweet Bird," in Milton's Pensorosa, "Myself I shall adore," and "The morning lark to mine attunes his throat," in Congreve's Semele, etc.' (Rees, *Cyclopedia*).

[26] And thus inviting comparison with one of the most popular Christian tragedies in 18th-c. England, Nicholas Rowe's *Jane Shore*.   [27] See LaRue, *Handel and his Singers*.

[28] Again, there seems no good reason for Sartori's assigning some of the *Didone* and *La ingratitudine* roles to Pavolo Sibilla of Rome. In both cases the libretto identifies the singer as 'la sig. Sibilla'.

[29] *The New Grove Dictionary*, 6th edn., s.v. 'Sibilla' by Winton Dean. She appeared as Mrs Pinto in 1750.   [30] Dean, *Handel's Dramatic Oratorios*, 551–3.

[31] Two more verses are given in *HG* I: p. 111:

> Bid the fierce vulture leave his prey
> and warble through the grove.
> Bid wanton linnets quit the spray,
> then doubt the shepherd's love.
>
> The spoils of war let heroes share,
> let pride in splendor shine.
> Ye bards unenvy'd laurels wear;
> be fair Susanna mine.

Ex. 10.4. First setting of 'Ask if yon damask rose' in *Susanna*, BL RM 20.f.8, fo. 55ʳ

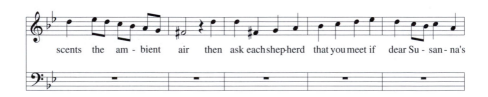

Ex. 10.4. (*cont.*)

ask each shepherd that you meet if dear Su - san - na's fair if dear Su - san - na's

forte   vn. colla parte piano

fair.   1. Ask if yon da - mask rose be sweet that

forte

scents the am - bient air ask if yon da - mask rose be sweet that

scents the am - bient air then ask each shep-herd that you meet if dear Su-san - na's

Ex. 10.4. (*cont.*)

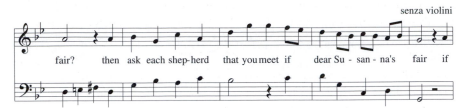

Da capo dal segno la 2da strofa
Da capo dal segno la 3za strofa
[Verses 2 & 3 in HG 1.3]

the opening ritornello, the voice enters with a phrase previously used in 'War, he sung, is toil and trouble' from *Alexander's Feast* (Ex. 10.5). This first setting modulates to the relative major, underscored by a medial ritornello, then moves back to the tonic in the second half, followed by the concluding ritornello.

Handel replaced this setting with a second one, inserted into the autograph score, which is a shorter, simpler aria, half as long as the original (Ex. 10.6). The opening ritornello is based on that in the first setting; he takes over the beginning and end, replacing its middle bars with a single bar. The vocal material appears at first to be entirely different from the original. Quite apart from the fact that the melody is a new one, there is no internal ritornello, and the mid-point of the song is in the dominant rather than the relative major. All in all, the second version is harmonically less adventurous than the first, fewer keys being tonicized, and the singer's lowest note is d' rather than c'; c' was apparently the lowest note of Sibilla's range, and sustaining it may have been a problem (though this could, of course, have been corrected without rewriting the entire piece).

But there are in fact similarities between the two settings. The end of the opening phrase from the original, for instance, has undergone diminution and has been moved to the middle of the aria, where it ends in the dominant before the repeat of the first line (Ex. 10.7).

Though nothing about the second setting (nor, for that matter, the first setting) is artistically amiss, Handel was to reset the aria once more (see *HG* 1: 110–11). There are two significant changes: first, the ritornello has been altered so that it previews a slightly longer stretch of the vocal material, which is almost identical with the second setting, apart from some simplification

EX.10.5. Comparison of (*a*) *Alexander's Feast*, 'War, he sung' (*HG* 12: 66, 1/2–2/1), and (*b*) *Susanna*, 'Ask if yon damask rose', first setting, BL RM 20.f.8, fo. 55ʳ

(*a*)

(*b*)

EX. 10.6. Second setting of 'Ask if yon damask rose' in *Susanna*, BL RM 20.f.8, fo. 56ʳ

Ex. 10.6. (*cont.*)

rose be sweet that scents the am-bient air? Then ask each shep-herd

that you meet if dear Su-san-na's fair if dear Su-san-na's

forte

fair?

Da capo dal segno due volte

(such as the elimination of the leap of a fourth from the first phrase). Second, and more important, the third setting has a fuller string accompaniment that includes second violin and viola. The decision to use a fuller orchestra may well have prompted Handel to create the third setting. As in the other settings, the first violin doubles the voice.

It is striking that two of these features characterize every aria Handel composed for Sibilla: all the solo numbers written for her in *Alexander Balus*, *Solomon*, and *Susanna* have melodic preview in the ritornello and a violin part that largely duplicates the vocal line. He may have tried to duplicate the sort

EX. 10.7. Comparison of first two settings of 'Ask if yon damask rose', BL RM 20.f.8: (*a*) fo. 55ʳ; (*b*) fo. 56ʳ

of popular ballads she so often sang, possibly at her own request, although this is impossible to establish.[32]

Another aspect of the two later settings of 'Ask if yon damask rose' is their brevity compared with the first. While shortening arias is typical of Handel's revisions, though not all his complete resettings, it is also true that he never gave Sibilla a long aria to sing. In addition to 'Ask if yon damask rose', Handel

EX. 10.8. 'Beneath the cyprus' in *Susanna*, BL RM 20.f.8: (*a*) fo. 58ᵛ; (*b*) fo. 59ʳ

---

[32] In 1745 Sibilla sang the role of Margery in a revival of Lampe's burlesque opera *The Dragon of Wantley*, a work Handel was said to have enjoyed (see the 19 Jan. 1738 letter of Lord Wentworth to his

Ex. 10.8. (*cont.*)

father, the Earl of Strafford, in Deutsch, *Handel: A Documentary Biography*, 449). It is instructive to compare Handel's music for Sibilla with Margery's music. Two of Margery's three arias offer first-violin doubling of the vocal part throughout, and all her arias eschew lengthy melismas. 'But to hear the children
mutter' is, like 'Beneath the Cypress' gloomy shade', a siciliano in two structural parts.

curtailed the ballad-like 'Beneath the cyprus' gloomy shade' in *Susanna* (*HG* 1: 112–13. The original is an ABB' form that never departs from the tonic. He revised the aria by shortening the ritornello (original transcribed in Ex. 10.8(*a*)) and then eliminating the final B' section altogether (Ex. 10.8(*b*)). The resulting AB form is more balanced, but a more pressing concern may have had to do with the drama. As Susanna's attendant, Sibilla sang a minor role. By and large her part is extraneous to the action of the drama, and for that reason Handel may have wished to truncate her arias. (Another possible reason for brevity, of course, might simply have been the quality of Sibilla's singing.)

Between them Sibilla and Frasi illustrate how different in nature the needs of individual singers—and consequently, Handel's revisions for them—could be. The participation of soloists with such different capabilities and qualities, from Italian-born opera-seria soloists to ballad singers, no doubt played a role in the diversity of aria style and form we find in Handelian oratorio.

The evidence from Handel's autographs, then, suggests first of all that Larsen's view of the role of the singers as insignificant in the aesthetic of Handel's oratorios is hyperbolic and, on a more profound level, that his stance dichotomizes too rigidly the interests of the composer (presumably towards musical and dramatic perfection) and the soloists (towards gratifying their 'whims'). Creating musical drama involves synthesizing many different components: oratorio is not a battlefield from which a single domain emerges victorious. The fact that the limitations and specific gifts of the soloists profoundly influenced Handel's creative process as well as his music does not undermine the dramatic integrity of oratorio. As we have seen, the composer's revisions not only serve to accommodate the singers' individual gifts, but at the same time transform and arguably often improve both the drama and musical setting. The fact that in his complex position as impresario, composer, and dramatist, Handel could achieve so exalted a level of dramatic integrity and musical content from such a mixture of abilities and styles adds weight to the measure of his creative accomplishments.

11

Conclusions

HANDEL composed with remarkable speed. What this tells us depends upon our own preconceptions, or as Philip Gossett would have it, upon the point we are trying to make. While Rossini has been criticized for writing quickly (unlike a 'serious' composer such as Beethoven), facility is often interpreted as merely another proof of Mozart's genius. As Gossett has noted, 'the aesthetic quality of a work of art, the extent to which it has endured or will endure, is not a function of its period of gestation. Let us purge this diction from our critical vocabulary'.[1]

If the longevity of its gestation bears no relation to the merit of a work, it might nonetheless tell us something about the place of a composer within his historical and cultural mileau. Thus Robert Marshall distinguishes between the compositional practices of composers who worked before and after the French Revolution:

Inspiration was more important in the baroque than in the post-revolutionary period. A composer like Beethoven enjoyed a 'luxury of time' which allowed him to experiment with and assemble a large number of ideas from which he would ultimately choose the best one. Bach and his contemporaries had to invent or 'discover' their ideas quickly. The hectic pace of production did not tolerate passive reliance on the unpredictable arrival of Inspiration.[2]

Admittedly Marshall's generalization applies best to the German 'mainstream'; early nineteenth-century Italian opera is an exception to the rule, as are such composers as the facile Frenchman Saint-Saëns. As a rough generalization, however, it helps us to understand Handel's relationship to Baroque composition.

Handel's place within this scheme depends upon the period of his life under scrutiny. While he was active as composer and impresario of Italian opera he worked with the speed expected of his generation, and first performances of

---

[1] Philip Gossett, *Anna Bolena and the Artistic Maturity of Gaetano Donizetti* (Oxford: Clarendon Press, 1985), p. xiv.   [2] Marshall, *The Compositional Process*, 235.

his operas often took place very shortly after composition was completed. When oratorio came to dominate his creative life, however, he could have enjoyed a 'luxury of time' not unlike Marshall's description of that of the post-revolutionary composer. Winton Dean goes so far as to suggest that some of this 'luxury of time' belonged to the period of 'precomposition' for the oratorios:

The popular notion of works like *Messiah* being composed in three weeks is an oversimplification. It is true that the commission of the oratorios to paper seldom took more than a few weeks; but that is a different matter. After 1740, when Handel composed most of the oratorios, he wrote very little other music . . . He generally set apart a period of one to three months in the summer for writing down new works . . . This scheme of work left him seven or eight months in every year free from creative or executive activity. Although no doubt his imagination profited from lying fallow, it is naive to suppose that it remained wholly idle. Much of the creative thought, and also a good deal of the sketching (which is not dated), must have taken place by the time he began the autograph score. Probably the spring and early summer months served as a period of gestation.[3]

Dean's contention—to use Marshall's paradigm a decidedly 'post-revolutionary' view of Handel's working methods—is, of course, speculative, and the balance of the evidence seems to tilt to the other side. Handel's correspondence with Charles Jennens (discussed by Dean himself) provides a more detailed account of the composition of *Belshazzar* than we have for any other oratorio. Handel did not receive the first act of *Belshazzar* from Jennens until 18 July 1744, the second act before 21 August, and he began composition on 23 August. Since he was occupied with the composition of *Hercules* from 19 July until after 17 August, it is unlikely that he took an extended period of time to sketch for *Belshazzar*. One wonders how much of *Belshazzar* or any other oratorio Handel would have conceived before receiving the text: with the obvious exception of instrumental numbers (and even so, for many oratorios the overtures often appear to have been composed last of all) many sketches seem often to have been conceived with the text in mind. Yet Handel completed Act I of *Belshazzar* on 3 September ('filled up' on 15 September), Act II on 10 September—twelve and nine days for each act. Although *Belshazzar* might not typify all the oratorios, the fact that he could compose such an oratorio, generally regarded as one of his very best, with only a brief period of planning with text in hand, it seems unlikely that more protracted periods of precompositional activity were usually needed. Although Dean is obviously correct

---

[3] Dean, *Handel's Dramatic Oratorios*, 87.

that many sketches might have been lost, there is no evidence that Handel normally sketched extensively.

In all, Handel's compositional habits in regard to time probably reflect those of his contemporaries. Like Bach, Telemann, and Vivaldi, Handel composed rapidly. It would be an odd thing, after all, if a Baroque composer's compositional method resembled that of the post-revolutionary period more closely than his own time. During the 1740s Handel continued to 'invent or discover' (an apt phrase for a prodigious borrower) his ideas quickly because it reflected his training, his lifelong practice, and his facility at composition.

Much of our knowledge of composition during the Baroque derives from studies of Bach. Although Bach's and Handel's working methods are alike in many aspects, this study has disclosed significant ways in which Handel's compositional process differs from Bach's, offering a broader view of early eighteenth-century compositional practices. One of the most obvious of these differences lies in Handel's tendency to curtail the length of arias and choruses upon revision. Bach's revisions normally extend his works: thus Handel's corrections conflict with Robert Marshall's contention, drawn from Bach's practice, that Baroque composers tended to expand pieces upon revision:

Corrections of the diminution type [i.e. ornamental changes in which elaborating notes of diminution have been added to the original] reflect a principal characteristic of Bach's composing scores, just as they reflect an essential element of baroque composition in general. The diminution principle as a principle of elaboration, extension, and enlargement is operative on many levels of Bach's compositional process. For Bach's tendency when changing his original idea was to expand upon it, and add to it rather than to reduce or contract it.[4]

Either Marshall's conjecture is not always true of Baroque figures other than Bach, or Handel's compositional process is more akin to that of later composers. I suspect that some truth lies in both statements.

On one side, it is dangerous to use Bach as a model for early eighteenth-century practice, and this apparently applies even to his methods of revision. Just as Handel's music differs profoundly from Bach's, so do his revisions, and it is possible that his revising process is more typical of his generation. Telemann's musical style, for instance, is much closer to Handel's than is Bach's, and this similarity enabled Handel to 'borrow' from Telemann with ease, manipulating Telemann's musical 'cells' just as he manipulated his own. Nonetheless, the music of both Telemann and Handel has a greater affinity with later styles than does Bach's art. It is well known (perhaps even exaggerated) that Telemann was

---

[4]   Marshall, *The Compositional Process*, 35–6.

a 'progressive' composer who did much to forge the so-called *galant* style. Handel's kinship with the new style is not as often discussed, and sometimes denied. Most recently Ruth Smith has maintained that his musical style in the oratorios is old-fashioned:

The complexity and elaborateness of much of Handel's aria writing had always distinguished him in the London opera public's view, not always favourably, from his fellow composers of Italian opera. Though he was capable of exquisite simplicity, he was evidently not inclined to adopt to any large extent the more homophonic style of Neapolitan composers writing for the Opera of the Nobility or the 'modern' *galant* style.[5]

Though Handel's style was more complex than that of many contemporaries, we must not straitjacket him into one side of a binary opposition. Scholars such as Gerald Abraham and Ellen Harris have suggested, with some justification, that his style remained, by his contemporaries' standards, complex and old-fashioned. On the other hand, Winton Dean has maintained that Handel's operas of the 1730s showed distinctly 'progressive' traits, and more recently others have has rightly attempted to trace *galant* elements in his late oratorios. Morever, it appears that Handel's interest in the new style might even have influenced his borrowing practice. The duet 'These labours past' in *Jephtha* (*HG* 44: 50–7) was in large part borrowed from the duet 'Cara, se madre' from Baldassare Galuppi's cantata *La Vittoria d'Imeneo*, composed for the wedding festivities of Maria Antonia Ferdinanda, daughter of the recently deceased King Philip V of Spain, and Vittorio Amedeo, son and heir of Carlo Emanuele III of Savoy.[6] Here one finds short, ever changing rhythmic figures, sometimes alternating from triple to duple divisions (bb. 71–3), as well as short syncopated figures (*HG* 44: 51, 1/1 and 1/3, etc.); an often symmetrical phrase structure, with frequent two- and four-bar phrases; pleasing, uncomplicated melodies; sweet-sounding thirds and sixths (1–7, 17–22, 63–76, etc.); a thoroughly homophonic texture; relatively simple, diatonic harmony; and even a harmonic rhythm that often moves at the rate of one chord per bar (8–12, 18–22, 27–9, etc.). In spite of some obviously Baroque features (such as the cadential formulae), this duet is a veritable textbook of *galant* traits.[7] Although these 'progressive' traits result in part from the use of Galuppi's music, none of these *galant* features, considered in isolation, is

---

[5] Smith, *Handel's Oratorios*, 21.

[6] Thomas Goleeke, ' "These Labours Past": Handel's Look to the Future', in *Göttinger Händel-Beiträge*, 6 (1996), 171–83.

[7] It is striking that Handel chooses periodic or nearly periodic phrase structures for final ritornellos in many of the arias in *Jephtha*. See e.g. 'Virtue my soul', 'Take the heart', and the chorus 'Welcome, thou whose deeds'. These perhaps constitute further evidence of modern trends in Handel's late music.

entirely new for Handel; all have their roots in his earlier music. In general, Handel was far less interested in fugue and far more interested in singable melodies than Bach, and these characteristics—gained, no doubt, from opera—point to the future.

Handel's compositional process, which has its own role to play in elucidating his musical style, seems to suggest that in some sense he 'straddles the fence', with one foot planted in *galant* soil and the other on Baroque ground. On the one hand—or, to be consistent, on one foot—just as his music sometimes shows progressive tendencies, so does his compositional process. We have seen that on a profound level Handel's music might be described as paratactic. Its basic building blocks are short, discrete, autonomous units, often with their own melodic and rhythmic identity: this typifies the material he tended to sketch or borrow. And we find such self-standing entities in larger spans of the music as well. Handel's manipulation of these materials on all levels manifests itself in simple reordering, insertion, and, more commonly, deletion: in short, processes akin to, though less rigorous and mechanical than, mid-eighteenth-century *ars combinatoria* techniques. It has been shown that Telemann was also interested in the *ars combinatoria*, at least in his sonatas with basso continuo.[8] The fact that *ars combinatoria* principles are generally discussed in relation to later composers (such as Mozart, Haydn, and Beethoven) may indicate that Handel's utilization of melodic reordering might be viewed as a pre-Classical trend. But such reordering was already common in the first half of the century.

It is, of course, in part Handel's harmonic practice that makes his method of revision possible. Brainard has identified one such precondition, which allows 'surgical' revisions to be made: 'successive phrases and sub-groups having the same tonal goal'.[9] But as we have seen, this is not the only harmonic precondition for insertions and deletions. Provided that phrases with contrasting tonal goals are relatively independent, as in Handel's bi-partite B sections, where discursive tonal organization reigns, such changes are easily implemented, as we have seen. This is simply another way of saying that his music is highly segmented or paratactic.

In some ways, Handel's additive method of composing resembles the process discussed in Koch's *Versuch einer Anleitung zur Komposition* of the 1780s and 1790s and exemplified by a composer who also began his musical training during the Baroque period, Franz Joseph Haydn.[10] Significantly, Koch's

---

[8] Jeanne Swack, 'Telemann and Permutation Technique: A Study in Compositional Process in the *Style Galant*', read at the 1988 meeting of the American Musicological Society in Baltimore.

[9] Brainard, 'Aria and Ritornello', 30.   [10] See Sisman, 'Small and Expanded Forms'.

method was based on that of Joseph Riepel. The affinity between Riepel's approach and Handel's composing method is revealed by Handel's expansion of simple phrases into whole pieces, as we saw in the Chapter 3. And his manipulation of form in some instances seems clearly related to processes described by Koch, as disclosed in Chapter 8. Riepel and Koch describe a process of musical expansion, however; to arrive at another of Handel's favourite methods of revision—deletion—the advice of Koch and Riepel should simply be reversed. But either way, the musical characteristics that allow such changes to be made are of necessity the same. Thus a direct line can indeed be traced, via Riepel and Koch, between Handel and Haydn, a lineage to which Bach, by and large, does not belong. Perhaps Handel, more than Bach, deserves to be labelled a 'progressive'.

Yet on the other hand, Handel's music remains profoundly Baroque in many respects, with a level of harmonic and melodic complexity and contrapuntal sophistication that is lacking in the music of his *galant* colleagues. These aspects of his music also influence his compositional revisions. While his music is paratactic on a number of levels, Handel knew how, in spite of that, to produce compositions with a seamless, or hypotactic, surface. His revisions tend to produce such continuous, seamless music by means of harmonic revisions that draw on functional rather than discursive harmony. Attempts to achieve smoothness are also manifested in the numerous corrections that delay or eliminate cadences. Such revisions are sometimes generated by the text, but on a more abstract plane the need to produce a hypotactic surface from paratactic elements was a routine compositional concern for Handel. Thus a mixture of styles lies at the very heart of his compositional process, which reflects the historical position of the composer, who worked at a time when Baroque and *galant* styles coexisted.

On another plane, a mixture of styles can be said to form the very essence of English oratorio as a genre—an amalgam of German Passion, Italian opera, and English anthem. In his preface to *Samson* Newburgh Hamilton described that work as a 'musical Drama . . . in which the Solemnity of Church-Musick is agreeably united with the most pleasing Airs of the Stage', a definition that suits many of Handel's oratorios. The common ground here is vocal composition, and evaluating Handel's compositional process has involved giving matters of text, drama, and voice their due. We have examined, for instance, how Handel's concern to create an expressive liaison between text and music in the realm of musical imagery manifests itself in new settings as well as in the process of recomposing old music to new texts.

Moreover, within the realm of vocal composition, the importance of the operatic component of the oratorio has stood out in this study. Although the oratorios were not staged, they were often dramatic works, and involved collaboration with living librettists, just as opera did. Handel apparently felt free to request changes in the text from the librettist, and his alterations of musical form as well as the final score illustrate that he was perfectly capable of overriding the structural dictates of the libretto. Furthermore, in his final years of oratorio composition, Handel regularly used Italian-born singers who had been active in Middlesex's opera company, and the late oratorios (after *Solomon*) become more operatic in character than any since *Hercules*, with the da capo again constituting the most common aria form. It is during this time that Handel's regular use of particular singers (Frasi, Guadagni, Lowe) makes its mark upon his composition. His concern that his music mirror the strengths of his singers, a characteristic that presumably belongs more to opera than oratorio, was seen in a series of revisions from *Solomon* and *Susanna*, both composed for Frasi's first season.

In the final analysis, many aspects of Handel's compositional process are mysterious. The respective roles of forethought and spontaneity, for example, must remain opaque. Nonetheless, this study has illustrated that the commonly accepted paradigm of spontaneity—borrowed ritornello as datum for improvisation—with its linear view of composition, has in spite of its basic truth misled us in certain regards. In fact, many aspects of Handel's composition were non-linear: the ritornello, far from always providing a precompositional datum, was frequently composed after material for the body of the aria had been decided upon. Similarly, Handel seems often to have decided first upon his melodic material and maintained it through the process of composition while improvising the form; at other times the form came first, and the melodic material could change. For such reasons this study has deliberately avoided putting forth a single, all-encompassing model for Handel's composition: the truth is too complicated to be captured by a single model.

The compositional process itself seems inextricably linked to the genre of oratorio, for at the heart of both lies a mixture—of procedures in the one and of styles in the other. The *stile antico*, the high Baroque, and the *galant* styles; the secular operatic style and the church style; the serious, the pastoral, and the comic can all be found, at times side by side, within the same works. It is perhaps no wonder, then, that Handel's composition embraced a wide variety of processes.

Robert Oppenheimer has argued for the necessity of maintaining both old and new theories in the sciences, and certain of his remarks are relevant for us:

To what appear to be the simplest questions, we will tend to give either no answer or an answer which will at first sight be reminiscent more of a strange catechism than of the straightforward affirmatives of physical science. If we ask, for instance, whether the position of the electron remains the same, we must say 'no'; if we ask whether the electron's position changes with time, we must say 'no'; if we ask whether the electron is at rest, we must say 'no'; if we ask whether it is in motion, we must say 'no'. The Buddha has given such answers when interrogated as to the conditions of a man's self after death; but they are not the familiar answers for the tradition of seventeenth- and eighteenth-century science.[11]

Similarly, if we ask whether Handel composed spontaneously, we must answer 'yes'; if we ask whether composition for Handel involved forethought and planning, we must answer 'yes'; if we ask if Handel composed in a linear manner from beginning to end of a given piece, the answer is 'yes'; if we ask if the beginning of a work was sometimes derived from thematic material from the body of the work, again we must answer 'yes'; if we ask if Handel's music is paratactic, we must answer 'yes'; if we ask if Handel's music displays hypotaxis, we must answer 'yes'. The fact that our overview of Handel's compositional acts between the creation of sketches and the final first performance score has revealed differing tendencies merely reflects the multiplicity of techniques and styles at his fingertips. Only with the help of different models extracted from analyses of individual pieces—models that, viewed from a certain distance, seem paradoxical—can we begin to capture the creative acts of such a versatile composer.

---

[11] J. Robert Oppenheimer, *Atom and Void: Essays on Science and Community* (Princeton: Princeton University Press, 1989), 31–2.

SELECTED BIBLIOGRAPHY

ABRAHAM, GERALD, 'Some Points of Style', in id. (ed.), *Handel: A Symposium*, 269–70.

—— (ed.), *Handel: A Symposium* (London: Oxford University Press, 1954).

AVISON, CHARLES, *An Essay on Musical Expression* (London: C. Davis, 1752; rev. edn., 1753).

BASELT, BERNDT, *Händel-Handbuch*, i: *Lebens- und Schaffensdaten. Thematisch-systematisches Verzeichnis: Buhnenwerke* (Kassel: Bärenreiter, 1978).

—— *Händel-Handbuch*, ii: *Thematisch-systematisches Verzeichnis: Oratorische Werke, Vocale Kammermusik, Kirchenmusik* (Kassel: Bärenreiter, 1984).

—— *Händel-Handbuch*, iii: *Instrumentalmusik, Pasticci und Fragmente* (Kassel: Bärenreiter, 1986).

BEST, TERENCE (ed.), *Handel Collections and their History* (Oxford: Clarendon Press, 1993).

BRAINARD, PAUL, 'Aria and Ritornello: New Aspects of the Comparison Handel/Bach', in Peter Williams (ed.), *Bach, Handel, Scarlatti Tercentenary Essays* (Cambridge: Cambridge University Press, 1985), 21–34.

BRETT, PHILIP, and HAGGERTY, GEORGE, 'Handel and the Sentimental: The Case of *Athalia*', *Music and Letters*, 68 (1987), 112–27.

BUELOW, GEORGE, 'The Loci Topici and Affect in Late Baroque Music: Heinichen's Practical Demonstration', *Music Review*, 27 (1966), 161–76.

—— *Thorough-Bass Accompaniment According to Johann David Heinichen* (Ann Arbor: UMI Research Press, 1986).

—— 'Handel's Borrowing Techniques: Some Fundamental Questions Derived from a Study of "Agrippina" (Venice, 1709)', *Göttinger Händel-Beiträge*, 2 (1986), 105–28.

—— 'The Case for Handel's Borrowings: The Judgement of Three Centuries', in Sadie and Hicks (eds.), *Handel Tercentenary Collection*, 61–82.

—— 'Mattheson's Concept of "Moduli" as a Clue to Handel's Compositional Process', *Göttinger Händel-Beiträge*, 3 (1989), 272–8.

BURNEY, CHARLES, *An Account of the Musical Performances in Westminster Abbey and the Pantheon in Commemoration of Handel* (London: Payne and Robinson, 1785).

—— *A General History of Music from the Earliest Ages to the Present Period*, iii–iv (London: by the author, 1789). Edited by Frank Mercer (London, 1935); repr. New York: Dover Publications, 1957.

—— *Memoirs of Dr. Charles Burney, 1726–1769*, ed. Slava Klima, Garry Bowers, and Kerry S. Grant (Nebraska: University of Nebraska Press, 1988).

BURROWS, DONALD J. 'Handel's Peace Anthem', *Musical Times*, 114 (1973), 1230–2.

—— 'The Composition and First Performance of Handel's *Alexander's Feast*', *Music and Letters*, 64 (1983), 206–11.

BURROWS, DONALD J. 'Paper Studies and Handel's Autographs: A Preliminary Report', *Göttinger Händel-Beiträge*, 1 (1984), 103–15.

—— 'The Autographs and Early Copies of *Messiah*: Some Further Thoughts', *Music and Letters*, 66 (1985), 201–19.

—— 'Handel's Last Musical Autograph', *Händel-Jahrbuch*, 40/1 (1994/5), 155–68.

—— *Handel* (New York: Schirmer Books, 1994).

—— (ed.), *The Cambridge Companion to Handel* (Cambridge: Cambridge University Press, 1997).

—— and RONISH, MARTHA, *A Catalogue of Handel's Musical Autographs* (Oxford: Clarendon Press, 1994).

CHISOLM, DUNCAN, 'New Sources for the Libretto of Handel's *Joseph*', in Sadie and Hicks (eds.), *Handel Tercentenary Collection*, 182–208.

CLAUSEN, HANS DIETER, *Händels Direktionspartituren (Handexemplare)* (Hamburger Beiträge zur Musikwissenschaft, 7; Hamburg: Verlag der Musikalienhandlung Karl Dieter Wagner, 1972).

DEAN, WINTON, *Handel's Dramatic Oratorios and Masques* (Oxford: Oxford University Press, 1959).

—— *Handel and the Opera Seria* (Berkeley: University of California Press, 1969).

—— 'Charles Jennens's Marginalia to Mainwaring's Life of Handel', *Music and Letters*, 53 (1972), 160–4.

—— and HICKS, ANTHONY, *The New Grove Handel* (New York: W. W. Norton & Co., 1982).

—— and KNAPP, J. MERRILL, *Handel's Operas: 1704–1726* (Oxford: Clarendon Press, 1987).

DERR, ELLWOOD, 'Handel's Procedures for Composing with Materials from Telemann's "Harmonischer Gottes-Dienst" in "Solomon"', *Göttinger Händel-Beiträge*, 1 (1984), 116–46.

DEUTSCH, OTTO ERICH, *Handel: A Documentary Biography* (London: Adam and Charles Black, 1955; repr. New York: Da Capo, 1974).

DREYFUS, LAURENCE, *Bach and the Patterns of Invention* (Cambridge, Mass.: Harvard University Press, 1996).

DUNHILL, ROSEMARY, *Handel and the Harris Circle* (Hampshire: Hampshire County Council and the Author, 1995).

Editionsleitung der Hallischen Händel-Ausgabe, ed. *Händel-Handbuch*, iv: *Dokumente zu Leben und Schaffen* (Kassel: Bärenreiter, 1985).

FISKE, ROGER, *English Theatre Music in the Eighteenth Century* (2nd edn., Oxford: Oxford University Press, 1986).

FULLER-MAITLAND, JOHN ALEXANDER, and MANN, A. H., *Catalogue of Music in the Fitzwilliam Museum, Cambridge* (London: C. J. Clay and Sons, 1983).

GOLEEKE, THOMAS, ' "These Labours Past": Handel's Look to the Future', in *Göttinger Händel-Beiträge*, 6 (1996), 171–83.

GOLDSMITH, OLIVER, 'On the Different Schools of Music', in *British Magazine* (Feb. 1760), repr. in *Collected Works of Oliver Goldsmith*, ed. Arthur Friedman, iii (Oxford: Oxford University Press, 1966), 91–3.

GOSSETT, PHILIP, *Anna Bolena and the Artistic Maturity of Gaetano Donizetti* (Oxford: Clarendon Press, 1985).

GRANT, KERRY S., *Dr. Burney as Critic and Historian of Music* (Ann Arbor: UMI Research Press, 1983).

GUDGER, WILLIAM D., 'Handel's Last Compositions and his Borrowings from Habermann (Part 1)', *Current Musicology*, 22 (1976), 61–72.

—— 'Handel's Last Compositions and his Borrowings from Habermann (Part 2)', *Current Musicology*, 23 (1977), 28–45.

—— 'Sketches and Drafts for *Messiah*', *American Choral Review*, 27/2–3 (1985), 31–44.

HARRIS, ELLEN T., *Handel and the Pastoral Tradition* (London: Oxford University Press, 1980).

—— 'The Italian in Handel', *Journal of the American Musicological Society*, 33 (1980), 468–500.

—— 'An American Offers Advice to Handel', *American Choral Review*, 27/2–3 (1985), 55–62.

—— 'Integrity and Improvisation in the Music of Handel', *Journal of Musicology*, 7 (1989), 301–15.

—— 'Harmonic Patterns in Handel's Operas', in Mary Ann Parker-Hale (ed.), *Eighteenth-Century Music in Theory and Practice: Essays in Honor of Alfred Mann* (Stuyvesant: Pendragon Press, 1994), 77–118.

—— (ed.) *The Librettos of Handel's Operas*, 13 vols. (New York: Garland Publishing, 1989).

HEINICHEN, JOHANN DAVID, *Der General-Bass in der Composition* (Dresden, 1728).

HICKS, ANTHONY, 'Ravishing Semele', *Musical Times*, 114 (1973), 275–80.

—— 'Handel's Music for *Comus*', *Musical Times*, 117 (1976), 28–9.

—— 'The Late Additions to Handel's Oratorios and the Role of the Younger Smith', in Hogwood and Luckett (eds.), *Music in Eighteenth-Century England*, 147–69.

—— 'Handel, Jennens, and *Saul*: Aspects of a Collaboration', in Nigel Fortune (ed.), *Music and Theatre: Essays in Honour of Winton Dean* (Cambridge: Cambridge University Press, 1987), 203–27.

HIGHFILL, PHILIP, *et al.* (eds.), *A Biographical Dictionary of Actors, Actresses, Musicians, Dancers, Managers and Other Stage Personnel in London, 1660–1800* (Carbondale, Ill.: Southern Illinois Press, 1978).

HILL, JOHN WALTER, 'Vivaldi's Griselda', *Journal of the American Musicological Society*, 31 (1978), 53–82.

—— 'Handel's Retexting as a Test of his Conception of Connections between Music, Text, and Drama', *Göttinger Händel-Beiträge*, 3 (1989), 284–92.

HOGWOOD, CHRISTOPHER, and LUCKETT, RICHARD (eds.), *Music in Eighteenth-Century England: Essays in Memory of Charles Cudworth* (Cambridge: Cambridge University Press, 1983).

HOULE, GEORGE, *Meter in Music, 1600–1800* (Bloomington: Indiana University Press, 1987).

HUDSON, FREDERICK, 'The Earliest Paper Made by James Whatman the Elder

(1702–1759) and its Significance in Relation to G. F. Handel and John Walsh',
Music Review, 38 (1977), 15–32.

HURLEY, DAVID ROSS, 'The Summer of 1743: Some Handelian Self-Borrowings',
Göttinger Händel-Beiträge, 4 (1991), 174–94.

—— 'Dejanira and the Physicians: Aspects of Hysteria in Handel's *Hercules*', *Musical
Quarterly*, 80 (1996), 548–61.

KING, A. HYATT, *Handel and his Autographs* (London: Trustees of the British Museum,
1967).

KOCH, HEINRICH CHRISTOPH, *Versuch einer Anleitung zur Composition*, 3 vols. (Leipzig:
Adam Friedrich Böhme, 1782–93; repr. Hildesheim: Georg Olms Verlag, 1969).

—— *Introductory Essay on Composition: The Mechanical Rules of Melody, Sections 3 and
4*, trans., with an Introduction by Nancy Kovaleff Baker (New Haven: Yale
University Press, 1983).

KUBIK, REINHOLD, *Händels Rinaldo: Geschichte, Werk, Wirkung* (Neuhausen–Stuttgart:
Hänssler, 1982).

LANG, PAUL HENRY, *George Frideric Handel* (New York: W. W. Norton & Co., 1966).

LARSEN, JENS PETER, *Handel's Messiah* (New York: W. W. Norton & Co., 1957).

—— 'The Turning Point in Handel's Career', *American Choral Review*, 26 (1989), 55–62.

LARUE, C. STEVEN, 'Metric Reorganization as an Aspect of Handel's Compositional
Process', *Journal of Musicology*, 8 (1990), 477–90.

—— *Handel and his Singers: The Creation of the Royal Academy Operas, 1720–1728*
(Oxford: Clarendon Press, 1995).

LESTER, JOEL, *Compositional Theory in the Eighteenth Century* (Cambridge, Mass.:
Harvard University Press, 1992).

LEVY, JANET M., 'Covert and Casual Values in Recent Writings about Music', *Journal
of Musicology*, 5 (1987), 3–27.

LONDON, JUSTIN, 'Riepel and *Absatz*: Poetic and Prosaic Aspects of Phrase Structure
in 18th-Century Theory', *Journal of Musicology*, 8 (1989), 505–19.

MACMILLAN, DOUGALD, *Catalogue of the Larpent Plays in the Huntington Library* (San
Marino: The Henry E. Huntington Library and Art Gallery, 1939).

MAINWARING, JOHN, *Memoirs of the Life of the Late George Frederic Handel* (London:
R. and J. Dodsley, 1760; repr. Amsterdam: Frits A. M. Knuf, 1964).

MANN, ALFRED, 'Handel's Succesor: Notes on John Christopher Smith the Younger',
in Hogwood and Luckett (eds.), *Music in Eighteenth-Century England*, 135–45.

—— (ed.), *Georg Friedrich Handel: Composition Lessons from the Autograph Collection in
the Fitzwilliam Museum Cambridge. Hallische Händel-Ausgabe Supplement*, i (Kassel:
Bärenreiter, 1978).

MARSHALL, ROBERT, *The Compositional Process of J. S. Bach* (Princeton: Princeton
University Press, 1972).

—— *The Music of Johann Sebastian Bach: The Sources, the Style, the Significance* (New
York: Schirmer Books, 1989).

MATTHESON, JOHANN, *Der vollkommene Capellmeister*, trans. Ernest Harriss (Ann Arbor:
UMI Research Press, 1981).

MILHOUS, JUDITH, and HUME, ROBERT D., 'Librettist versus Composer: The Property Rights to Arne's *Henry and Emma* and *Don Saverio*', *Journal of the Royal Music Association*, 122 (1997), 52–67.

MILLNER, FREDERICK L., *The Operas of Johann Adolf Hasse* (Ann Arbor: UMI Research Press, 1979).

NIEDT, FRIEDRICH ERHARDT, *The Musical Guide Parts 1 (1700/10), 2 (1721), and 3 (1717)*, trans. Pamela L. Poulin and Irmgard C. Taylor (Oxford: Clarendon Press, 1989).

PARKER-HALE, MARY ANN, 'Handel's Choral Recitatives', *Göttinger Händel-Beiträge*, 2 (1986), 170–7.

—— *G. F. Handel: A Guide to Research* (New York: Garland Publishing, Inc., 1988).

POWERS, HAROLD, 'Il Serse trasformato', *Musical Quarterly*, 47 (1961), 481–92; 48 (1962), 73–92.

RATNER, LEONARD, '*Ars Combinatoria*: Chance and Choice in Eighteenth-Century Music' in H. C. Robbins Landon (ed.), *Studies in Eighteenth Century Music: A Tribute to Karl Geiringer on his Seventieth Birthday* (London: Allen & Unwin, 1970), 343–63.

—— *Classic Music: Expression, Form, and Style* (New York: Schirmer, 1980).

REES, ABRAHAM, *The Cyclopedia; or Universal Dictionary of Arts, Sciences, and Literature*, 41 vols. (Philadelphia: Samuel F. Bradford and Murray, Fairman, & Co., *c*.1820).

ROBERTS, JOHN, 'Handel's Borrowings from Telemann: An Inventory', *Göttinger Händel-Beiträge*, 1 (1984), 147–71.

—— 'Handel's Borrowings from Keiser', *Göttinger Händel-Beiträge*, 2 (1986), 51–76.

—— 'Handel and Charles Jennens's Italian Opera Manuscripts' in Nigel Fortune (ed.), *Music and Theatre: Essays in Honour of Winton Dean* (Cambridge: Cambridge University Press, 1987), 159–202.

—— 'Handel and Vinci's "Didone Abbandonata": Revisions and Borrowings', *Music and Letters*, 68 (1987), 141–50.

—— 'Why did Handel Borrow?', in Sadie and Hicks (eds.), *Handel Tercentenary Collection*, 83–92.

—— (ed.), *Handel's Sources: Material for the Study of Handel's Borrowings*, 9 vols. (New York: Garland Publishing, 1986–8).

ROGERS, PATRICK J., *Continuo Realization in Handel's Vocal Music* (Ann Arbor: UMI Research Press, 1989).

ROSAND, ELLEN, 'Operatic Madness: A Challenge to Convention', in Steven Paul Scher (ed.), *Music and Text: Critical Inquiries* (Cambridge: Cambridge University Press, 1992), 241–87.

SADIE, STANLEY, and HICKS, ANTHONY (eds.), *Handel Tercentenary Collection* (Ann Arbor: UMI Research Press, 1987).

SARTORI, CLAUDIO, *I libretti italiani a stampa dalle origini al 1800*, 6 vols. (Cuneo: Bertola & Locatelli, 1993).

SHAW, WATKINS, *A Textual and Historical Companion to Handel's Messiah* (London: Novello, 1965).

SIEGMUND-SCHULTZE, WALTHER, 'Zu Händels Schaffensmethode', *Händel-Jahrbuch* (1961/2), 169–36.

SIEGMUND-SCHULTZE, WALTHER, *Georg Friedrich Händel: Thema mit 20 Variationen* (Halle, 1965).

—— 'Georg Friedrich Händel als ein Wegbereiter der Wiener Klassik', *Händel-Jahrbuch*, 27 (1981), 23–36.

SISMAN, ELAINE, 'Small and Expanded Forms: Koch's Model and Haydn's Music', *Musical Quarterly*, 68 (1982), 444–75.

—— *Haydn and the Classical Variation* (Cambridge, Mass.: Harvard University Press, 1993).

SMITH, RUTH, 'Intellectual Contexts of Handel's English Oratorios', in Hogwood and Luckett (eds.), *Music in Eighteenth-Century England*, 115–33.

—— 'The Achievements of Charles Jennens (1700–1773)', *Music and Letters*, 70 (1989), 161–90.

—— *Handel's Oratorios and Eighteenth-Century Thought* (Cambridge: Cambridge University Press, 1995).

SMITH, WILLIAM C., *Handel: A Descriptive Catalogue of the Early Editions* (Oxford: Basil Blackwell, 1970).

SMITHER, HOWARD E., *A History of the Oratorio*, 3 vols. (Chapel Hill: University of North Carolina Press, 1977–87).

SQUIRE, WILLIAM BARCLAY, *Catalogue of the King's Music Library*, i: *The Handel Manuscripts* (London: Trustees of the British Museum, 1927).

STROHM, REINHARD, *Essays on Handel and Italian Opera* (Cambridge: Cambridge University Press, 1986).

TAYLOR, CAROLE, 'Handel's Disengagement from the Italian Opera', in Sadie and Hicks (eds.), *Handel Tercentenary Collection*, 165–81.

TAYLOR, SEDLEY, *The Indebtedness of Handel to Works by Other Composers* (Cambridge: Cambridge University Press, 1906).

TELEMANN, GEORG PHILIPP, *Musikalische Werke* (Kassel and Basle: Bärenreiter, 1950–).

TOBIN, JOHN, *Handel at Work* (London: Cassell, 1964).

TROWELL, BRIAN, 'Congreve and the 1744 *Semele* Libretto', *Musical Times*, 111 (1970), 993–4.

TYSON, ALAN, *Mozart: Studies of the Autograph Scores* (Cambridge: Harvard University Press, 1987).

WEIMER, ERIC, *Opera Seria and the Evolution of Classical Style 1755–1772* (Ann Arbor: UMI Research Press, 1984).

WINEMILLER, JOHN, 'Handel's Borrowing and Swift's Bee: Handel's "Curious" Practice and the Theory of Transformative Imitation' (Ph.D. diss., University of Chicago, 1994).

—— 'Recontextualizing Handel's Borrowings', *Journal of Musicology*, 15 (1997), 444–70.

YOUNG, PERCY, *The Oratorios of Handel* (London: Dennis Dobson Ltd., 1949).

ZIMMERMAN, FRANKLIN, 'Händels Parodie-Ouverture zu *Susanna*: Eine neue Ansicht über die Entstehungsfrage', *Händel-Jahrbuch*, 24 (1978), 19–30.

—— 'Purcellian Passages in the Compositions of G. F. Handel', in Hogwood and Luckett (eds.), *Music in Eighteenth-Century England*, 49–58.

INDEX OF HANDEL'S COMPOSITIONS

GENERAL INDEX

DATE DUE

DEC 1 6 2004			

DEMCO 38-296